Maintenance Reinvented

and

Business Success

Everything is about business

By Richard G. Lamb, PE, CPA
Cost Control Systems, LLC
www.cost-controls.com

ISBN 978-0-615-33440-0

Information contained in this work has been obtained from sources believed to be reliable. Neither the author nor publisher guarantee the accuracy or completeness of any information published herein and neither the author nor publisher shall be responsible for any errors, omissions, or damages arising out of the use of this information. The work is published with the understanding the author and publisher are supplying information, but not attempting to render professional legal, accounting, engineering or any other professional services. If such services are required, the assistance of an appropriate professional should be sought.

Trademarks: Microsoft, Microsoft Office, Excel, Access, InfoPath and Visual Basic (VB), Oracle, SAP,Crystal Reports, Adobe LiveCycle and Maximo are registered trademarks in the United States and other countries.

Table of Contents

iv

Chapter 1
This Book: Maintenance Reinvented

From this book you will discover how to make maintenance a part of your firm's business success. This is in contrast to what you already know about improving business-driven maintenance efficiency and equipment effectiveness.

This begs an answer to single question. What is business success? The answer lies in a simple principle. Your firm competes to win returns that are above its industry's average. All things, including our jobs, are decided by the final score.

The returns of interest to this book are profit, profit margin, return on investment and cash return on investment. Maintenance has always taken a toll or tax on these returns. This is because, until only recently, we have not known how to make maintenance a part of business success, The purpose of this book is to explain how to bring maintenance to grow, rather than shrink, your firm's returns.

Overview: The reinvention is in the chapters

We have all been around long enough to know that salespeople, consultants and authors make big claims; meaning you should test this author. Chapter 2 will submit the book's claims to its readers to test. The test begins with establishing that the historical intent of maintenance improvement has been business performance but explains why its methods are limited to improving maintenance efficiency and equipment effectiveness rather than designing for business returns. Chapter 2 will introduce the methods that are being newly brought to the puzzle of maintenance because they are the difference with which the firm can make maintenance a part of business success.

The chapter will introduce the concept of executing returns rather than strategies and their practices. What this means is that business success is the outcome of maintenance strategies, but is executed by working back from the returns they are to increase to the exact actions we must take now to trigger and sustain them.

The discussion of new methods and executing returns will bring to the forefront that accounting principles and financial statements are foundational to developing and measuring maintenance as part of business success. The point will thread itself throughout the chapter. With the firm's financial statements we determine how the firm's returns are sensitive to maintenance strategy. Subsequently, we will form strategies that hit the exposed nerves and then measure their impact on returns. Both are determined with dash-board-type, what-if financial models that are built on the firm's financial statements.

The explanation of financial models will introduce what the book calls "interface measures." They give us the ability to initially tie maintenance strategies to business returns through the firm's financial statements. Just as important, they are the pivot point at which the firm will subsequently be able to budget, measure and deliver the returns that are the known and quantified outcomes of the formed maintenance strategies.

Finally, Chapter 2 will explain how the process to make maintenance a part of business success creates a surgical focus that causes a program to naturally downsize itself. This is important. Without such a focus, any program has a high probability of collapsing before it reaches full term. The explanation of downsizing will be tied to the final topic of the second chapter which is the stages of conducting a program or smaller initiative to increase the firm's returns.

The book's remaining chapters will get down in the weeds we fly over in Chapter 2. We will begin by getting our arms around the competitive environment in which the firm struggles against its rivals to realize returns above the industry's average.

Accordingly, Chapter 3 will provide a structure with which the practitioner would survey the firm's competitive situation. The objective is to form maintenance strategies that fit and enhance the firm's overall business strategies. The chapter will offer a method to map strategies upon the firm's competitive situation. They are tested and expanded by subsequent financial analysis.

Chapters 4 through 6 will drill into accounting principles and financial statements. This is an absolutely necessary topic. A firm's financial statements must be the basis on which "being part of business success" is determined, quantified, managed and controlled.

The field of maintenance has long held itself back because it has overlooked the absolute need to think in terms of accounting and returns. Accordingly, Chapter 4 will explain the fundamental accounting principles and financial statements maintenance practitioners must understand. Otherwise, they will not be able to guide their firms and clients to the business success that is possible through maintenance strategy.

Chapter 5 will structure the accounting principles and financial statements as business models and with them explain how to construct a returns sensitivity analysis model. Sensitivity analysis determines where the firm's returns would be sensitive to maintenance strategy. Recall that Chapter 3 will explain how to draft strategies upon competitiveness. Sensitivity analysis may eliminate some of these earlier formed competitiveness-based strategies. This is because, based on the financial-statements-driven findings for sensitivity, the practitioner will link all strategies to the firm's sensitivity to maintenance strategy. As this is done, additional strategies may also emerge that the competitiveness-based analysis did not think of.

Because of competitiveness and returns sensitivity analysis, we will know that the firm's returns are "conceptually" sensitive to the strategies now on the table. Chapter 6 explains how to evaluate the formed strategies in the context of what the firm's financial statements and returns will look like when each is fully operational. Some strategies will be eliminated even though they fit the nature of the firm competitiveness and sensitivity.

This will happen if financial analysis finds that they will not significantly increase returns.

In the process of explaining the model to evaluate the financial worthiness of candidate strategies, Chapter 6 will introduce and explain how the extremely important interface measures are formed to fit the firm's unique competitive, operational and financial case. They are used to evaluate the strategies and then become part of the permanent processes to measure and control the returns the strategies are to deliver.

A section in Chapter 2 will have introduced the principle of executing returns rather than strategies and their practices. Historically, maintenance efficiency and equipment effectiveness programs have focused on executing practices and then searching for the resulting returns.

The method is to start with the returns to be expected from the formed maintenance strategies. We then trace back to the elements of the collective strategies that will predict and influence the returns. Chapter 7 will explain the process in depth.

Making maintenance a part of business success does not end when the formed strategies are executed through their returns. The returns must be sustained by ongoing corporate and plant level maintenance management. It is hard to envision how that is possible without a system to budget and then control and forecast variance. In fact, it is hard to envision the possibility of reaching the returns, let alone sustaining them.

The field of maintenance has never been able to effectively budget and control variance. This is because we have always been limited to the structure and reports of the traditional accounting system. Chapter 8 will introduce and explain a budgeting and variance system that matches the case of managing maintenance. This is an important breakthrough because without it we have to question the feasibility of any maintenance initiative. This is because regardless of what we intend to achieve the reality is that we cannot effectively deliver it.

The budget and variance method for maintenance-driven returns complements the traditional accounting system as it operates parallel to it. It is based on measuring and controlling the maintenance workload and the resources it engages or consumes to sustain returns. As nonfinancial measures, the earlier mentioned interface measures sit at its core. In contrast, the traditional budget and variance system is built upon the accounts of the accounting system. With them it is impossible to link much of any maintenance action to returns because variances tell us almost nothing with which we can take action.

Regardless of the claims made for business performance, historically the mission of maintenance programs has been limited to improving maintenance efficiency and equipment effectiveness. A set of best practices has emerged over the years that are engaged in these programs. A firm's practices are measured against them and the recommendation is usually to bring them up the standard.

Organization design for maintenance has largely been process of design by shooting from the hip. However, now returns are at stake. Consequently, organizational structure and roles must be designed with a larger view than only the execution of the maintenance work. Chapter 9 will explain the principles and process for deriving organization structure and roles, but with focus on five business subsystems.

Maintenance is a little about maintenance and a great deal about audit and control. This is highlighted by the recognition that many of the topics introduced up to this point are actually subtypes within audit and control.

Competitive and financial analysis, maintenance strategy, and budgeting and variance control are its upstream elements. The "standard" best practices and organizational development are also types of controls. For example, the process to manage maintenance work orders falls into the category of "feed forward" controls.

There are overarching principles of audit and control that must be alive and well in the firm. This includes tying all elements together as a system; including auditing the audit and control system. Chapters 9 will explain the principles and practices of audit and control and the process to layout an overall system.

At the mention of technology our thoughts leap to computerized maintenance management systems and hand-held devices. However, there is much more.

Information technology has evolved from rocket science and high-priesthood to tools that are user friendly, lurking on our computers, waiting for us to put them to work. An example is Microsoft Access, as a part of the Microsoft Office suite, which gives us the means to almost effortlessly reach into the firm's data and put it to use.

Most firms have these modern technologies available on the computers of almost every employee engaged in maintenance and reliability functions. Through them we can grab and put data to work. We can automate work management, give a front-end to processes, build high grade budget and variance control systems, and automate audit and control procedures and notices. Chapter 11 will introduce and explain these technologies in the context of generating returns through maintenance.

The discussion has changed

What is so striking about the previous section is that it is immediately noticeable that these are not the paragraphs we have all read over and over. Maintenance has been reinvented and the discussion of maintenance has expectedly changed tremendously. The change is forever because it does not make good business sense to go back.

The important thing is that firms can now change their discussion of maintenance. The discussion will begin differently; kicking off with how do we make maintenance part of our business success? The discussion is no longer much about evaluating and improving the standard maintenance and reliability best practices.

This is a huge shift. Instead, of best practices the discussion will be driven by how the firm competes to win returns above its industry's averages. Evaluation, as feedstock to the discussion, will be directed to understanding the firm as a competitive, operational and financial beast.

Out of that, all discussions will be centered on maintenance strategy as part of the firm's competitive strategy. More specifically, the discussion will be how the strategies fit the firm competitively and what the firm's financial statements will look like as a result. The discussion of maintenance and reliability best practices will still not have emerged as the epicenter of discussion: in fact never will.

As the discussion progresses, it will continue along a completely different beam. It will shift to executing specific increments of returns. Furthermore, it will not be an open-ended discussion as in the past. It will be a discussion of those elements that must be in place to ensure that the returns are actually generated, measured and sustained.

In the discussion of executing returns standard best practices will emerge. Rather than a discussion of improving them, they will be discussed in the context of all elements that are molded to fit the firm's determined maintenance strategies.

The discussion of elements will be much broader than the historical best practices. It will be extended to include the elements of disciplines that have never been part of the discussion of managing maintenance. These disciplines will include strategic planning, budgeting, variance control and forecasting, audit and control, organizational development, and modern information technologies.

Not only is the discussion changed forever, but it is changed immediately. This shift has proven to occur beginning with this book, specifically this chapter. Rather than bragging on the book, it is a testimonial to the need to shift that we have all sensed. We can finally put our finger on the question that haunted me ever since entering our field in the late 1980's and publishing a book in 1995.[1] At the gut level I knew I was missing the point, but could not figure out what it was.

Why are we all ready for the discussion to change? It is because, through the firms that engage us, we all strive to be part of something worthwhile to our families, and local and global communities.

---

[1] Lamb, Richard. *Availability engineering and management for manufacturing plant performance*. Englewood Cliffs, NJ. Prentice Hall, 1995.

Chapter 2
Can We Get to Business Success?

This chapter confronts head-on the three challenges one CEO said he poses to all propositions, "Does it make good businesses sense, can it be measured and when do we get our money?" The answers are heck yes, big time and quickly.

The proposition being put forth by the book is to make maintenance a part of your firm's business success: measured by returns greater than the industry's average. This is in contrast to improving maintenance efficiency and equipment effectiveness; something that cannot safely make promises for increased returns.

However, you have been around long enough to know that salespeople, consultants and authors make big claims. Therefore, you are going to want to see some proof in the form of new methods: something new under the sun.

As you inspect the methods you will want to see in them proof that both the drivers and outcomes for returns can be measured. Passing the inspection you will want to know when your firm will get its money and see evidence that doing so has some type of driving force making it happen.

You have seen too many programs collapse under their own weight. Accordingly, your final sanity-check will question how victory can be reached without sucking all of the air out of the place.

This concern has two dimensions. First is how can your firm increase its returns with the least effort, cash and time? Second, which is closely related to the first, is how the onion is peeled. More specifically, how will people be engaged, what are the steps and deliverables, and what is the timeline?

The purpose of this chapter is to offer up the explanations on which the book's readers can make these judgments.

What's new under the sun

What is being newly brought to the management of maintenance that would make it a viable player in a firm's business success? There are classic disciplines that are almost always active and visible in ongoing business success. If missing in action, solutions for business performance are questionable for the simple reason that they have not stepped through all of the traps. Therefore, let's answer the "what's new" question with respect to these classics.

Figure 2-1 shows the business classics as they are related to maintenance. Each is a dimension on the radar chart. The chart contrasts qualitatively how the mission to make maintenance a part of business success and how the mission to improve maintenance efficiency and equipment effectiveness engage the classic disciplines. The inner boundary depicts the dimensions and the extent they are engaged in the mission to improve maintenance efficiency and equipment effectiveness. The contrast is immediately obvious as is the answer to the "what is new" question.

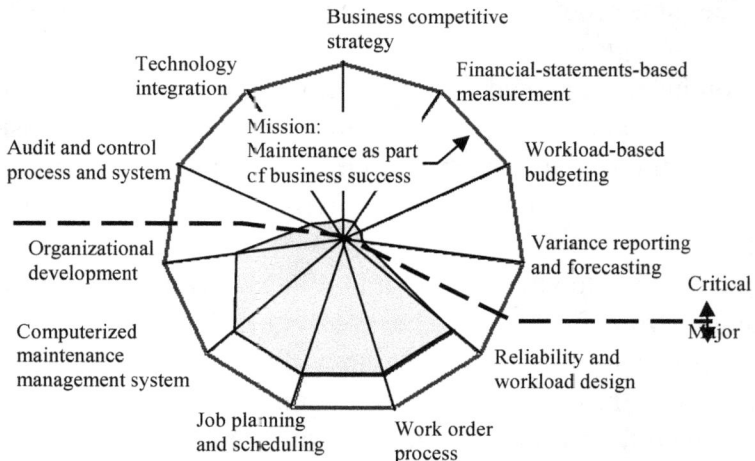

Figure 2-1: Contrast of disciplines engaged in making maintenance part of business success and improving maintenance operations.

Let's distinguish the disciplines as critical and major with respect to making maintenance part of business success. A discipline is classified as critical when its weakness or absence eliminates the rational possibility of a targeted outcome. If done without the advantage of the major disciplines, the critical ones can still deliver the returns and competitiveness that are possible through maintenance strategy: albeit not as efficiently.

Alternately, a dimension is major if the competitiveness, as returns, it makes possible are dependent upon the critical dimensions to succeed. Programs with the sole mission of improving maintenance efficiency and equipment effectiveness place all of the major dimensions in play but incorporate almost nothing of the critical disciplines.

It is very important that we make this distinction. This is because missions to improve maintenance efficiency and equipment effectiveness cannot be expected to increase business returns to the extent it is possible through maintenance strategy. Many good programs have been justified on the promise and later shut down when the returns were minimal and difficult to measure.

The next two of the absent five critical disciplines determine if the plant is actually succeeding at its maintenance strategies. They are also the means by which the plant will steer itself to success.

The first of the two is workload-based budgeting. It puts in place the many faceted details upon which the firm is able to measure if it is reaching and sustaining business success. The budget is critical because it sets the measurable relationship between all work and all resources to accomplish it. Furthermore, the relationship cannot be measured through the traditional accounting system.

The second of the two "are-we-succeeding" disciplines is workload-based variance reporting and forecasting. Through it, the plant will confirm that the relationship between work and resources is occurring in fact and take action if it is not on beam.

One of the six critical disciplines, audit and control, is weak. Internal audit and control ensures that the plant is consistently complying with the processes it has implemented for specific competitive advantages. Audit and control has historically had only a weak presence in the field of maintenance and reliability. This is because reports on "key performance indicators" have incorrectly become regarded as audit and control.

The last of the critical disciplines is technology integration. It is critical because it is the difference between knowing how to increase returns, thus, competitiveness and being actually able to do so. The criticality of the discipline is so much the case that reinventing maintenance to be a part of business success did not emerge until certain technologies and their integration with maintenance and reliability management were understood.

Among the five major disciplines of Figure 2-1 the field of maintenance and reliability has considerable history. However, rather than targeted on increasing returns, they have developed to improve maintenance efficiency and equipment effectiveness. The disciplines are reliability and workload design, work order management, planning and scheduling, computerized maintenance management system (CMMS) and organizational development.

The reliability design methods potentially increase gross profit through equipment effectiveness. Through workload design they can also decrease a plant's required maintenance expense by determining the most effective set of maintenance tasks to sustain the effectiveness of individual assets. However, without the critical disciplines they are not able to effectively find and focus on exactly where and how the firm's returns are sensitive to maintenance strategy. Consequently, rather than returns they are largely focused on individual equipment and one failure at a time.

Without the six critical disciplines, the work order management process will not be molded to increase and sustain returns. There is nothing to guide it to such an end. It is instead aligned and molded by standard best practices rather than the firm's sensitivity to maintenance strategy. With the critical disciplines the process will be molded to be the conduit through which strategies formed to touch the nerve will be conducted. This is equally the case for how the computerized maintenance management system is configured and engaged in the plant.

Job planning and scheduling also succumb to the same shortcoming. In fact there are many variations for planning and scheduling and how they draw upon current technology. They are far from one-size-fits-all practices.

Historically, in the field of maintenance and reliability the dimension of organizational development has been present. However, the inclusion of analytical disciplines in its solutions is weak.

Therefore, the claim for making maintenance a part of business success is backed by the fact that this book is not claiming a different outcome while continuing to propose that we do the same things. Once we are aware of what is newly being brought to the puzzle of maintenance, we cannot envision maintenance becoming part of business success without them.

Execute returns rather than strategies

As mentioned and bears repeating, competitiveness is defined as a firm's ability to win returns above the average of its industry. Since this is the goal, it makes sense that we think in terms of executing returns rather than strategies. When management is introduced to the firm's specific strategies for making maintenance a part of business success, they will want to know when they will get their money. We should focus on getting it for them.

Executing returns calls for a different model of project management. The traditional model is represented by its Gantt-chart-type horizontal project plans that define the tasks to implement each strategy and the resources and schedule to do so. The distinction is important because Gantt-type project management has proven to be marginally effective for all but a relatively small number of cases. The common characteristic is that they are projects that follow a well traveled path. Every maintenance strategy is essentially a one-off and, accordingly, requires a different project management approach.

The new model of "project management" is based on the concept of lag measures and lead abilities. A return, as a lag measure, is influenced by upstream abilities that can predictably influence the return. For example, a lead ability to manage some aspect of productivity will cause a change in returns. Sandwiched between them are the returns and downstream from lead abilities are the line items of the financial statements.

The new model defines and executes lead abilities by tracing backward from specific returns to precisely focused abilities that will not only directly change them, but can also be influenced. Therefore, executing returns begins with a process to identify and define lead abilities connected to returns.

Figure 2-2 shows the hierarchy of project planning as top-down from returns and execution as bottom-up to returns. At the top are the returns for which the firm competes. How they change will be decided by the degree the chosen maintenance strategies will ultimately affect the three areas of the income statement and balance sheet.

The three areas are as follows:

- **Gross profit:** Sold product times price less the direct labor and materials to produce it.
- **Overhead expense:** Working, material, manufacturing and general support resources, and capital assets as depreciation incurred to sustain returns.
- **Assets:** Current assets and property, plant and equipment engaged in plant productive capacity.

The mission to make maintenance a part of business success designs and crosses over a bridge between the maintenance strategies and the three areas of the firm's financial statements. This is done by forming a set of what we will call "interface measures." Through them the strategies will affect the three areas of the financials. Gross profit, overhead expense and assets of the financial statements will be predictably influenced by maintenance strategies through one or more of the interface measures.

An example is fixed expense. Improvements in the interface measure of the number of equivalent jobs per period per asset base will affect parts of the financial statements besides overhead expense. There may also be ramifications for cash flow through working capital balances in current assets and liabilities. In the longer terms there may also be ramifications for plant property and equipment. Interface measures must be formed for all cases.

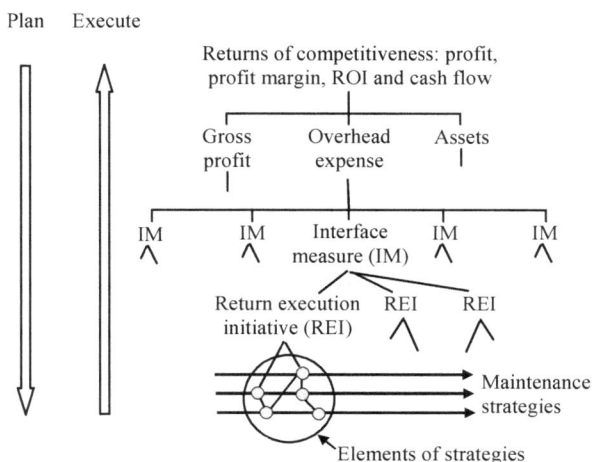

Figure 2-2: Hierarchy for executing returns.

The mention here of interface measures is the tip of a large iceberg with immense implications. They are formed when the strategies are being subjected to financial-statements-based analysis. Once formed, they are used daily, weekly, monthly and annually to actually measure and ensure that the returns of the maintenance strategies are occurring in fact. If not, the interface measures give us the wherewithal to determine why.

Because they are nonfinancial measures we can easily track back to what is happening and how they are affected. Modern information technology makes the ability to trace and compute easily possible. This means that we can put pencil to paper and compute exactly how the financials are being moved during the period of interest. Interface measures are discussed in depth by a later chapter, but deserve mention here because of their importance to returns.

The mission to make maintenance a part of business success will determine maintenance strategies that fit the firm's overall competitive strategies. Financial-statements-based financial analysis will have determined which of the strategies, as candidates, are return-significant and have eliminated those that are not. In the process of doing so returns sensitivity analysis will also have determined through which of the three areas of the financials and their related interface measures there is the greatest potential to move the plant's competitive returns.

This insight will provide focus to the next steps of planning for execution. The next step will determine very specifically how the returns will be executed. Accordingly, to execute returns we continue downward from each interface measure.

A business strategy for maintenance is actually a collection of elements that eventually join with others within the strategy and other strategies to cause returns to increase. The problem solved is that strategies do not directly and traceably drive returns. It is how their collective interrelated elements eventually come together that do. Consequently, the program planner will work through and package interrelated elements of disparate strategies for the express purpose of incrementally executing increases to returns.

This is done by defining the individual, unique lead abilities that will move each interface measure. For each, the planner will work backward to identify elements from across and between strategies that must be resolved, built and in place to make each unique ability operational with respect to moving the returns.

Execute a lead ability and we execute incrementally increased returns. Consequently, each ability as a package of elements is called a "return execution initiative" (REI). They are so precisely focused that the resulting affect on the targeted competitive returns will most often begin to flow within 100 days of go; possibly weeks.

The contrast between the new and old models of project management is shown in Figure 2-3. The figure shows that the traditional-type project approach of the old model is horizontal. By comparison, the REI model of execution cuts across the horizontal strategies rather than moves along them.

As they do, the vertical REIs will unearth elements that have fallen unrecognized and lost in the white space between Gantt bars because nobody owns a crystal ball. For the same reason they will concurrently reveal and integrate all of the elements along the Gantt bars that are relevant to the ability being put in place; linked to a specific measurable result for returns. They will also reveal events and obstacles that would not have been foreseen by traditional project planning.

The challenge that was thrown down at the beginning of the chapter was to show how to know when your firm will get its money. Accordingly, there is the need to see evidence that getting to the money has some type of driving force making it happen.

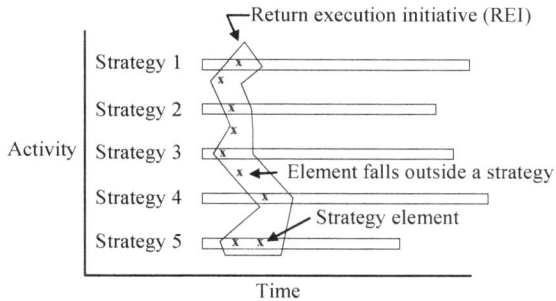

Figure 2-3: Vertical and horizontal approaches to project management.

Both are very evident in the process to execute returns rather then strategies. Furthermore, the drivers continue to be part of the normal processes of managing maintenance in a manner to ensure continuing returns and actually be able to report them to management as part of the firm's normal business tracking processes.

Focus and downsize

One concern for the feasibility of maintenance programs is that the energy, treasure and timeline to implement and get the money back are prohibitive. Any program that sucks all of the air out of the place has a low probability of going full term. This means that much that is done before the wick burns out has minimal business value: much like a costly, but half built bridge.

The good news is that a program to make maintenance a part of business success naturally downsizes itself; immensely. This is driven by the surgical focus on returns and how exactly the firm's returns are sensitive to maintenance strategy. This surgical focus occurs at six levels, each downsizing the total program while accelerating the rate that returns occur and build up.

Figure 2-4 shows that the new model of maintenance has six levels of focus. At each the program downsizes itself driven by the work done at the stage of the program. Consequently, the magnitude of energy and cash cost to reach increased returns is much less than it is for programs with the mission to improve maintenance efficiency and equipment effectiveness.

The six levels of focus and downsizing that determine program success are as follows:

- Determining the maintenance strategies that will contribute to the firm's business-level competitive strategies and advantage.
- Confirming which candidate maintenance strategies will significantly increase returns.
- Planning to execute the returns of the strategies rather than the elements of the strategies.
- Compressing the design and execution stages into one stage.
- Cutting the program when remaining unexecuted returns would be less than what the engaged resources could accomplish elsewhere for the firm.
- Leaving untouched the surplus elements of the program's maintenance and reliability strategies.

Level 1: Strategic relevance. The first level of focus and self-directed downsizing grows out of acquiring an in-depth understanding of the firm's current competitive strategies and then determining the maintenance strategies that will strengthen or extend them. This creates focus for the simple reason that it determines what is strategically relevant. It downsizes the program as it eliminates all others.

Level 2: Significant returns. The second level of focus and downsizing is the accounting-based financial measurement of the strategies that passed the test of competitive relevance. When the program puts pencil to paper on these strategies, some will be found to appear far more attractive than they actually are.

The program is downsized as financial-statements-based analysis eliminates some strategies and prunes others. This happens because the purpose of accounting-based analysis is to confirm that each strategy will noticeably improve profit, profit margin, return on investment and cash return on investment. Otherwise, we cannot answer one question a CEO used to stump many a proposition, "Why bother?"

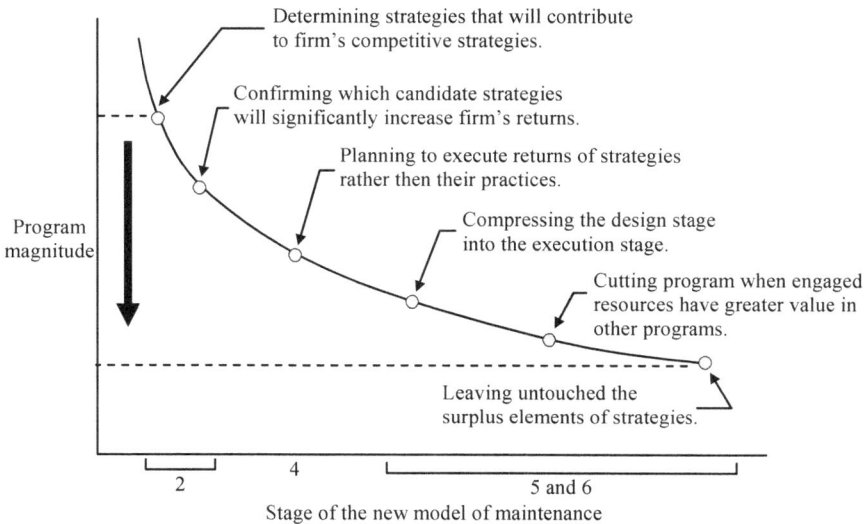

Determining strategies that will contribute
to firm's competitive strategies.

Confirming which candidate strategies
will significantly increase firm's returns.

Planning to execute returns of strategies
rather then their practices.

Compressing the design stage
into the execution stage.

Cutting program when engaged
resources have greater value in
other programs.

Leaving untouched the
surplus elements of strategies.

Program
magnitude

2

4

5 and 6

Stage of the new model of maintenance

Figure 2-4: The six levels of focus and self-directed downsizing.

Level 3: Execute returns. The third level of focus and self-directed downsizing is how the plant executes the strategies that have successfully navigated the gauntlet of the first two levels. The program will execute returns of strategies rather than execute the practices of strategies. The previous section explained what is meant by "executing returns" and how it is done with what we call "return execution initiatives" (REI).

Generating returns through strategies is actually a blanket approach to winning returns. Furthermore, until returns emerge in fact they can only be classified as a hoped for outcome. This is because maintenance strategies are synergistic with respect to returns rather than directly and measurably linked to specific increments of return. They are also mutually dependent on common elements.

Focus and downsizing is caused as cross-strategy elements are pulled into a specific REI as a set of actions that will tangibly increase one or more returns. All other elements remain on the shelf until proven relevant by being drawn into another REI.

Level 4: Compress two stages into one. The fourth level of focus and downsizing results because the surgical focus on returns compresses the largest and longest stages of any program: design and execution. Executing returns drives the program to do so.

A program with the mission to make maintenance a part of business success is downsized considerably because the design stage only continues as standalone until enough is known of the details to identify and define the elements of strategies that are pulled into individual REIs. Design is more precise and, in turn, much quicker when done in the context of reaching a result.

Level 5: Fight for life. The fifth level of focus and self-directed downsizing is that the program to increase returns is required to "fight for life." As the program progresses, it must continuously prove that it still deserves to live. This too is made possible through the principle of executing returns rather than strategies. The result is that program results are quantified and ranked as incremental returns.

There will be a point in time that the resources engaged by the program have greater potential for profit, profit margin, return on investment and cash flow if engaged in other programs. At this point the program will lose the fight. Downsizing will occur because the program provides the facts on which this point of demise can be identified when reached. The firm may choose to tackle the returns that remain as an alternative program, i.e., continuous improvement.

Level 6: Eliminate surplus elements. The final level of focus and downsizing reveals its results when the program comes to an end. Each REI pulls cross-strategy elements into the REIs at hand. It follows that such an approach will leave on the shelf all elements that were not relevant to the accomplished REIs.

Going into the program, it is not practical to attempt to identify and screen out all irrelevant elements. This is a reason that the design stage is transformed to execution; to avoid wasting energy, time and treasure designing what may never be relevant. The process of executing returns through REIs decides what must be designed by the program.

The six levels are cumulative. As the program progresses, it will naturally trigger them. This makes focus and self-directed downsizing an extremely effective force for shrinking the program to a feasible size. Just as important the forces are the result of targeting what reigns supreme in business success: returns and cash flow.

The stages to reach business success

This section will summarize the stages to reaching the state that maintenance is an important player in business success. It will address three aspects. First, how are plant personnel engaged in the program in a manner that is sensitive to the reality that they also have a real job? Second, what are the stages and their purpose? And third, what are the deliverables and timeline?

A firm may not wish to undertake a full program. Accordingly the next section will speak to the alternative: strategic initiatives. Initiatives tap into all of the principles; but do so in a way and order that fits a narrow pursuit; but still for business returns.

Engaging personnel

Programs that are too large may be unfeasible as a business strategy for some firms. The previous two sections explained how the focus on returns allows programs to overcome this fatal obstacle. Feasibility is enhanced by how the firm elects to engage its personnel in the program.

There are two extremes. At one extreme is to recruit outside consultants to conduct the program's or initiative's stages. The consultant does most of the heavy lifting.

At the other extreme is to form teams of firm personnel to conduct the stages. Outside consultants are engaged as mentors and facilitators to the team as they do most of the heavy lifting.

In between is to utilize consultants whose role is to do the heavy lifting to the greatest practical extent. As they do, they are to collaborate heavily with the firm's personnel; so much so that the personnel own the outcome abilities of each REI. There are teams, but they are very fluid and largely informal.

This book calls the strategy "eagle teams" because eagles do not flock and neither should teams. The eagle model recognizes an almost universal truth. Firms employ only enough people to do its work. Therefore, solutions by flocking are not always feasible because they pull personnel from their day jobs. Instead, the program works through informal teams and the consultant behaves in the style of an entrepreneur.

This is appropriate because the entrepreneurial philosophy strives to reach a result. Entrepreneurs also know that they must have a deal with the players to reach it.

Getting a deal engages players in reaching five points of agreement; usually in sequence. They must agree that the program is tackling the right problems and taking the right approach to solving them. They must agree that the solutions are correct, the obstacles to the solution have been recognized and how to overcome the obstacles is included in the solution.

The initial program stage to understand the firm as an enterprise prepares and positions the program for the eagle strategy. As the consultant surveys and understands the firm as a competitive, operational and financial beast, who must be engaged in specific stages, aspects and results of the program becomes increasingly apparent. Through informal teams, they are involved frequently in short blasts as needed, catch-as-catch-can and mostly one-on-one.

As entrepreneurs, the consultant's task is to draft, promote and refine solutions until the eagles have a deal. The consultant as the entrepreneur is like the ball in a pinball machine. The consultant bounces off the players as "bumpers" until a solution is formed, agreed to and executed.

Through "dynamic team rosters" the eagle strategy draws all relevant players and necessary perspectives into the solution as their attention is needed. The model converges rapidly on a solution and its execution. Just as importantly, the solutions are much better because collaboration is unfettered by formality and organizational lines. Meanwhile, the disruption to the work of the firm is insignificant.

Therefore, answering the question of engagement should begin with the eagle strategy as the point of reference. From it the firm can determine its need or desire to move in the direction of greater formal engagement or less overall engagement. Programs will typically have multiple cases. The program manager will recognize them as the onion is peeled and select the best engagement strategy.

Program stages

This section will summarize the program stages for making maintenance an important player in the firm's business success. As it does it will tie together all of the concepts that have been introduced and summarized up this point in the chapter.

Plotted in Figure 2-5, the generic stages that would be tailored for each firm are as follows:

1. Evaluate the approach to making maintenance a part of business success.
2. Understand the firm's competitive, operational and financial case.
3. Form candidate maintenance strategies.
4. Select the final strategies with financials-statements-based measurement.
5. Develop the details of each strategy.
6. Define and execute REIs.

Stage 1: Evaluate the approach to reaching business success. The first need for any firm is to determine if the approach to making maintenance a part of business success make sense. In other words, can that dog hunt? The purpose of the first stage is for the firm to inspect the approach and its methods to confirm that it can. Consequently, the meat of this stage is presentation to different groups across the firm.

The stage is additionally important. The history of programs limited to maintenance efficiency and equipment effectiveness has given industry a very limited perspective of its possibilities through maintenance strategy. Understanding how the dog hunts will change greatly and permanently the plant's discussion and expectations of maintenance.

Stage 2: Understand the firm's competitive, operational and financial case. The stage is accomplished over three to six weeks. It is done by interviewing people across the firm; largely one-on-one. At the same time it will reach into the firm's databases to confirm and gather facts. The goal is to gather in one place the depth of understanding and facts on which maintenance strategies will be formed, evaluated, downsized and executed by subsequent stages.

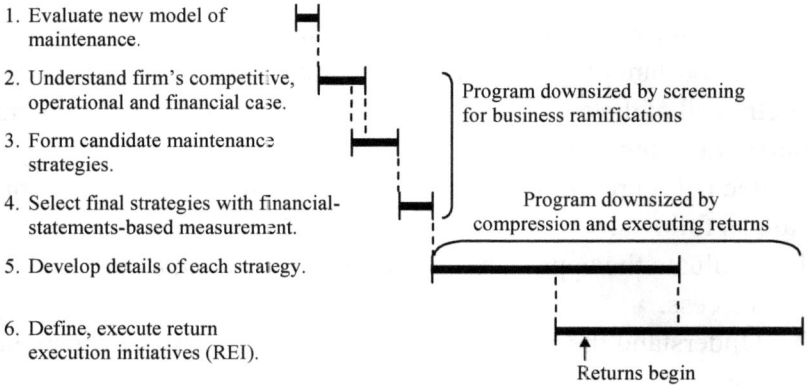

1. Evaluate new model of maintenance.

2. Understand firm's competitive, operational and financial case.

Program downsized by screening for business ramifications

3. Form candidate maintenance strategies.

4. Select final strategies with financial-statements-based measurement.

Program downsized by compression and executing returns

5. Develop details of each strategy.

6. Define, execute return execution initiatives (REI).

Returns begin

Figure 2-5: Stages of the new model maintenance program.

The stage will focus on the enterprise and its industry, how it competes and operates, and its financial statements. Rather than largely concerned with maintenance and reliability practices the current state of maintenance and reliability will be surveyed in this much larger context.

The stage ends with conducting returns sensitivity analysis. Based on the collective insight gained by the stage, its purpose is to quantify how and the extent that the firm's returns are sensitive to maintenance strategy.

Stage 3: Form candidate maintenance strategies. The stage draws upon the understandings, insights, findings, and returns sensitivity analysis of the previous stage. The meat of the stage is to form a set of maintenance strategies that will measurably increase the firm's business returns through its overall competitive strategies.

Strategies are first generated with a method called competitive mapping. Through it we map the firm's competitive makeup through to maintenance strategy as an extension or addition to the makeup. Consequently, we know the strategies we put on the table have a strong strategic fit with how the firm competes for returns above the industry's average.

Rather then stop here; we will search for maintenance strategies from a different vantage. It is to search in the context of the returns sensitivity analysis. As we muck around in the accounting details of the financials we will gain an increased sense of the firm as a whole. Doing so may jog us to think of possibilities that were not so apparent through competitive mapping. This is because in the process of sensitivity analysis a view of the numbers for a specific element may cause us to recognize a sensitivity for which maintenance can touch its nerve endings.

These tools will be used to brainstorm across the organization. In other words, they give the firm the opportunity to pull many people with different perspectives and sensitivities into the activity to determine the future of maintenance in the firm.

There is something else that takes place at this stage. It downsizes the program to only those things that fit the firm's competitive strategies. That all else drops out is in direct contrast with the historical programs to improve maintenance efficiency and equipment effectiveness. For them almost everything appears to be worth doing.

Stage 4: Select final strategies with financial-statements-based measurement. At this juncture the plant has in hand a list of maintenance strategies that fit the firm's business-level competitive and financial picture. However, coming into the stage they are considered only as candidate strategies. This is because the plant cannot yet safely assume that the strategic fit will also be financially significant. They must still be measured with respect to how businesses are judged; by their financial statements and returns.

Interface measures were introduced in the earlier section of the chapter that explained how the returns rather than maintenance strategies and their practices are executed. They are formed at this stage in order to measure the degree that each strategy will increase competitiveness as measured by returns. With them the stage will determine how much one or more returns would be moved by each strategy. In other words, the meat of the stage is to confirm that the needle on the return meters will actually move in an amount that matters.

Just as the previous stage, this stage will further downsize the pro-gram. The previous stage screened out those things that would not fit the firm's competitive strategies. This stage will, in turn, screen out those things that do not have financial significance even though they have competitive fit.

Stage 5: Develop the details of each strategy. The plant now has in hand its maintenance strategies. It will need to design them to some degree before actions to execute the returns they affect can begin.

The traditional view in project management is that the object of interest is fully designed and then executed. The view here is that something is designed until enough is known to begin the execution of returns.

For maintenance strategy the traditional view of design is not effective. It wrongly presumes that we can foresee everything that must be designed for; which we cannot. Trying to do so chews up time and energy which comes at hard-cash cost and lost time until first returns. At some point, design is most accurate if it is conducted in the process of reaching a return.

During the design stage, management and program leadership will watch for the break point when the program has come to know what it needs to know to begin executing returns. When the point is reached, the plant will shift from a program in the conduct of designing strategies to a program increasingly engaged in executing returns; the next stage.

This philosophy is the fourth level at which the program creates sharp focus, thus, further downsizing itself. It does so by compressing the design and execution stages. Along with compression it brings the first returns on line as soon as it is possible to tap into them. In effect, the design and the execution stages converge to become one stage; striving to reach specific increments of return.

Stage 6: Define and execute return execution initiatives (REI). As mentioned, at some point during the design stage the program shifts from design to executing REIs. "Executed" is defined as an ability that is fully functional and self-sustaining. The process of defining and executing REIs was explained by an earlier section.

Both the shift to execution from design and the definition of execution are important. Planning and design becomes doing, and doing becomes planning and design. An REI reveals and acts on what must be done, the obstacles that must be overcome, the full understanding of roles in the solution and many other things that cannot be fully known or fine tuned until we actually drive to the target returns.

Think of REIs as a list of relatively small, but important, initiatives for which a certain rule applies. Only several, if more than one, are taken on at a time by a team or consultant. As one is accomplished, another is pulled from the list. This allows the plant to execute returns surrounded by business as usual.

This approach creates a fifth and sixth level of focus as plant returns are increased incrementally in rank order. The fifth level of focus kicks in if management decides to cut off or place the program on hold in favor of other propositions to the plant with greater competitive significance than what remains on the list. In other words, the best propositions for competitiveness have been tapped.

The sixth level of focus is the case because maintenance strategies build up as their elements are increasingly pulled into operations by REIs. At cut-off or full execution some elements will no doubt be left untapped. The program has again downsized itself. It has essentially narrowed the original maintenance strategies by dropping elements.

Program deliverables, decisions and timeline

A program to make maintenance part of business success has only three deliverables. This is because from the start, the program is focused on the final deliverable; increased returns. The three deliverables are organizational knowledge, maintenance strategies and returns. Along the way to each deliverable, management will frequently make decisions for go/no-go, direction, and focus and downsizing.

Deliverable 1: Organizational knowledge. The first deliverable is the organization's acquired knowledge of how to build business returns through maintenance strategy.

The deliverable positions the firm to make its first decision. The decision is whether or not the means and methods of program can be expected to increase the firm's competitiveness. This is also a conclusion for whether or not maintenance is actually an important part of the firm's overall competitive possibilities.

The time to reach the deliverable may be days to several weeks. Time is a function of the range of presentations, as discussions, that must take place and when the firm's members are available to engage in them.

Deliverable 2: Maintenance strategies. The second deliverable is a set of maintenance strategies. They will be defined with respect to their ability to enhance or add to the firm's returns through its competitive strategies.

The strategies will have been drafted, screened and downsized by three stages of the program over four to eight weeks. The stages developed an understanding of the firm's competitive, operational and financial case, formed candidate maintenance strategies and evaluated them based on principles of financial-statements-based measurement.

With the delivered strategies, management will further confirm its conviction that the program will increase the firm's business-level competitiveness through its returns. Management will make a decision whether to continue, reshape or abandon the program. If the decision is to continue the program, management may make decisions that further shape and sharpen it.

Deliverable 3: Returns. The third deliverable is executed individual abilities that have begun to contribute incremental increases to profit, profit margin and return on investment and cash return on investment. In other words, the third deliverable is measurably increased returns.

There are intermediate points to the delivered returns. Detailed design of strategies will evolve until enough it known about the collective strategies to begin planning and executing the return execution initiatives (REI) that deliver returns.

Ultimately the program will boil down to executing returns through its REIs. Strategy design will continue within the process of executing returns. As a base of reference for timeline, if the strategies were fully designed before execution begins, up to two business quarters would be required. Transition from standalone design to REIs should take place well within that timeframe.

Management will make decisions for the scope and execution of REIs. As it does, management will frequently reconfirm that the program makes good business sense and redirect it if it drifts out of its power zone.

The timeline to completing all REIs will depend on several factors. One factor is how quickly the firm reaches a point in strategy detailed design that it can transition to executing returns through REIs. As mentioned, this is the point at which enough is known about the collective strategies that REIs can be planned and commenced.

A second factor is the plant's capacity to absorb REIs in the midst of all else that is going on. The philosophy of execution is to do a few REIs well in a short period of time. When one is done, it is replaced with next ranked REI on the list. Most REIs will be completed within 100 days; some within weeks or even days.

A third factor is management's decision at some point that enough is enough. At that point REIs will still contribute competitiveness. However, the resources engaged to execute them could contribute more to competitiveness through some other program. This decision essentially decides where the program ends or becomes a continuous improvement program or a to-do list.

Initiatives: the alternative to programs

The previous section summarized the stages and deliverables of a program linking maintenance through strategy to the firm's returns and cash flow. However, the reality is that few firms take on maintenance or other programs; except rarely. They are just too much. The more realistic expectation is that the firm will take on focused strategic initiatives for returns. This does not make the program approach less relevant. Instead, it provides a starting point to determine how to identify strategic initiatives for returns through maintenance and how to actually skin the cat.

There is a pattern for these initiatives. As the firm comes to understand maintenance as part of business success, discussions seems to reveal and give a name to a primary strategic thrust or concept. Through it, maintenance will be managed to increase the firm's competitiveness.

As the team puts meat on the strategy, competitive perspective will be mapped and woven into it either formally or informally. The financial models will be built to evaluate the strategy and reflect the operational nature of the enterprise as it responds in a unique way to the competitive challenges of its industry and markets. With it, all of the possible ramifications of the initiative will be defined as the interface measures in the model. They will be the link between the firm's financial statements and the strategic initiative.

From there the team will define what must be done with respect to all other facets of the reliability and maintenance functions and then accomplish it driven by the principle of executing returns. A primary component to reach the result is to define and build the structure of the budget and variance system aligned to the strategy. If not the first initiative, the system will be expanded or modified as necessary to encompass it.

The reliability and maintenance work management process, including planning and scheduling, will be subjected to surgical refitting. The use of the computerized maintenance management system will also be subjected to surgical reconfiguration.

Organizational development will also be subjected to surgical revision. The focus will be what it must be to sustain the returns of the strategy once reached.

The audit and control aspect of the strategy will be developed as an integral part of the initiative. If this is the first initiative for making maintenance business worthy, just as for the budget and variance system, it too must be designed and put in play for the first time; but largely limited to the initiative. As additional strategic initiatives are taken on, the audit and control system will be expanded or modified to absorb the needs of each.

In all cases, the readily available software and database tables making the strategy possible will be put into play. All firms have considerable off-the-shelf software and data available to automate the processes being built by the strategic initiative.

The point is that the program-oriented explanations will all be reflected in the strategy. However, they will be engaged in a unique sequence and configuration to reach an innovative result for business returns and cash flow.

Chapter 3
Strategy for Competitiveness and Returns

Maintenance reinvented to be part of business success is a complete shift in thinking and approach. Rather than improve maintenance efficiency and equipment effectiveness through highly replicable standard best practices, the purpose is to, instead, arrive at an outcome for cash, profit, profit margin and return on investment that the firm's rivals cannot easily and soon replicate. The trail for arriving at such a competitive advantage begins with forming a set of maintenance strategies that fit, enhance and add to the firm's business-level competitiveness.

This chapter will explain the "what, how-to and why" of arriving at competitive advantage through the possibilities of business strategy for maintenance. It will approach the explanation in two sections.

The first section will identify and explain several basic principles on which any firm forms strategy. The second will describe the approach that applies the principles to form the firm's unique set of business strategies for maintenance.

Principles of competitiveness

A set of principles are fundamental to arriving at competitive strategy. This section will introduce and explain them.

The principles of interest are as follows:
- Financial performance is competitive performance.
- Concurrent and next business cycle thinking.
- Cross-industry platform competitive strategy.
- Cross-industry five competitive forces.
- Strategy and competitive fit.

Chapter 3

Financial performance is competitive performance

Firms compete for profit, profit margin, return on investment (ROI) and cash return on investment (CROI). The winners realize returns above the average for all competitors in their industry. The losers fall below the average and suffer all of the trials and tribulations that come with it.

Behind these results of competitiveness are the results that move them. Accordingly, competitive strategy must recognize them and build strategies to affect them.

One underlying basis of performance for strategic focus is cash position and generation. This area of performance is subjected to great attention because cash is the blood of the business. A firm with high profits but no cash is out of business. A firm's sources and uses for cash is a primary basis on which it is judged and its outlook is assessed.

Other background measures to be affected by strategies are gross margin, direct and fixed expense, turnover or velocity, and current and capital assets. The ratios between line items in and across the income statement, balance sheet and cash statement are also an issue for competitive attention.

The firm's reward for doing well is that it is expected to do better yet. Therefore, growth in the primary measures is also an overarching competitive thrust of business strategy.

A purpose of a business enterprise is to create wealth for its owners. A measure for competitiveness that reflects the judgment of a firm's outlook for creating wealth is the P-E ratio (price per share divided by earnings, profit or income per share). The ratio reflects a collective judgment of the firm's ability to excel competitively as measured by its returns, financial reports and ratios.

As the firm's P-E ratio goes so goes its opportunities and threats for the future. For example, firms with a low P-E ratio compared to their industry are frequently devoured by others with a better ratio. Others are no longer around. Need we say more?

These matters do not just apply to publicly traded companies. All privately held firms must also pay homage. Competitiveness is judged one way or another always by the same or equivalent measures. In other words, there is always closure: a prize for success and penalties for lack of success.

The point is that designing successful strategies includes the principles and practices of financial measurement. In other words, all good strategy is set solidly in the principles of finance and accounting. Consequently, it is not surprising that the approach to strategy begins with getting our arms around the financials. Doing so is a primary step to revealing the firm's competitive strategies for maintenance.

Concurrent and next business cycle thinking

Successful firms concurrently think and take action with respect to two time frames: current and next business cycle. Most industries are subject to bust and boom cycles as shown in Figure 3-1: even the funeral business.

When the industry is in its down-cycle, rivals will compete to stay in the black. At the same time, the toughest rivals will also prepare to compete in the next cycle. During a down-cycle, the firm will prepare itself to shift gears and tap all profitability that is available to it when the business environment goes the other way. This may mean that during the down-cycle the rival must prepare to grab more profit than it had the capacity to do so in the last up-cycle.

When the up-cycle does begin, the firm's competitive focus will change to capturing it. As the cycle has flipped, the rival will also begin preparing its weapons for the next down cycle. Such a perspective is doubly important when the timing for shifts in cycles cannot be foreseen with much accuracy.

Figure 3-1 shows the ramifications. When the cycle turns up, without dual-cycle thinking the firm will lose a substantial portion of its opportunity for growth in profitability. This lost opportunity would often have done much to heal the wounds of the down cycle.

In some industries, there is another loss from not preparing for the up-cycle while struggling with the down-cycle. The competition amongst firms is to stay abreast of growth. The firm that does will end up with a greater, possibly permanent, market share. Lost market share may be permanent or only regained at a tremendous cost to profitability.

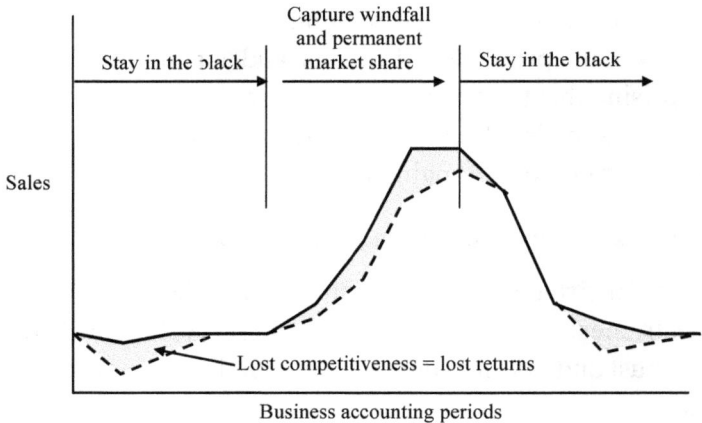

Figure 3-1: Strategy formed for the current and next cycle.

At the other end of the cycle, avoiding or shortening the devastation of the downturn has all sorts of ramifications. In some cases this may be the opportunity to gobble up the rivals most heavily hit by the down turn. This alone has all sorts of ramifications for returns. For example, the firm will be able to grow its market, thus, its business even though the market is not growing.

The importance for dual-cycle thinking is especially relevant to maintenance strategy. This is because the thinking behind the current-term decisions is often limited to the current cycle. For example, in good times it is hard to capture and motivate attention for building the firm's ability to manage the resource strategies that will drive maintenance expense. When the cycle flips, usually quickly, the firm is months away from being able to take its expense in hand and goes into the red for some time before returning to the diminished, but possible, black of the down cycle.

This is one of many reasons why the principle of business returns, as the measure of competitiveness, is fundamentally important to forming business strategy for maintenance. As strategy calls for spending cash and human energy with respect to the next cycle, the strategies have to be explicit and sharp. In other words, the ramifications for the returns of competitiveness must be clearly identified, understood and measured.

Platform competitive strategies

At a high level, competition within an industry tends to base itself on a platform strategy. Upon it each firm has a unique strategy set. Consequently, the total possible elements of competition within an industry are an almost infinite number of variations.

There is a widely held belief that the platform competitive strategy of each industry falls into three cases. The philosophy is that a firm must choose to compete as one of the three types. If the firm straddles the fence it will dilute its resources and not be able to reach and exceed the industry average returns.

The three platform competitive strategies are as follows:
- Cost leadership.
- Differentiation.
- Focused.

The distinction is useful for maintenance thinking. This is because maintenance practitioners tend to view their practices as if the cost leadership strategy is always the case. Reliability practitioners tend to view the world as if there is a perpetual market growth and, consequently, more capacity is always better. Recognizing the three strategy types causes us to step back and determine the true case and proceed accordingly.

Cost leadership. The nature of an industry in which cost leadership is the primary strategy is demonstrated by Figure 3-2. In such an industry price is essentially set by the high cost producer at the current level of demand. Plants are the stair steps. Those whose costs places them to the left of the demand line will receive profit to the degree their costs are lower than the high cost producer. To the right of the demand line, the plant may be shut down for "inventory control."

In such an industry firms have a range of strategies. The firm may concentrate on efficient-scale facilities, build their ability for availability performance, build the ability to optimize and sustain cost through tightly managing production and overhead cost, and many other possibilities.

Essentially, the thrust in a cost leadership driven industry is total cost per unit of product and revenues divided by total assets (turnover or velocity).

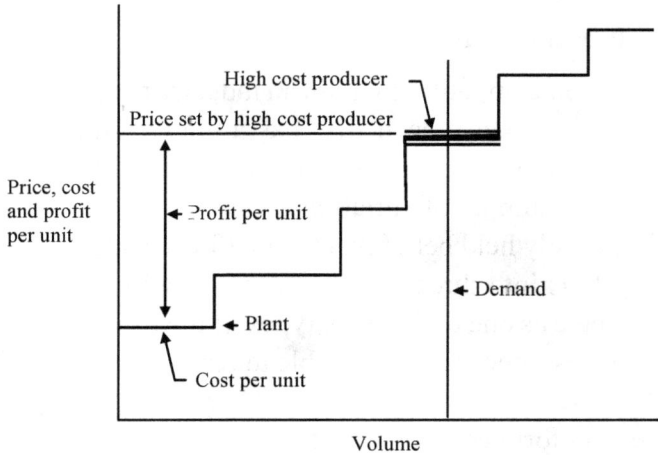

Figure 3-2: Cost leadership platform strategy.

The nature of competitive advantage can be seen in the payoff of cost leadership against the five competitive forces that will be the topic in the next section. The firm or plant will still make returns after their higher cost rivals have competed their profits down or away. Powerful buyers can only pressure the prices of the higher cost rivals. The firm will be in a better position to absorb the price increases of powerful suppliers. A firm's ability gained over time to sustain and improve its cost leadership will be a barrier to new entrants into the industry. Cost leadership also gives the firm a weapon to counter substitute offerings or better absorb their damage than its rivals.

Differentiation. Differentiation as a platform strategy is defined as the case for industries in which what is being offered by its individual rivals has important or significant characteristics such as service, quality, and features. Most telling is that the differences are considered by the buyers to be unique and important. Cost is not ignored. It is not the primary strategic focus.

Differentiation pays off differently than cost leadership. The demand for product and its impact on prices still affects the fortunes of the competitors. The difference in outcome is which competitors suffer the most as market demand falls. This is shown in Figure 3-3.

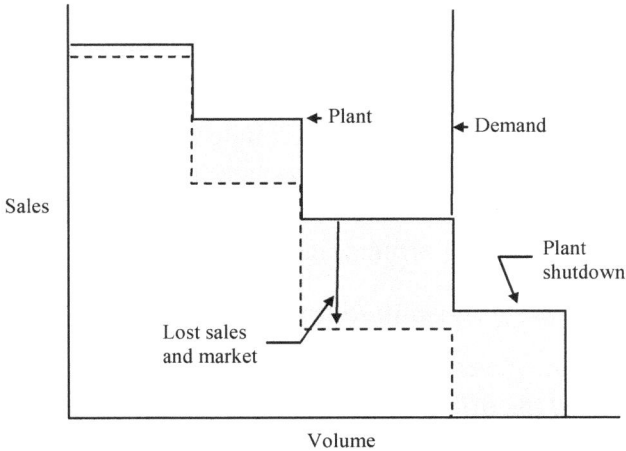

Figure 3-3: Differentiation platform strategy.

The relative market share of the rivals at current demand declines to different degrees. The most strongly differentiated rivals will experience much less loss of sales volumes than the weakest of the differentiated competitors. This will result in a much larger drop in market share. The difference may be so great that the firms with the least differentiation of importance will be forced to shut down their plants and remove capacity from the market until demand increases and pulls its production or service capacity back into the market.

The firm in an industry for which the platform strategy is differentiation will counter the previously mentioned five competitive forces in different ways then cost leadership. The firm is protected against rivals as customers are loyal due to the differences, thus, their market share and price is less sensitive to the economic cycle. The loyalty is also a barrier that new entrants must overcome. The firm, due to less price and demand sensitivity, will be better able to deal with the power of suppliers to raise prices. The ability to deal with suppliers carries over to be the ability to counter the power of buyers as they lack a comparable alternative product or service. For the same reason, the firm will be in a position to compete against substitute offerings.

Focus. The platform strategy of focus recognizes that in some cases neither cost leadership nor differentiation reigns supreme industry-wide. By comparison a firm may work both. There is still focus on one of the two competitive types.

The difference is that the firm will isolate market segments and compete with one or the other in each segment. The focus strategy may be built around the nature or relative magnitude of the five competitive forces. It may also be built around the characteristics within the forces.

Cross-industry five competitive forces

From one of the platform strategies, returns are decided by five competitive forces and the offensive and defensive strategies the firm takes in response to them. The combinations of platform, forces and response to them are almost infinite. Therefore, the chapter will not attempt to describe cases. Instead, it will identify the five competitive forces and their aspects. The purpose is to give the practitioner an ear with which to pick up the firm's competitive case, recognize how it is reflected in its operations and form maintenance-based strategies to deal with them.

In other words, the practitioner cannot guide a firm to business success with a tin ear to the competitive forces. When maintenance professionals interview to understand the firm they must have the antennas to pick up the forces in action.

The five competitive forces are a widely accepted framework that was developed by Michael Porter.[2] The forces cause us to recognize that competitiveness does not just take place amongst rivals, but is decided within a larger competitive environment. Accordingly, to understand the firm's competitive strategy and how the firm and its plants are the operational response to them; the practitioner must listen for the nature of the following competitive characteristics (Figure 3-4):

- Rivalry within the industry.
- New entrants into the industry.

---

[2] Porter, Michael E., *Competitive Strategy*. The Free Press, New York, NY. 1980

- Substitute products and services to the industry's offering.
- Power of buyers to pressure prices.
- Power of suppliers to pressure costs.

Rivalry among competitors. Rivalry is the competition amongst firms to gain an upper hand in the industry and, in turn, win returns that are about their industry's average. Competition is driven as the rivals feel pressure on their returns or see an opportunity to increase them. Each move by one rival usually has an effect on all others.

Rivalry will be greater to the degree that the following factors are the case in the industry:

	Power of buyers	
Threat of substitute products	Rivalry among industry competitors	Threat of new entrants
	Power of suppliers: labor, materials, services	

Figure 3-4: The five competitive forces confronting the firm.

- The number of rivals is great and none have dominance.
- Growth is limited, causing the rivals to fight for market share instead of focus their resources on staying abreast of growth along other dimensions of returns.
- Fixed cost is a large percent of price; causing the rivals to drag prices down as they do what ever they can to utilize excess capacity.
- Difficulty and cost of storing and holding various inventories is high; causing rivals to pressure prices as a means to move inventory off their balance sheets.
- There are limited barriers to grabbing market share from a rival because of switching cost and differentiation.
- Capacity increases are made in large increments causing the industry to experience the travails of chronic over capacity.
- Break-even point is high because large-scale capacity is characteristic of the industry.

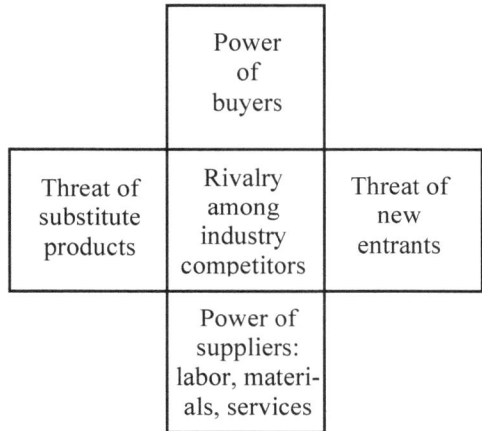

- Rivals are diverse such that rules of the game are never established.
- Some of the rivals have very high stakes in the industry.
- There are barriers for capacity to exit the industry giving rivals no choice but to stay and fight when the business cycle turns down.

Threat of new entrants. New entrants may be a considerable threat in some industries. They will bring new capacity, quest for market share and possibly considerable resources to make it happen. The result will be that prices may be driven down and cost increased; resulting in a price-cost squeeze on profit.

The threat is the greatest if the following is the case:

- Economies of scale are not table stakes of the industry.
- Product differentiation is limited such that the entrant will not have to invest considerably to overcome the buyers' resistance to switching.
- Need to invest heavily in productive capacity and other aspects such as front-end cost is not prohibitive or of a magnitude that would push up the entrant's overall cost of capital.
- Costs to buyers of switching are not significant, thus, not requiring the entrant to offer a considerable price advantage to overcome rivals.
- Distribution channels are open or not limited to the capacity they can receive from the industry.
- Cost advantages do not exist that cannot be easily replicated by entrants: proprietary technology and know-how, favorable access to raw materials, location, government supports, and learning and experience curves.
- Government policies do not present barriers to entrants.
- Retaliation is not expected as indicated by history, from firms with resources and commitment, and slow growth that would trigger retaliation by the current rivals.

Substitute products. In most industries, the firms are competing with industries that produce products that can or do substitute for the firm's offering. This places limits on prices. This is increasingly so the stronger the price-performance characteristics of the substitute offering. The limit on profit through price occurs across all business cycles.

Two cases are most threatening. First is if the price-performance relationship of the substitutes is improving with time. Second is if substitutes are offered by industries with high profits and profit margins.

Power of buyers. Buyers actually compete with an industry. They do so by forcing prices down or making it mandatory to deliver greater quality or service without offsetting price increases. Buyers can also play one rival off against another.

Their power in the subject industry is greatest if the following is the case:

- The buyer's business looms large in the firm's success; especially if the industry has a large fixed cost making it necessary for the firm to sustain high capacity utilization.
- The industry's product is a large part of the buyer's cost motivating the buyer to shop amongst rivals and substitute goods, and generally play hardball.
- The degree of differentiation is limited giving the buyer the position to exercise power over the rivals.
- The firm and its rivals have switching cost between buyers.
- The buyers' margins are tight and the firm's sales to them as a cost are a significant part of the buyer's total cost.
- Buyers could choose to produce the firm's product such that even the threat gives them power.
- The firm's product is not a significant factor in the quality of the buyer's product or offering.
- The buyer has a deep understanding of the firm's industry, demand, operation and cost.

Power of suppliers. Suppliers exert power with threats to raise prices or reduce the quality or service of their offerings. The power to do so is especially tough on firms that cannot pass the results of supplier power through to its buyers.

Suppliers have power to the extent that the following characteristics prevail:

- The number of suppliers is relatively concentrated; especially if there is a dominant leader able to influence price, quality and service across the supplier's industry.
- The supplier is not threatened with triggering a substitute good by exercising power.
- The industry or firm is not a significant part of the suppliers' business.
- The supplier's product is important to the firm's manufacturing process or quality; especially if the supply cannot be stored to offset the suppliers' power with a position in inventory.
- The suppliers' differentiation and switching cost is not of the magnitude to prevent playing the rival firm's off against each other.
- The supplier may be able to produce the firm's product and, thus, represents the threat of a new entrant.

Power of labor as supplier. The points made regard suppliers as a source of products, materials and services. However, labor is often a supply. Furthermore, labor often has great power within an industry or a region.

There are two measures of the power of labor. One is the degree of organization. The other is the degree that the types of labor can match the need for labor as it changes.

Strategy and competitive fit

What is competitiveness has already been defined, but bears repeating. It is the ability or advantage that allows a firm to win returns that are above its industry's average. The returns, as the ultimate measures of profitability are profit, profit margin, ROI and some measure of cash returns such cash return on investment (CROI). At this juncture we need to define strategy and competitive fit.

Strategy. Strategy is how the firm as a chain or network of operations or processes deals with the competitive forces that conspire to prevent them from receiving returns above the industry's average. A firm's strategies are actually a unique set of activities.

Firms and their value chain, including the plant, may seem to be similar. However, their set of strategic activities will always be unique. This is because their business goals, values, strengths and weaknesses, opportunities and threats, and social issues are a unique combination. The uniqueness drives them to choose or evolve to do activities differently and perform different activities.

Competitive fit. This brings us to competitive fit. The firm's unique set of activities must fit together to create competitiveness. Fit has three characteristics. First is which activities will be performed. Second is how the activities are configured. And third is how the activities relate to each other.

Competitive fit is, therefore, a system of entwined activities. They provide competitive advantage because they cannot be easily or rapidly imitated by competitors. If imitated they would actually prove to be toxic to the imitator.

The perspective of strategy as a unique set of activities is an important point of reference for how maintenance has been reinvented. The overall reinvention regards the critical and major disciplines of maintenance and reliability that were introduced by Chapter 2 as basic activities. Maintenance strategy is the result of determining how their elements should be molded to fit the firm's overall a competitive fit with respect to "which, how and relationship." Accordingly, they will be collectively transformed to a unique set of fitting activities.

Furthermore, the fit of maintenance and reliability elements of greatest importance is not to each other. It is the fit with their firm's business-level set of unique activities that matters most. Through the business-level fit, their fit with each other takes form.

Approach to form business strategy for maintenance

The previous section introduced a set of principles with which the practitioner can survey the firm's competitive situation and accordingly recognize why the firm's operations are what they are. This section will describe how the principles are applied in the approach to arrive at maintenance-based business strategies for the firm's competitiveness and the returns that come with competitiveness.

The approach begins with gathering insight, details and data with which the firm will form its strategies. In other words, the thrust is to understand and describe the firm as a competitive, operational and financial beast striving to realize returns that are better than its rivals. From there we will continue on to form, evaluate and design the firm's maintenance strategies.

The section will introduce the methods to form strategies by mapping. Mapping is done from two directions: competitiveness-operational and returns sensitivity.

Competitiveness-operational mapping will be demonstrated in this section. However, returns sensitivity analysis is explained in Chapter 5. This is because an important part of forming strategy is financial-statements-based analysis. The next three chapters will provide the practitioner with the knowledge and tools to do the financial work of forming maintenance-based strategy; including returns sensitivity analysis.

This section will describe how the stages and their parts come together as maintenance strategy for execution. The stages to reach a final set of maintenance strategies for execution are as follows:
1. Gather insight, details and data.
2. Map candidate strategies.
3. Select final strategies with financial-statements-based analysis.
4. Detail the strategies for execution.

Stage 1: Gather insight, details and data

The first stage is to gather insight, details and data. It is not a stepwise process as much as it is a single activity with three dimensions. The three dimensions of interest are explored or surveyed concurrently. However, for the purpose of explanation we will view them distinctively.

Shown in Figure 3-5, the three dimensions of interest to be surveyed are as follows:

- Firm's financial case.
- Firm's competitive case.
- Firm as a business operation.

Figure 3-5 shows that each aspect provides insight to the others. This goes so far that the strategy, once formed, may direct our attention back to our insights for further explora-tion; or cause us to better under-stand what we already know. The figure also suggests that the power of the firm's maintenance strategy depends upon how well we explore the firm as a competi-tive, operational and financial beast.

Figure 3-5: Three areas of insight, details and data.

It may be worthwhile to make a point about what we are doing and not doing in this stage. We are not evaluating the firm. We are surveying and understanding the firm. Based on the survey, we will ultimately generate maintenance strategies. In other words, we are not here to tell the managers how to run their business divisions and depart-ments. The rule of maintenance reinvented is to determine how to make maintenance a part of the firm's overall business success and make it a reality.

Survey the financial and accounting case. Accountants refer to the financials: AKA financial statements. The financials include the income statement, balance sheet and statement of cash flow.

The line items and accounts of the financials are the basis on which the firm computes its returns as measures of business success. Returns include, but are not limited to profit, profit margin and return on invest-ment. The firm may also track and publish some kind of return related to cash. This book will base its explanation on cash return on investment.

Firms also look at their financial position and strength with ratios. Ra-tios compare line items and accounts against each other. These may be within the same statement or between statements. An example within a statement would be ratios that reflect the firm's ability to cover its debts with cash. An example between statements may be revenues divided by assets.

Firms format and utilize the financial statements, returns and ratios in different ways. What they are, and why, must be understood by the surveying practitioner. This is because the answers are always powerful messages for forming maintenance strategy. They strengthen our understanding of "what matters" to the firm.

Accordingly, the strategist will engage the appropriate personnel in discussion of the financials. One purpose is to establish or confirm the definition of each line item and account. It is to also understand how and why the firm evaluates and responds to its financials, core measures and ratios as it does. The discussion will also cover the firm's current and foreseen financial positions and its expected competitive response to them.

More than merely "looking at the books," understanding the firm's financial details discovers how the firm thinks as it conducts its business. How it thinks says a great deal about what the firm's maintenance strategies must accomplish for the firm competitively.

Survey the business competitive case. The second dimension for survey is the firm's competitive case. This will pull into the survey the previously introduced principles of competitiveness: industry platform competitive strategies, five competitive forces, competitive fit and business cycle.

The strategist will establish with the firm's appropriate personnel which overarching platform strategy typifies the industry: cost leadership, differentiation or focus. Just as importantly the discussion will also define the nuances of the overarching platform strategy with respect to the firm and its industry.

Figures 3-2 and 3-3 depicted the general nature of cost leadership and differentiation. However, through the discussion, the depictions will be molded and refined to be an accurate picture of the firm's industry as we explore its drivers.

Also as part of the discussion of drivers, we will come to determine and understand which aspects of the five competitive forces (rivalry, entrants, substitutes, suppliers and buyers) are actually the case for the firm. Forming our exact depiction of the platform strategy pulls the forces into the discussion. As it does, the strategist will form a description of each force as it is exactly relevant to the firm. In turn, the strategist will learn how the firm deals with each aspect of the five competitive forces.

A business does not compete in a static environment. Over time there is change in the industry. Unfortunately, these are rarely easy to foresee in timing and exact nature.

Whatever the change is; change is also cyclical. These are normal cycles to the industry, but often each comes with something unique each time the cycle comes around. Consequently, the survey will gather an understanding of the basic business cycles and how the basis of competition changes in each. Meanwhile, the maintenance strategist will seek to spot the unique characteristics of the current and next business cycle.

This suggests a point of interest. Although a bit off beam, let's give it a quick "eyes right." As this book explains reinvented maintenance it becomes apparent that there is a new role for managing maintenance as part of business success in the firm. The role is to periodically conduct strategic planning for maintenance as the business and its environment change.

This is no different than what businesses do as a whole. However, in the past strategic planning for maintenance did not emerge because our field was limited ability-wise to improving maintenance efficiency and equipment effectiveness. Defining the role in the firm will be dealt with by the chapter on organizational development.

Survey the firm as a business operation. The third area of interest is the firm's operations at the corporate and plant levels. The purpose is to grasp how the business works.

In the past, the default strategy for maintenance has been to improve maintenance efficiency and equipment effectiveness. Consequently, the survey of operations has been largely limited to the plant's maintenance and reliability practices. Now that maintenance is reinvented to be a part of business successes the survey must regard the workings of the entire enterprise; including maintenance and reliability within it. The survey of operations must take this larger view because it recognizes that business and plant operations are a functional response to the firm's competitive and financial case.

Consequently, the strategist will isolate and explore all operations that fit two criteria. First, they are relevant to competitiveness and returns. Second, they would be touched either directly or indirectly by maintenance strategies. These determinations will be made by engaging appropriate personnel in putting boundaries around the operational scope of interest.

The survey will also seek out all relevant corporate and plant management information systems. Such systems are integral to how the business works. Just as important, they also generate data. The survey of the systems results in identifying what data is available to the ultimately designed maintenance strategies and how it can be made available to their processes.

Stage 2: Map candidate maintenance strategies

The first stage was to gather the information and perspective on which maintenance strategies will be defined, designed and ultimately executed through returns. The purpose of Stage 2 is to form, by mapping, a set of candidate maintenance strategies with the findings. They are candidates until tested for their direct significance to the firm's returns.

As maps, the steps of the stage are as follows:
1. Map maintenance strategies from competitive-operations.
2. Map maintenance strategies to returns sensitivity.
3. Map the final set of candidate maintenance strategies.

Figure 3-6 shows how we move through the steps to map strategy. There are two paths which work the firm's case along two dimensions. One is from the direction of competitiveness. The other is from the direction of how the firm's returns are sensitive to any type of strategy; including maintenance. Both lead us to maintenance strategy, but cause us to seek it out from two directions of business success.

Both trails are interrelated. If a strategy does not emerge along one of these trails it is obviously irrelevant to the firm. Ultimately, we harvest both maps and, in turn, form a unified set of maintenance strategies by mapping. Each strategy and its mapped substrategies are considered to be candidates until screened for financial significance by the next stage: financial-statements-based analysis.

Step 1: Map strategy from competitiveness. The first step is to map the firm's business competitiveness in a hierarchical framework.

The map is a powerful tool, so much so that all maps are confidential. This is unfortunate for the

Stage 1:
Gather insight, details and data

↓

Stage 2:
Map candidate maintenance strategies.

Map strategy from competitiveness	Map strategy to sensitivity
Map business competitiveness	Conduct returns sensitivity analysis
↓	↓
Extend map maintenance to strategy	Map strategy on sensitivity

↓

Form unified map of maintenance strategies

↓

Stage 3:
Select strategies with financial-statements-based analysis

↓

Stage 4:
Detail the strategies for execution.

Figure 3-6: Steps to map maintenance strategies for business success.

book. Even a representative map is still to some degree a representation of some firm's actual case. To provide an example that does not inadvertently violate confidentiality let's look to materials found in the public domain. That we must take this tactic is a testimonial to the power of maintenance when mapped for business success.

Figure 3-7 shows the beginning of Southwest Airline's competitive strategy as a map of operations in competitiveness. The figure shows that the map is comprised of statements of competitiveness that are operational in nature. Each block is a competitive-operational response to the surrounding platform strategy and five competitive forces in the industry.

The top box states a very distinctive, clear overarching competitive strategy for winning returns in excess of the industry's average. It is to be a low fare, convenient and high reliability air carrier.

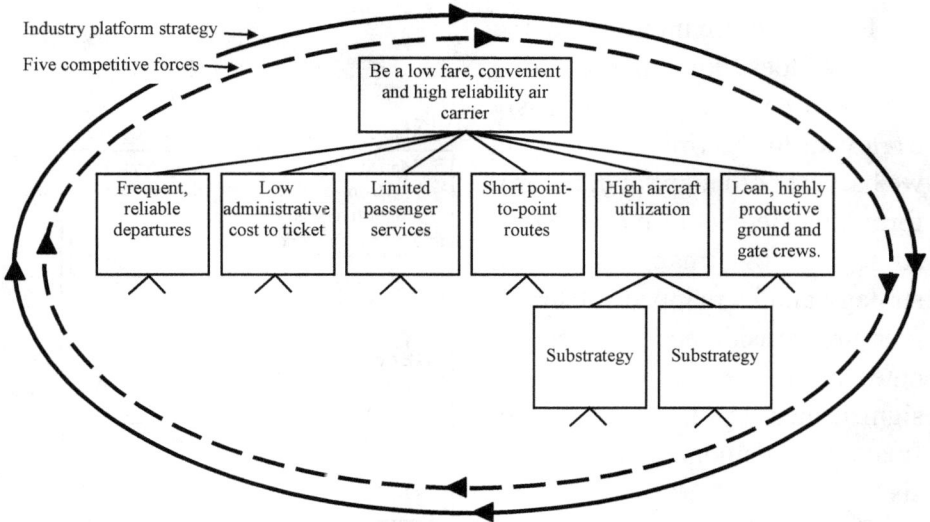

Figure 3-7: Example of a competitiveness map.

The second level of the map shows six sub-strategies. They are frequent, reliable departures, low administrative cost to ticket, limited passenger services, short point-to-point routes, high aircraft utilization, and lean, highly productive ground and gate crews. Notice that they have an operational nature as they state how Southwest Airline has chosen to compete.

The mapping process continues downward from each to its multiple levels of substrategies. Some paths will be longer and wider than others. At each level of mapping the practitioner must ask himself or the mapping team a simple set of questions. What role does maintenance have in the success of each location on the map? How would the role be operationally described? As answers emerge they are placed in the next level and then subjected to further downward mapping until each trail plays out.

Of several of the second level strategies in Figure 3-7, it is apparent that maintenance strategies have many roles in competitiveness. As these paths are extend, exactly what the roles are will take form as a unique operational statement of competitiveness. There will be surprises and new perspectives of maintenance as the roles emerge. For some of the strategies, practitioners will be surprised to find that maintenance has relevance that they have never before considered. When we change the way we look at things, the things we look at change.

The competitive operations map gives the firm an opportunity to think through the strategic relevance of maintenance for competitiveness and, therefore, business returns. The drafted map is used as a platform to engage firm personnel in the discussion by asking them to explore and validate it with the team that formed it. These individuals will include executives who are accountable for returns and middle and frontline managers, staff and trades who are responsible for delivering the returns of competitiveness.

The review, revision and confirmation process sets in place an important milestone for ultimately executing and sustaining the returns possible through maintenance. It is the platform from which personnel across the firm can confirm that the overall program for maintenance is working on the correct business goals. It also demonstrates that frontline managers and workers are not going to be deluged with a boatload of best practices that are only justified on general principle.

A case tells the story. A standard and major maintenance improvement program was underway in a leading chemicals firm. An executive was presented with the first draft. Excitedly, he made the comment, "This is the first time I have really understood why we are doing this." He then ordered his reports to brainstorm the map with its drafters.

That the executive made this comment with the force that he did revealed that the program was in trouble. To that point it was largely fueled by faith based on a belief system. However, until the details of the map were put on the wall it was on borrowed time. Before maintenance was reinvented to be part of business success it was normal for programs to unknowingly be in such a predicament. Their only hope was to outrun the posse: and they usually did not.

Step 2: Map strategy to returns sensitivity. What is described in this step is the subject of Chapter 5. Chapter 4 presents the principles of accounting and finance that underlie what is explained in that chapter. Therefore, we limit ourselves here to a summary view of the step. The goal is to establish a sense of the method although it is explained in depth by later chapters.

Returns sensitivity analysis converts the firm's financial statements to a business model of financial returns: profit, profit margin, return on investment and cash return on investment. The first stage has put the practitioner in a position to establish a list of firm-specific assumptions around which the model is made a what-if analysis tool for decision-making. For example, what if we could improve the ratio of material to product by some percent; how much would our returns change?

As the what-if assumptions are varied we can see the degree that returns will increase in response: sensitivity. In turn, we can trace through the line items and accounts of the financial statements to the pressure points where the firm would be sensitive to maintenance strategy; or any strategy for that matter. It falls to us to determine exactly what strategies would touch the nerve at the pressure points. "Standing" at the pressure point the strategies we think of are expressed in financial-operational terms.

Therefore, this step is somewhat similar to the first step. We are working our way down from the top; which is business success as measured by returns. At some level we naturally flow to the matter of how maintenance strategy can affect the outcome. And the "how" points to the "what."

Step 3: Map the set of candidate maintenance strategies. The previous steps have revealed two things. First, exactly how maintenance strategy would fit the firm's overall competitive ability to win returns greater than the industry's average. Second, how the firm's returns are sensitive to maintenance strategy.

In both cases, maintenance strategies are mapped to the competitive and returns cases. Just as important the emerging strategies are stated in operational terms; making them executable, measurable and manageable. It is becoming increasingly clear what must be done to make maintenance an important part of the firm's business success. Now we need to finish off the tackle.

This step extracts or harvests the details from both maps and brings them together. The goal is to reframe them as a system of core maintenance strategies and their substrategies.

We begin the process of extraction by inspecting the competitiveness and returns sensitivity maps to form an expression of what maintenance within the firm's overall business operations is to accomplish. In other words, what is the mission or overarching business purpose of maintenance? The airline's competitive strategy map (Figure 3-7) is an example. Its top box is a statement of business purpose or mission. In our case we are stating a mission which will drive and guide all maintenance strategies.

The statement should be inspiring, short and meaningful as it expresses the exact nature of maintenance that would make it an important player in the firm's business success. It should be of a nature that when ever it comes time to zig or zag; we would be caused to choose one over the other. Just as important, it is a statement that guides the day-to-day actions with respect to the firm's currently standing maintenance strategies.

The next step of the process is to map the firm's core maintenance strategies as they are related to the statement of purpose. This would be the equivalent to the second row of Figure 3-7. The core strategies will always be a short list.

A principle that begins with this level and applies to all others is that each core strategy must be mutually exclusive. Accordingly, we must inspect the boxes of each to confirm that two or more strategies are not tackling the same aspect or saying the same things differently. We may also find that one should be a substrategy to another.

One red flag for mutual exclusivity is if the number of core strategies is greater than five: the rule of fives. The rule says that when identifying strategies we will seldom exceed five and it is a red flag when we do. If we inspect Figure 3-7 we can see that the rule of five is exceeded. However, the strategies are mutually exclusive and the list is still short.

From there the core strategies are mapped downward to constituent substrategies. There will be multiple levels of substrategies. Substrategies will also be mutually exclusive between and across levels. As mentioned before, how we describe them operationally drives them to comply with the principle of mutual exclusivity. The better they are worded operationally to be aligned to the next higher strategy level, the more unique they will be and, thus, mutually exclusive.

As the map continues to expand downward we are essentially generating some of the details of each core strategy. This too is a reason that the wording at each junction in the map is important.

The skeletal hierarchy of a maintenance strategy map is shown in Figure 3-8. Unfortunately, for this book we cannot offer an example to inspection. As mentioned earlier, this is because the maps are the type of detail a firm would regard as confidential. Furthermore, the book does not offer a make-believe case because they would invariably be influenced by actual cases. This book will not run the risk of inadvertently revealing how a surmiseable firm has chosen to compete with its rivals.

It is noteworthy that the core strategies and substrategies are not of the ilk of improve availability performance, improve the work order process, increase proactive maintenance, achieve world class planning and scheduling, install a new computerized maintenance management system, etc. As the map progresses downward, these aspects

Figure 3-8: Hierarchy of the maintenance strategy map.

as disciplines will emerge. However, when they do they will be as elements taken from one of many management disciplines and not a set of practices. Accordingly, they will be expressed as operational substrategies and molded in the context of the higher-level strategy.

Just as the two maps that precede it, the maintenance strategy map is reviewed across the organization. The most effective approach is for an individual to draft a map as a starting point in then engage others in brainstorming. This continues until the map is no longer changing.

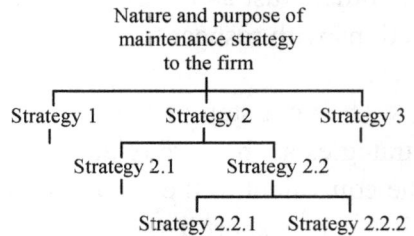

It is important that the people be engaged in mapping who that the firm must depend upon to advocate, execute and sustain the substrategies as part of their normal responsibilities. Consequently, the review, brainstorm and refinement process allows everyone to confirm that the program is still working on the right business challenge, is going about it in an effective way, and is coming up with the correct solution. One reason is that, by brainstorming, they joined in forming the strategies as solutions to making maintenance a part of business success.

At this juncture we have a set of business strategies for maintenance which fit the firm's overall competitive strategies. Up through the firm's competitiveness, the identified maintenance strategies will generate returns. As mentioned earlier, the next stage is to determine which of the strategies and their substrategies will actually move returns: their outcomes will not be lost in the rounding.

We earlier cast an eye to periodic maintenance strategic planning. What we are doing now is the first planning cycle. Furthermore, the set of three maps are the starting point to the next strategic planning cycle. Much further into the future the collective sets of maps will be an archive with which the planning team can both learn from and improve on the past. The full ramifications of the archive are fun to ponder. The fact that we can is a mark of having reinvented maintenance to take its rightful place in business success.

Stage 3: Select strategies with financial-statements-based analysis

At this point we have a detailed map of maintenance strategies which are directly aligned with making maintenance an operational part of the firm's business success. Going into this stage we consider them to be candidates rather than final.

The mapped strategies fit the firm competitively and financially. However, we cannot safely assume that they will significantly increase the firm's profits, profit margin, return on investment (ROI) or cash return on investment (CROI).

If they fit, but are insignificant to returns, we are just putting another log on the fire that must be attended to. For every green, wet log, the firm is precluded from adding one that is dead, dry and ready to burn.

Therefore, the stage is to evaluate the mapped strategies rigorously with respect to profit, profit margin, ROI and CROI. When we are finished, the map of maintenance strategies will have been pruned to those that both are a competitive and financial fit, and will also significantly increase returns.

We do this with financial analysis based on the firm's financial statements. Because of the detail of the strategies map, we can clearly tie each core strategy to returns.

We do this by converting accounting principles and financial statements to business and returns sensitivity analysis models. In fact, this has already been done as an action for determining how the firm's returns are sensitive to any strategy generally and to maintenance strategy specifically. Now we extend the models to evaluate each of the maintenance strategies we have generated by mapping.

The extension is what we call "interface measures" and a subject of Chapter 6. These are nonfinancial measures that rest between the financial statements and the maintenance strategies. In fact, they are a key piece to making it possible to increase business success through maintenance strategy. This is not only with respect to design, but applies to execution and day-to-day management.

Interface measures are designed by looking at each core strategy and its substrategies and then asking ourselves what relationships are affected by them. A simple is example of a relationship is trade days per equivalent job. Its denominator and numerator are nonfinancial. Consequently, we can easily measure both through the data normally collected in the firm's databases. Furthermore, we can subdivide the measure into categories.

At this point we should speak to a matter that may undermine the credibility of the previous paragraph if we do not. Few people understand the basic concepts of data and databases, how data gets into databases, how we get it out and what we can do with it. Consequently, maintenance practitioners walk past what can be done easily with modern technology.

This is doubly devastating because so much is done in the field of maintenance based on assumptions and beliefs that are not supported by facts that are easily obtainable. The problem is that practitioners do now seek facts if they do not know how to get them short of a big undertaking.

Building the sensitivity model and now the interface-driven models for evaluating and selecting the final core strategies and substrategies is a big subject; not to be confused with difficult. It rests upon the principles of finance and accounting. Consequently, the work of this and the previous step is covered by the next three chapters. The purpose here is to highlight the locations of financials-statements-based analysis within the process of forming maintenance strategy.

Stage 4: Detail the strategies for execution

The strategy map has formed core strategies and their multiple levels of substrategies. The financial-statements-based analysis has removed the tag of "candidate" as it has pruned the map to strategies that will increase the firm's competitiveness and returns. Strategies are also pruned if too difficult to be reasonable: would take a building of rocket-surgeons to design, execute and sustain.

The last stage of developing maintenance strategy is to form their final details. In this case, we will inspect the map and determine what details should be attached to the strategy with respect to functional details. For example, work scheduling will at some level may be molded within a substrategy. It will accordingly take on unique characteristics; i.e., exactly how available scheduling technology will be configured to control a particular aspect of productivity.

Another example may be a decision process. For example, the firm may have a strategy for a decision process to make failure-driven maintenances cost or production loss decisions to reflect the business impact on the current and next business cycle. There may also be a process to form tactics for a small accumulating inventory of such cases to be done in a manner that takes the least current-time hit on profitability.

The point is that these details would be designed by this step. Chapter 2 spoke to the need to downsize programs to be feasible. It pointed to the recognition that we cannot see every detail. Some will only become clear when we execute the returns of the strategies. Consequently, as we are engaged in detailed design we must be alert to spotting the point at which it is time to stop design and allow the remaining details to emerge as we execute returns.

Recall that Chapter 2 also introduced the principle of executing returns rather than strategies. The approach will be explained in depth by a later chapter. However, the reminder here is that the final details for the strategies will emerge as they are pulled along by triggering off explicit increments of returns.

Maintenance reinvented

Maintenance has been reinvented. This chapter is another strong demonstration that it has. Everything it presents and explains is about business success.

The chapter begins by tackling the problem of how businesses achieve success through their business strategy; not maintenance best practices. When the chapter evolves to speak of maintenance it is still a discussion of business success; not the discussion of best practices that is normal to the old version of maintenance.

As the chapter progresses, it becomes apparent that the best practices are not strategies. Furthermore, rather than applied in standard form, their elements are engaged selectively as they are molded to maintenance-based business strategies designed to enhance the firm's business success.

Ultimately the strategy development process of the chapter produces a set of business-stated maintenance strategies. They have the power to be part of the firm's business success because they fit the firm's competitiveness and will significantly increase its returns. Any strategies not meeting these criteria have been pruned out.

Before reinvention, the quest to increase returns was often questioned by practitioners. The belief was that maintenance efficiency and equipment effectiveness would be undermined. Maintenance reinvented does not treat these as conflicting goals for the simple reason that, if they are undermined when relevant, we have not succeeded at increasing the firm's business success as it is possible through maintenance.

Chapter 4
Finance and Accounting for Maintenance

We only have to experience recession to be reminded how important successful businesses are to societal well being. Furthermore, all businesses have a purpose that has some fundamental role in the well being of society; locally, regionally and globally.

Therefore, it is important to realize that the firms that most successfully fulfill their purpose from the societal perspective are the ones that compete for and win returns that are above the average in their industry. In fact, this may decide which rival firms within an industry will survive to fulfill their purpose. This highlights the absolute necessity of reinventing maintenance to be part of business success as measured by profit, profit margin, return on investment and cash return on investment.

Pinning maintenance to financial ramifications has two dimensions. The first dimension is to determine exactly which line items and accounts in the firm's financials will be affected by maintenance.

The second dimension is whether the magnitude of the effects will be significant with respect to returns. In business, many propositions meet the test of competitive fit, but many fewer survive the second test. This is why business strategies for maintenance formed and passing the competitive fit test are classified as candidates until they pass the second test. This and the next two chapters will deal with the test of financial feasibility.

Before reinvention, maintenance programs dealt poorly with the financial and accounting side of maintenance. Consequently, it is not surprising that our field was also weak in its regard for business competitiveness. As maintenance was reinvented to be a part of business success, the disciplines of competitive strategy and accounting-based financial analysis emerged as critical and were made a normal part of the field of maintenance and reliability.

The purpose of this chapter is to explain finance and accounting principles to a lay person. These are deep, complex subjects. However, the explanation does not need to be.

Accordingly, the chapter will provide the depth of explanation that will enable maintenance practitioners to take a place at the table in the serious on-going discussions and planning for winning the returns of competitiveness. Finance and accounting principles will be explained in the context of the ramifications of maintenance as part of business success. Stated another way, what we must know if we are to bring maintenance to increase the firm's returns rather than tax them.

The chapter will begin the process by introducing and defining the core principles of finance and accounting that every practitioner must know. It will subsequently introduce and explain the three core financial statements because the purpose of reinventing maintenance is to change them.

The next chapter will transform the financials statements to business and returns sensitivity analysis models. Through them the practitioner can trace and evaluate the consequences of any maintenance strategy. The subsequent chapter will explain how to rigorously evaluate the returns from specific strategies.

Principles and definitions

The principles and definitions for finance and accounting are wide and deep. However, for the purpose of dealing with maintenance reinvented to be a part of business success there are core principles and definitions to understand. This section will deal with some of them. Others will emerge later in this and the next two chapters.

The principles and definitions to be addressed in this section are as follows:

- Accrual basis of accounting and the matching principle of accounting.
- Models of accounting and related financials.

- Generally accepted accounting procedures.
- Cost and expense.
- Fixed and variable expense
- Cost of goods sold.

Accrual basis of accounting and matching principle

Businesses are measured by the accrual-basis of accounting. This is compared to cash-basis accounting.

However, neither the accrual or cash approaches can effectively measure all aspects of business success. This is true for managing maintenance expense. However, all types of basis of accounting converge on the same numbers; just with a different perspective, serving different purposes. Accordingly, all things and consequences roll up to the firm's accounting system and the system is accrual-basis. Furthermore, the accrual-basis system incorporates cash-basis accounting through one of its core financial statements: statement of cash flow.

The principle of accrual-basis is simple; especially when referenced against cash-basis. In accrual-basis accounting, all sales are recorded as revenue or sales when they are made as compared to when cash is received. For cash-basis the transaction would be classified as a sale when cash is received.

The other side of the coin is that all expenditures, as a cost or expense, are recorded when incurred. This is compared to recognizing them as such when cash is paid. Cash-basis accounting would record a cost or expense when a cash transaction actually takes place.

Hand in hand with accrual-basis accounting is the matching principle. The principle is that revenues must be matched to the costs that generated them. This is regardless of that time at which cash is paid or received.

This matching relationship can be somewhat messy because it is subjected to the individual firm's accounting policies or rules. Accordingly, costs that are very directly connected to the sold product, and others that are not, must somehow be related to the generated revenue. Consequently, we should never make assumptions about the linkage, but should seek out the firm's policies. As they say in journalism, "Think your mother loves you? Then check it out."

The absolute necessity of accrual-basis accounting is demonstrated by an actual case. An oil field supply firm always managed with cash-basis accounting. During the current boom cycle in oil exploration they were generating cash hand over fist and spending it like a drunken sailor on leave.

Some smart aleck accountant convinced the CEO to install an accrual-basis accounting system. When started up, they found that the firm was heavily in the red. It is no wonder we all hate accountants: they cause trouble.

Shortly afterwards the business collapsed from what could not be seen by cash-basis accounting: how well it was doing and what was its true financial position. Until the system, they were essentially managing according to their bank account. "How could we be out of money, we still have money?"

Model of accounting and related financials

Once upon a time there was a movie in which the young heron planned to become an accountant because, as she occasionally gushed, "Accrual-basis accounting is the greatest of all human inventions." It is ironic that engineers are so averse to accounting because, as the young lady had discovered, the accrual-basis system is an incredible mechanism.

The accounting model comprises three submodels. There is a financial statement associated with each submodel. The models and statements are as follows:
- Financial position model and balance sheet.
- Results of operation model and income statement.
- Change in financial position model and statement of cash flow.

Financial position model and balance sheet. A firm measures its financial position as Equation 4-1. By financial position we mean, at a point in time, what is our financial standing or condition.

$$\text{Assets} = \text{Liabilities} + \text{Equity} \qquad 4\text{-}1$$

The equation can be seen clearly in the structure of the firm's balance sheet. Its line items are subjected to all sorts of analysis which determine how ready the firm is to compete in the accounting periods to come. An example of the importance of the balance sheet is reflected in a commonly heard reference to the strength of the firm's balance sheet.

Firms compete with respect to the strength of the balance sheet. Ones with a strong position are literally a competitive threat to those in a weak position.

Results of operation model and income statement. At the end of each round, the balance sheet tells us whether the firm is hanging on the ropes or will able to get back in the ring ready to jab, move and work combinations. The "results of operation" model tells us how well the firm has done in the previous rounds.

The financial statement that paints the firm's picture of results is the income statement. The income statement is typically called the Statement of Operations. The model and statement are built on Equation 4-2.

Profit = (Revenue – Cost of goods) – Overhead expenses   4-2

Position, as the balance sheet, and results, as the income statement, are linked across the accounting model. Profit for the period is added to what is called retained earnings in the equity section of the balance sheet. The line item is essentially the total of all income ever made by the firm less every payment made to shareholders in the form of cash and dividends.

The statements are also linked through inventory and property, plant and equipment (PP&E). As inventory is removed when sales are made, the cost of the inventory is linked to sales. At the same time, the inventory accounts of the balance sheet will change.

Depreciation, depletion and amortization (DD&A) is an expense in the income statement. It reflects the using up of capital assets, whereas, the above case was the withdrawal of current assets. As there is DD&A expense in the income statement, the balance sheet account for PP&E will decrease.

Cash flow model and statement of cash flow. The previous submodels told us if the firm is winning on points. Cash flow and changes in cash position give us insight for whether the firm has the juice to go the full fifteen rounds.

The submodel is concerned with whether the firm has well utilized its cash and is ready to go forward in an aggressive, highly motivated manner. Is it generating cash from operations? Has it used well its generated cash in its investment and financing?

Accordingly, the submodel is represented by Equation 4-3. The associated financial statement is the Statements of Cash Flows. Both cash-in and cash-out of the equation include cash involved in operations, investments and financing.

$$\text{Cash flow} = OP + ARO + CFI + CFF \qquad \text{4-3}$$

Where: OP = Operating profit.

ARO = Adjustments to reconcile operations to cash.

CFI = Cash expended or recovered from investments.

CFF = Cash expended or received from financing activities.

The submodel through its statement has linkages to the income statement and balance sheet. The cash statement begins with operating profit and then backs out, or reconciles, the line items of income that did not entail cash. An example is DD&A.

The reconciliation also adjusts the cash from operations for changes in current assets such as inventory and accounts payable. This may be shown as a line item that refers to changes in working capital: current assets less current liabilities.

The CFI and CFF variables of the equation account for the cash activities that run parallel to operations. Respectively, they are the expenditures or proceeds for new or divested capital assets, and the payments and proceeds for borrowing.

The relationship in the statement of cash flow is demonstrated by Figure 4-1. The elements of the waterfall chart will vary by firm and period, but always interplay as shown. Whatever the combination, the net result is cash flow.

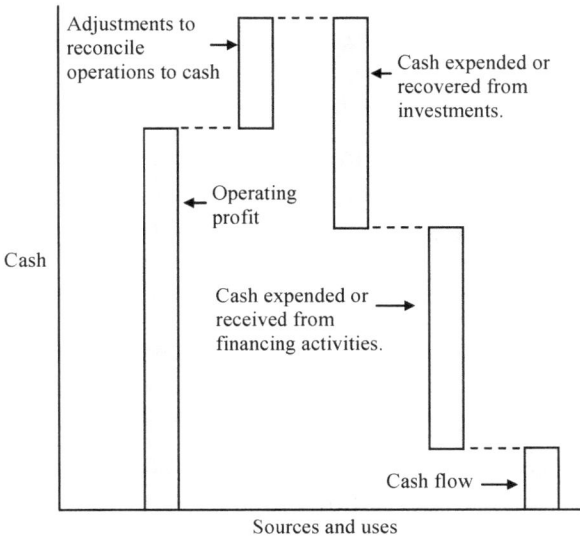

Figure 4-1: Schematic view of the statement of cash flow.

The final evident link between the balance sheet and cash statement is that the result for cash for the period, as cash flow, is added to the beginning balance of the current report period. It then becomes the cash account in the period's balance sheet.

Double-entry accounting

The internal mechanics of accrual-basis accounting works based on the mathematical concept of "double entry." This means that accounting entries or transactions are always subjected to the algebra of equality. Because of double entry it is difficult to create or destroy matter; to quote physics. The disasters we periodically see are more typically the result of finding a loophole allowing vague reporting rather than breaking the physics rule of matter.

This is especially apparent in the balance sheet. If an asset increases, liabilities or equity must also increase, thus, holding the books in balance.

It is also possible that there will be change in one of the three balance sheet sections that does not change the other two sections. In such a case, a line item change will be offset by the change of another within the same section. For example, the firm may buy materials with cash and place them in inventory. Within current assets the double entry would be to reduce cash and increase materials inventory. Each case is called a transaction.

We have all seen double entry in the form of the infamous "T" accounts that scare everyone; including engineers and many accountants. Each transaction is literally a small puzzle. General Bradley used to entertain himself by doing algebra problems. We could entertain ourselves with "T" account puzzles.

The confusion of double entry is doubly so because the inventory transaction and income recordation are actually made at different times: before and after closing the books on the accounting period.

There is an original set of double entries affecting at least two balance sheet accounts. Later in the monthly closing process there are additional double entries to convert many initial entries to their place on the income statement. For example, at this time the change of inventory level from transactions that add and subtract inventory becomes cost of goods sold in the income statement.

This complexity can be bridged for the sake of understanding and thinking finance and accounting in the context of forming and measuring maintenance strategies. The key is to think post-closing. For example, a maintenance expense can be considered as a double-entry outcome for affect to the balance sheet and income statement. This will, in fact, be how the topic is presented in this book.

The point of double entry is simple. The practitioner, in pondering the ramifications of a maintenance strategy, must think through its nature as a transaction with a double-entry cause and effect relationship across the financial statements. This is absolutely necessary because correctly computing business returns is based on correctly recognizing the impact of an action on the three financial statements and then upward to business returns. The book later provides models making this much easier than it sounds.

Generally accepted accounting principles

The system of generally accepted accounting principles (GAAP) is continually in the process of being refined to prevent vagueness and the creation and destruction of matter in managing, measuring and reporting business performance. GAAP ensures that all firms report their situation within a uniform set of standards that generally mean the same thing to all of us. Otherwise, there would be chaos in our economic world resulting in much less wealth and individual well being.

Having said this, GAAP allows firms a degree of discretion in its policies and the timing by which it recognizes revenues and expenses. This discretion also allows for the format of presentation. For example, a firm has the choice of combining and showing both period direct and indirect expenses as the cost of sales. Alternately, some direct expenses may be placed with indirect ones.

This suggests that the practitioner may need to reformat the financials to match the analytical, design and measurement of maintenance actions. This is because firms present their performance in formats that serve a different purpose; financial performance and position.

The reformat of the financials must also be consistent with GAAP; able to roll up and be consistent with the principles. Otherwise, the practitioner will not be able to link maintenance strategies and actions to the returns they affect.

Another point is that the analyst must make sure that he or she knows exactly what is covered in the firm's standard presentation. This will be done with the accounting department. That same discussion will provide the details the practitioner needs to reformat the financial statements. Recall that Chapter 3 speaks to this need as part of the first step to form business strategy for maintenance.

Cost and expense

How reference to cost is made amongst practitioners is too imprecise to be particularly helpful in thinking through the relationship of maintenance strategy to business returns. Sometimes we can even see sales lost due to availability performance referred to as a cost; or loss avoided with availability performance is some times presented as a savings.

A cost in accounting is an expenditure. It only becomes an expense when it is matched to the revenues it generates directly as cost of goods or indirectly as a period cost such as payroll. Recall that revenue is recognized as the time a sale is made. In other words, a cost in the purest sense is not an expense. A cost only later becomes an expense as it is matched to actual sales.

So where does the rest of the expenditure go if not an expense? Until a cost becomes an expense it is an asset. For example, an expenditure for materials that not yet matched to sales becomes an inventory asset. When the inventory is withdrawn by a sales transaction it becomes an expense.

Another example of the difference of cost and expense is property, plant and equipment. At the time of expenditure, the cost becomes a capital asset: property, plant and equipment. The cost becomes an expense as it appears in the income statement as depreciation, depletion and amortization.

Variable and fixed expense

Then there is the confusion of variable and fixed expense. It is almost funny. What is variable is fixed and what is fixed often varies.

The key is that what is categorized as variable and fixed expense does not refer to whether or not the expense charged each month is constant or varying. It refers to its driver and its relationship to the accounting period.

Variable expense is also called direct expense. It is the direct labor, materials and services engaged to produce the firm's product or services. Consequently, it will stay generally fixed with respect to each unit of product. Alternately, the expense will vary in the accounting period as sales volume varies. This is because it appears as cost of goods sold which will be explained later in the chapter.

A fixed expense is generally constant from period to period. It is, therefore, indirect with respect to the produced product. An example in manufacturing is maintenance. Yes, it varies somewhat from period to period. It may even vary as production level changes. However, each month spending is expensed in the period. By comparison, most direct costs pass through inventory.

What is variable and fixed expense is a matter of policy. However, for maintenance strategy the practitioner must make the distinction between direct production expense and maintenance as factory or manufacturing overhead. This is because maintenance-based business strategy affects returns differently through them.

Many of us are associated with firms whose policies do not typically include all direct costs as cost of goods sold. For example, oil refiners typically include direct operator payroll in fixed overhead expense.

Within maintenance, we can also isolate variable and fixed expense. Direct may be labor, materials and service of actual work. Other such as staffing or site service may be overhead.

Cost of goods sold

Then there is cost of goods sold (COGS). This is a powerful example of the difference between a cost and an expense. It is also the point at which we move our perspective from production thinking to income thinking.

Just as important it pushes us to look at plant availability performance in a different light. This could, in turn, cause us to define a different set of parameters for the subject plant's availability performance. Rather than maximum production and productive capacity, availability performance must be linked to the firm's opportunities to make sales and the profit margin of the sales.

In its purest sense, COGS is the direct expense associated with each unit of sold product. It is not the direct cost of the month's production. This would only be the case if production and sales matched.

Accordingly, COGS will either be based on a one-to-one relationship of a unit of product to its direct cost or by an inventory-based calculation. The inventory-based calculation is shown in Figure 4-2.

All new expenditures are added to the beginning balance. The balance at the end of the accounting period is subtracted and the difference is in

COGS. There are complexities to valuing the four components of the calculation; however, the concept is what is important at this juncture.

Calculation of cost of goods sold	
Period of May 20X1	
Beginning inventory: April 30, 20X1	$ 20,000
Add: Additions to inventory May 20X1	$100,000
Less: Ending inventory May 31, 20X1	$ 40,000
Cost of goods sold	$ 80,000

Figure 4-2: The basic flow of expenditures to cost of goods sold.

This pattern will apply to a chain of inventories such as materials, work in process and finished goods. The difference is what is added in the case of each. For example what is the cost of goods in the calculation may be the cost of materials to production flowing to the "add" line item of the work in progress inventory.

As mentioned earlier, firm's have leeway for how they record and recognize cost and expense. For example, it is conceivable that an indirect manufacturing expense could be included in the cost of goods sold. Likewise, it is conceivable that direct costs could be treated as overhead. For example in refining and chemicals, direct production labor may be treated as indirect manufacturing. The difference is that wages, rather than included in inventory balances, will be included as an expense of the period regardless of the match between units sold and produced.

This brings us back to a core point. The practitioner must determine with the accounting department exactly what is included in the various expense categories. In other words, locate all of the costs and establish when they become period expenses that will appear in the income statement. What is found may change how we look at the matter of business returns and, in turn, maintenance strategies.

Income statement

The purpose of the Statement of Operations, AKA income statement and profit-loss statement, is to measure how well the firm performed during the reporting period. For clarity this book will call it the income statement.

From the vantage of business strategy for maintenance, the income statement presents the pathways through which the firm's business returns can be improved. With it we can identify the top-level and underlying line items that are within the ability of maintenance strategy to affect. Once we have finish the search, the objective is to put pencil to paper to determine how and how much the southeast corner of the income statement can be improved through maintenance strategy.

We practitioners are tempted to limit our business thinking to this statement. However, maintenance-based business strategy has sweep across all of the financial statements. Accordingly, maintenance as reinvented is intent upon seeking them all. The exploration begins with the income statement because the results of operation flow to the balance sheet and statement of cash flow.

Simple view of the income statement

The concept of the income statement is very simple. Let's step over the pointy-headed explanation and go straight to the arithmetic.

Figure 4-3 shows a simple income statement. At the top are sales or revenues. Then there is the cost of goods sold (COGS). COGS is the direct cost of producing the sold product.

Direct cost of sales, as introduced earlier, is a variable expense. This is because, as sales vary in the short term, the direct cost of the sold product varies along with it in terms of units sold. In this way the expenditures incurred to initially produce the good are recognized by accrual-basis accounting as a period expense.

What COGS includes can vary from firm to firm. An earlier section explained the basic math of COGS as inventory is withdrawn and sold. However, the direct cost line can range much wider. Expenses not included in the cost of sales would be included in the fixed expense line farther down in the statement.

Income statement: Period of 20X1

Sales	$	1,000
Less: Cost of goods sold (direct cost).	$	600
Gross profit	$	400
Less:		
Fixed expense	$	150
Depreciation	$	60
Operating profit	$	190
Less:		
Interest	$	50
Taxes	$	70
Net profit	$	70
Profit margin		7.0%

Figure 4-3: Simple income statement.

Sales less COGS (direct cost) is gross profit. This is an important line. It tells the story about the profitability of sales. A product can have high sales volume and revenues but the associated variable cost may be such that the gross profit is small.

Below gross profit are the fixed expenses; AKA overhead or indirect expense. One line item is typically presented: sales, general and administrative (SG&A). What else is included is decided by the firm's accounting policies. Ideally the fixed expense section of the format would present maintenance expense as a line item amongst all other manufacturing fixed expense. If not, the practitioner will need to reformat fixed expense to make the distinction.

The expenses of the fixed expense section of the income statement tend to be fixed, approximately, in the short-term. Thus, it is called a fixed expense. As sales volume varies from period to period the expense continues to be reported. This is the case unless a change is made directly to the firm's business operation to change a fixed expense in a generally permanent manner.

This is an important distinction. As gross margin is increasingly narrow, how well the fixed expense is managed is increasingly germane to the bottom line and returns. We practitioners are widely engaged in industries with tight margins and a large maintenance expense. In fact, the relationship is a quick test for the importance and urgency of forming business strategy for maintenance and the degree of sophistication of those strategies.

Figure 4-4 shows the arithmetic of gross margin and fixed expense with respect to the ramifications of managing the fixed expense. For two extremes of margin we can see the difference for profit from a 10 percent reduction in maintenance expense. The same change in expense has three times the improvement in profit for the small margin case than for the large margin case. As fixed expense is a greater portion of the cost of operations, the percent change would ratchet up further.

| | Firm margin | |
	Large	Small
Sales	$ 100	$ 100
Direct cost: Cost of goods sold	$ 40	$ 60
Gross profit	$ 60	$ 40
Fixed expense including maintenance	$ 30	$ 30
Profit	$ 30	$ 10
Profit margin	30%	10%
Fixed expense reduced 10%	$ 27	$ 27
Profit after 10 percent reduction	$ 33	$ 13
Percent change for profit and profit margin	10%	30%

Figure 4-4: Relative significance of fixed cost to profit.

The simple income statement (Figure 4-3) includes depreciation also know as depreciation, depletion and amortization. The line item reflects the theoretical concept of converting a cost initially recorded as an asset, to an expense recognized in the period's operation.

Another line item of concern is interest expense. Whereas, depreciation is a measure of "using up" assets, interest reflects the use of capital to acquire assets and cover other needs. Because of the enterprise-wide nature of debt management, as part of the firm's overall debt and equity strategy, interest expense is often shown below the operating profit line.

Because maintenance can affect the asset base, maintenance strategy is an indirect driver affecting the firm's debt and equity strategy. Also as the cost of operations is improved by maintenance strategy, interest expense may be touched as less debt is required to support the same level of business performance.

Finally, the income statement will include a line item for tax. Taxation is a field in its own right with many complexities. To minimize the firm's tax bite, it is managed at the business-level rather than directly connected to any one operating strategy. Of course, maintenance strategy does have indirect ramifications through its affect on profit, and property, plant and equipment. However, the best approach to financial thinking in maintenance strategy is to limit the analysis of cause and effect to income before taxes.

Figure 4-3 shows two primary measures of competitiveness; profit and profit margin. Profit, AKA earnings or income, is a primary return. The income statement also distinguishes profit at multiple levels; the most obvious is bottom line or the southeast corner of the statement. At a higher level, profit may be presented as operating profit. Another distinction is profit "before interest and taxes."

The level of interest to the practitioner can vary. It is driven by the level of profit that maintenance-based business strategy can potentially affect. Ultimately, the firm's selected final maintenance strategies will decide the level of focus.

Profit margin is the second primary return on which firms are judged. Margin is profit divided by sales and presented as a percentage.

Profit should always be accompanied by profit margin to be meaningful information. The reason is demonstrated by the response of the news media each time the oil and gas exploration and production industry experiences its own boom cycle as all industries periodically do. When it does the news media whips itself into a populist fury over the profits and politicians call for windfall profit taxes.

However, it is a false picture. First, the basic monetary amounts involved are always greater than ever before due to normal inflation of the dollar and demand over time. Second, the E&P industry includes firms of extremely large size, thus, producing large numbers. And third, if profit margin were computed it would reveal that the industry is actually only experiencing profitability a bit above average for all industries. However, publishing profit as dollars without accompanying percent profit margin makes a much better news story.

Income statement at full complexity

Now that we have looked at the basic concept we can build and understand a more rigorous view of the income statement. As a starting point; Figure 4-5 shows contrasting formats appearing as annual reports to the SEC. There are several points to note.

One is that the formats from firm to firm are different. Some offer more information than others. When we search for some details it is obvious we would have to go to the accounting department to get them.

Case A: Statement of Income	20XX	Case B: Statement of Income	20XX
Operating revenues	$ 110,000	Net sales	$ 97,000
Cost and expenses		Cost of goods sold	$ 69,000
Cost of sales	$ 100,000	Gross profit	$ 28,000
Plant operating expenses.	$ 5,000	Selling, general and administrative expense:	$ 18,000
Selling expenses	$ 500	Research and development costs	$ 5,500
General and administrative expens	$ 650	Profit from continuing operations	$ 4,500
Depreciation and amortization.	$ 1,300	Interest expense	$ 1,400
Total costs and expenses	$ 107,450	Provision for income taxes	$ 950
Operating income	$ 2,550	Net income	$ 2,150
Interest and debt expense	$ 420		
Income from operations	$ 2,130		
Income tax expense	$ 560		
Net income	$ 1,570		

Figure 4-5: Two formats for the income statement appearing in public.

The detail of Case B gives us little with respect to pure COGS and, instead combines everything as the cost of sales. The only common distinction among the fixed expense of the two statements is sales, general and administrative expense. In one case, DD&A is not shown as a line.

Compare this to Figure 4-6; the text book ideal. In this format we can see very explicitly what the case is.

Statement of income: "Text book"	20X2		Schedule of cost of goods sold	20X2
Sales	$ 210,000		Direct materials	
Cost of goods sold (see schedule of cost)	$ 107,500		Inventory: Dec 31, 20X1	$ 11,000
Gross profit	$ 102,500		Purchased direct materials	$ 73,000
Sales, general and administrative expense	$ 80,000		Direct materials available to production	$ 84,000
Operating profit before interest and taxes	$ 22,500		Inventory: Dec 31, 20X2	$ 8,000
Interest expense	$ 3,400		Direct materials used in production	$ 76,000
Income tax expense	$ 4,300		Direct labor	$ 18,000
Net income	$ 14,800		Factory overhead	
			Indirect labor	$ 4,000
			Supplies	$ 1,000
			Heat, light and power	$ 1,500
			Depreciation	$ 4,000
			Factory overhead	$ 10,500
			Manufacturing cost period 20X2	$ 104,500
			Work in process at Dec 31, 20X1	$ 6,000
			Period total manufacturing cost	$ 110,500
			Work in process at Dec 31, 20X2	$ 7,000
			Cost of goods manufactured	$ 103,500
			Finished goods at Dec 31, 20X1	$ 22,000
			Cost of goods available at Dec 20X2	$ 125,500
			Finished goods at Dec 31, 20X2	$ 18,000
			Cost of goods sold	$ 107,500

Figure 4-6: The "Text book" income statement.

This brings to the surface an essential step in developing maintenance strategy. We must develop "working purpose" financials that provide the details with which we can effectively design and manage maintenance strategy in the subject firm.

The previous chapter spoke of reformatting the financials. The actual and text book income statements of both figures demonstrate why. In that spirit Figure 4-7 is the text book case reformatted to better suit the needs to develop, measure and manage maintenance strategies.

Notice that the statement has been reformatted in the simple structure of Figure 4-3. Also shown is the detail of calculating the cost of goods sold. The method will be revisited in the discussion of the balance sheet.

It is noteworthy that the format of Figure 4-7 would not include direct labor in some industries and firms in the cost of goods sold. Oil refining and petrochemicals are examples. Instead, direct labor is most typically recognized under factory overhead.

Statement of income: "Reformatted"	20X2	Schedule of cost of goods sold	20X2
Sales	$ 210,000	Direct materials	
Cost of goods sold (see schedule of cost)	$ 97,000	Inventory: Dec 31, 20X1	$ 11,000
Gross profit	$113,000	Purchased direct materials	$ 73,000
Factory overhead		Direct materials available to productio	$ 84,000
Maintenance labor	$ 3,000	Inventory: Dec 31, 20X2	$ 8,000
Indirect labor	$ 1,000	Direct materials used in production	$ 76,000
Supplies: maintenance	$ 750	Direct labor	$ 18,000
Supplies: indirect	$ 250	Manufacturing cost period 20X2	$ 94,000
Heat, light and power	$ 1,500	Work in process at Dec 31, 20X1	$ 6,000
Depreciation	$ 4,000	Period total manufacturing cost	$100,000
Sales, general and administrative expense	$ 80,000	Work in process at Dec 31, 20X2	$ 7,000
Operating profit before interest and taxes	$ 22,500	Cost of goods manufactured	$ 93,000
Interest expense	$ 3,400	Finished goods at Dec 31, 20X1	$ 22,000
Net income before income tax	$ 19,100	Cost of goods available at Dec 20X2	$115,000
		Finished goods at Dec 31, 20X2	$ 18,000
		Cost of goods sold	$ 97,000

Figure 4-7: The ideal income statement for supporting maintenance strategy as part of business success.

Strategy by line item

The previous chapter described the process to survey the firm and its overall operations as a competitive beast. The objective is to determine which strategies will sustain, advance or create competitiveness.

A step in that process is to reformat the firm's available accounting information such that strategy development for maintenance can isolate the line items within its sphere of influence. With the transparency the practitioner can describe very specifically how maintenance and reliability actions can move each line item. At this step every part of maintenance strategy will be tied explicitly to business returns. It follows that we can then identify what we must do to put pencil to paper and quantify the significance of each element of strategy to returns.

The cause and effect relationships of maintenance-based business strategy to the income statement will be unique to each firm. The possibilities and their uniqueness are so great that it is not feasible to identify and explain them. However, we can point to the line items for which maintenance strategy will be relevant and the generic ways that it will. However, in an actual setting there are surely many possibilities that a book's author cannot imagine.

The line items in the income statement of Figure 4-7 for which there are so many possible are as follows:

- Sales volume and price.
- Cost of goods sold.
- Maintenance expense.
- Depreciation and interest expenses.

Sales volume and price. As mentioned earlier, what is produced is not what is sold. Production as a cost goes to inventory that later appears in the income statement as cost of goods sold when the product is sold. Therefore, the issue for the sales line is to determine the nature of production performance correlated to the challenge of having the appropriate inventory level to respond to sales.

The seemingly obvious purpose of maintenance strategy is to produce more and, thus, punch up the sales line. However, this is not a good assumption. Instead, we must ask ourselves what the firm must be able to do through its productive capacity or how we should actually measure maintenance capacity with respect to the sales line.

The point is that how the utilization of productive capacity ties to sales is a unique competitive case for each firm. It will also very likely reflect competitive issues tied to inventory control and other aspects across the firm's operations. The maintenance strategies developed for the firm must be consciously aligned to exactly what that is.

Maintenance strategy may also speak to the average price realized over the accounting period. The strategy may reflect the ability of the plant to survive or recover from short-period, full-capacity sprints when there is a disruption of supply. If this were American football we would call it the take-away, give-away ratio. Strategy affecting price may also reflect matters of sustained quality levels. There are always possibilities.

Cost of goods sold. Maintenance strategy presents a wide range of possibilities for returns. For some firms, profitability of sales may be a target rich environment for business performance. Therefore, the search for breakthrough maintenance strategy will be directed at the COGS line item; rather than just sales volume. The most fundamental area of interest is the ratio of direct labor and materials to unit of product.

Too often practitioners attempt to excite management with the prospect of improving productive capacity through availability performance. However, when availability performance is already high and gross margin is tight; the greatest opportunities for availability-driven strategies may be the cost of goods sold line.

Maintenance expense. This is an important line item because it is persistent to the firm's bottom line and cash case. Cost improvement through the ratio of COGS is only maximally beneficial as there is a market for product, thus, capacity utilization. However, an optimized fixed expense is reflected in all business cycles; only the magnitude of the affect changes. How true this statement is for each firm is a function of its gross profit margin and the percentage that maintenance expense is of gross profit.

A chosen business strategy may reduce the maintenance expense to its optimal with respect to the firm's business plan for the year. Alternately, the decision may be to limit its growth to inflation rather than allow its drivers to creep. In both cases, the affect is to prevent the cost of maintenance from offsetting gains the firm works hard to achieve elsewhere across its business operation.

The possible list for improving the maintenance expense is long and its items are unique to the firm's case. However, the opportunities have categories. One is maintenance strategies that apply reliability techniques to reduce the annual workload and materials and parts to maintain the plant and its facilities. Another case is strategies that design work management to get the year's work done at higher productivity.

Depreciation and interest expense. Maintenance strategy will eventually roll up to affect the firm's DD&A and interest expense. The most direct cause would be if the firm is successful at improving the productive capacity of the existing production system.

Over time such outcomes may cause the firm to reduce the rate at which it invests to add capacity and the incremental size of each addition.

As it does the plant and equipment asset base will not grow as rapidly and, in turn, constrain the growth of the DD&A expense. This may also decrease the debt overhanging the firm.

The chapter on competitiveness defined one competitive issue as the incremental size that capacity is added in the industry. The issues driving DD&A and interest expenses are tied to incremental increases.

However, this also reveals another issue for the sales line. The ability to add capacity short of major capital investment can be a factor in the pricing that underlies sales. This is because the firm's expansion will not cause it to drive down prices in its own market. This can happen as the firm is forced to utilize the new capacity it has brought into the market; creating an oversupply case.

We could point to hundreds of strategic ramifications for maintenance through the line items of the income statement. This is equally so for the two other financial statements. The point is that maintenance, as reinvented, surveys the firm and seeks them out. Otherwise, we have to ask ourselves if programs to improve maintenance are justified vis-à-vis the other opportunities the firm has to improve its returns.

Balance sheet

The balance sheet, also known as the statement of financial position, reports the firm's current position. Is it hanging on the ropes or ready for the next round? Does it have the energy to sustain its attack throughout the next and subsequent rounds?

Before it was reinvented, our field has had little regard for the balance sheet. However, the fact is that maintenance strategy has wide ranging implications for the balance sheet. Furthermore, the balance sheet is reflected heavily in return on investment and cash return on investment.

Simple balance sheet

Figure 4-8 provides a view of a balance sheet. It is a real-world case with the unusual and minutia removed. Notice that assets and liabilities are subdivided by current and long-term. The distinction for what is "current" is that assets will be expended largely within the next accounting period and liabilities are expected to roll over in the same period.

As a point of reference consider the purpose of a financial audit. It is to confirm that assets and equity are not overstated and liabilities are not understated. We could easily say that the purpose of business strategy for maintenance is to increase equity as worth (assets minus liabilities) as it reduces the balances of assets and liabilities needed to sustain the firm's competitiveness.

The balance sheet has two "double-entry" relationships with the income and cash flow statements. Recall that an earlier section distinguished that we could simplify our perspective by looking at transactions as single stage; bridging statements.

One such relationship is that between inventories and COGS. The inventory balance reflects the rate that productive capacity has made product available for sales and product is withdrawn from inventory as sales occur. The relationship will be explored in greater depth later in this section.

It is noteworthy that we can see at this point of double-entry-type thinking why more is often not be better with respect to plant availability performance. As actual availability performance overshoots marketable capacity, the inventories grow and reduce return on investment and cash return on investment. In such a setting a practitioner who dwells on the wonderment of availability engineering and management may be speaking to the hand.

The second interconnection is property, plant and equipment. The linkages are how the book value of production assets is reduced by recognition of "using up" production assets as depreciation and depletion. As DD&A is recognized in the income statement, the net balance for assets declines in the balance sheet.

The third interconnection is financing. The debt incurred around short and long-term assets will generate interest expense. As interest payment is due, it becomes an expense on one side and cash reduction or a payable on the other side.

Consolidated statement of financial position

	As of December 31	
	20X2	20X1
ASSETS		
CURRENT ASSETS		
Cash and cash equivalents	$ 2,145	$ 2,947
Receivables, net	$ 1,716	$ 1,939
Inventories, net	$ 948	$ 943
Other current assets	$ 195	$ 224
Total current assets	$ 5,004	$ 6,053
Properly, plant and equipment, net	$ 1,551	$ 1,811
Goodwill	$ 896	$ 1,657
Other long-term assets	$ 1,728	$ 4,138
TOTAL ASSETS	$ 9,179	$ 13,659
LIABILITIES AND SHAREHOLDERS' EQUITY		
CURRENT LIABILITIES		
Accounts payable and other current liabilities	$ 3,267	$ 3,794
Shorl-term borrowings and current porlion at long-term debt	$ 51	$ 308
Accrued income and other taxes	$ 144	$ 344
Total current liabilities	$ 3,462	$ 4,446
Long-term debt, net at current portion	$ 1,252	$ 1,289
Pension and other postretiremenlliabilities	$ 2,382	$ 3,444
Other long-term liabilities	$ 1,122	$ 1,451
Total liabilities	$ 8,218	$ 10,630
SHAREHOLDERS' EQUITY		
Common stock.	$ 978	$ 978
Additional paid in capital	$ 901	$ 889
Retained earnings	$ 5,879	$ 6,474
Accumulated other comprehensive (loss) income	$ (749)	$ 452
	$ 7,009	$ 8,793
Treasury stock, at cost	$ (6,048)	$ (5,764)
Tolal shareholders' equity	$ 961	$ 3,029
TOTAL LIABILITIES AND SHAREHOLDERS' EQUITY	$ 9,179	$ 13,659

Figure 4-8: Simple balance sheet.

The fourth double-entry-type interconnection is retained earnings The definition of retained earnings is all income incurred since start up minus dividends and payments made to owners. Consequently, the maintenance strategies that improve the income statement will be reflected here.

A firm's net worth is assets less liabilities. Therefore, strategies that increase the performance reported by the income statement also increase stockholder wealth. As maintenance strategies reduce the firm's assets and liabilities relative to the reported performance, worth will increase through the increase of retained earnings; if not paid out in dividends or used to reacquire the firm's stock. This worth will be rewarded by the stock market as the P-E ratio increases: creating wealth for the stockholders and lower weighted cost of capital available to the firm.

Strength of the balance sheet

Firms are always concerned with the strength of their balance sheet. But what does that mean? It follows that maintenance strategy should inspect the drivers of strength for opportunities to increase competitiveness. This is especially so since the strength of the balance sheet says a great deal about the firm's opportunities to grow its business.

The strength of the balance sheet is measured by three relationships within the balance sheet and a fourth between the balance sheet and income statement.

They are as follows:
- Current ratio.
- Cash-to-debt ratio.
- Debt-to-equity ratio.
- Working capital to sales and operating profit.

Current ratio. The current ratio measures short-term liquidity. It is simply current assets divided by current liabilities. It tells those who judge the firm how well it could cover its current liabilities with its current assets.

A ratio of less than one means that a firm cannot pay its bills. A ratio over one means the company can. However, if too high the firm may be tying up cash that could be used for other purposes; such as paying down debt, making new investment or buying back the firm's stock. As this is rectified the firm's return on investment and cash return on investment increase.

This makes a point for analyzing the financial ramifications of maintenance strategy. The strategist should assume that the gains will not be allowed to languish as excess current assets. This is reflected in the returns sensitivity analysis that will be explained in the next chapter.

As a standalone number, the current reading may not mean much. What is happening with the current ratio over several accounting periods may be the greater point of interest.

Cash-to-debt ratio. Investors like to see companies funded by a large degree of cash generated through operations rather than a high percentage of debt in the capital structure. The cash-to-debt ratio is determined by adding cash and short-term investments, and dividing the result by total short and long-term debt.

Debt-to-equity ratio. The debt-to-equity ratio measures the amount of long-term debt financing relative to equity in a firm's capital structure. It is measured by dividing long-term debt by stockholder equity. A firm will have a target debt-to-equity ratio, but the degree of leverage varies significantly across industries.

Some debt can be good, but it also a business risk. As debt to equity is greater the firm will experience much greater returns in a boom cycle. However, there is considerable risk going the other way. A principle of judo is to use the opponent's momentum to slam him to the mat. This is what happens to a high-ratio firm when the business cycle flips from boom to bust.

Is this relevant to maintenance strategy? It may be if maintenance expense is a large part of manufacturing overhead and in a tight gross margin enterprise. Constraining a fixed expense at its optimal would cushion the "slam."

Working capital to sales and operating profit. Working capital is current assets less current liabilities. The working capital to sales ratio and working capital to operating profit ratio measure the balance sheet relative to the firm's performance.

The ratios reflect how much current assets and liabilities the firm engages to produce sales and operating profit. As such it places a primary aspect of strength, working capital, in the context of the profitability it generates. In other words, is the firm doing more with less?

It is likely that there are strategic possibilities for maintenance to affect working capital. For example, as strategies are built to manage the various costs of maintenance, the cash required to run the business should be reduced. When a strategy is formed, it will be tested for many ramifications; including this one.

Note one mathematical aspect of computing the ratio. The income statement presents performance over a period of time. Consequently, current assets and current liabilities are computed as the average of the year's beginning and ending balances.

These and other ratios can be used to evaluate the balance sheet and the other financial statements. By doing so the practitioner may find that there are key relationships that require special focus given the firm's circumstances.

A tool that may be used is the Dunn and Bradstreet ratios for industries. With it the practitioner can check for ratios that are stronger or weaker than the average. Once discovered, the practitioner should inspect for the possibilities or need for maintenance strategies relative to the findings. This once again highlights the definition of competitiveness which is for the firm to win returns in excess of the average of its industry.

Inventories and cost of goods sold

The explanation of the income statement pointed to cost of goods sold (COGS) as the outcome of the sequence of cost to asset to expense. Inventory, as an asset, is the way station between cost and expense. In manufacturing, it is actually a set of production inventories: materials, work in progress and finished goods.

It is important that we understand the structure of inventories. Equation 4-4 is the basic equation for all inventories. It is used in the calculation of the cost of labor and materials in the cost of goods produced. The formula reflects the flow of cost to asset to expense.

$$RI = AI + BI - EI \qquad\qquad 4\text{-}4$$

Where: BI = Beginning inventory.

AI = Added inventory.

RI = Removed inventory.

EI = Ending inventory

This relationship is significant to maintenance strategy for several reasons. One is that we can view the match between the utilized capacity and sales. For the maintenance practitioner this is an important window into business returns because the match can be potentially influenced by maintenance strategy.

Through the window we can evaluate and confirm that maintenance strategy to sustain plant productive performance is effective and also matches the nature of the market demand, and service and quality levels. The relationship will also test and confirm the success of maintenance strategy if one of its targets is the ratio of product to the direct cost to produce it. There are many possibilities that will be found in actual practice.

For the practitioner, the focus is not the dollars. It is the drivers behind the dollar amounts of the inventory. More specifically, for which of the drivers could maintenance strategy make a difference to inventory level.

To see the case, Figure 4-9 is a schematic view of Equation 4-4. The figure shows the pathways along which the development of maintenance strategy will seek out opportunities to improve competitiveness. There are at least two important relationships along the paths or flow of cost.

First is the ratio of materials and direct labor flowing into the work in process and finished goods inventories. Along the path are the relationships the practitioner can evaluate for opportunities to improve gross profit and, therefore, operating income.

Second is the relationship around which maintenance strategy can be developed to improve the match between sales and the utilization of productive capacity. There are questions to be asked as we seek strategy. Are the maintenance strategies in force proving to be effective? Are they correctly focused on the nature of market demand and associated quality and service levels?

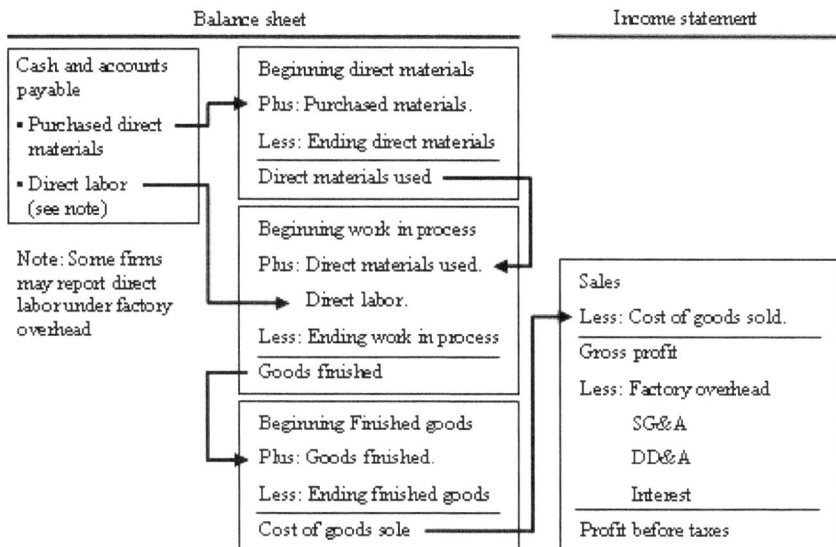

Figure 4-9: Flow of cost to inventory asset to expense.

The matter of capacity utilization is often treated by measuring and increasing the percent of time that the plant can perform at specified level of production: availability performance. However, the section suggests that the measure is simplistic and does not tell the story. We have to get into the details of competitiveness and returns to determine what matters and define availability performance accordingly.

What matters will have a great deal to do with strategies we may seek to optimize the related production inventories. Although not a manufacturing case, we all know of one that highlights the importance of inventory strategy as it is possible through maintenance.

WalMart realizes a small profit margin: only around 3 percent. Consequently, a great part of their business strategy is pinned on logistics and what is on the shelf. This is because to do so greatly reduces retail goods inventories on the books. This, in turn, increases the ratio of sales over total assets. The result is greater than one. The ratio time profit margin results in a business return on investment greater than 3 percent.

Chapter 4

Formatting the balance sheet for strategy

The ramifications of maintenance strategy are threaded throughout the typical balance sheet shown in Figure 4-8. However, the stitching is hidden. To overcome that, the balance sheet can be reformatted to analyze and then manage the ramifications of maintenance strategy to the balance sheet.

Reformatting the income statement meant that we had to move line items to different locations in the statement. We also had to break the line items apart into their subitems.

Reformatting the balance sheet requires that we gather the backup details to several of its accounts. Once done it is relatively straight forward to identify which accounts could be affected by maintenance strategy and then estimate to what degree they can be moved.

Because of this, it will be possible to see how the balance sheet will changed by the strategy. This is important because the firm's return on investment and cash return on investment would be increased by the resulting strategy.

What distinctions in subaccounts we are interested in will be decided by what we are looking for. Some maintenance strategies will have the effect of reducing the cash needed to be held. Consequently, the model balance sheet should isolate which portion of the cash and near-cash balance is affected by maintenance strategy and, in turn, estimate the impact.

Inventories are another set of accounts that will require expansion. We are not just interested in maintenance inventory. In fact, the significance of strategies that reduce maintenance inventory's often too small to be of interest. When it is the case it would most often appear as a substrategy or detail of a higher level, more consequential strategy.

The bigger question is whether maintenance strategy could somehow reduce the plants' largest inventories. For example, the certainty of productive capacity in critical circumstances may reduce the need to carry as large an inventory of materials, work in progress or finished products. Accordingly, reformatting the balance sheet will subdivide the inventories to the categories and levels to which maintenance strategy can be linked to changing them.

The alter ego to cash and inventories in the balance sheet is accounts payable. Will the firm carry a lower accounts payable balance if various maintenance strategies were put in place? Just as for cash and inventories, the balance sheet will be reformatted to reflect which portion of total accounts payable is reasonably apt to be affected by maintenance strategy.

Property, plant and equipment (PP&E) and its alter-ego, long-term debt is the next primary area for reformatting the balance sheet. Maintenance strategy may have a longer-term affect on the PP&E balance in the balance sheet. Accordingly, reformatting will be for the purpose of extending the details by categories of assets. When done, the analyst will be able to estimate the magnitude of change with time as the result of maintenance strategies.

Furthermore, the result will roll over to the income statement as DD&A expense and, possibly increased sales. Accordingly, as PP&E is categorized as necessary to estimate cause and effect of strategy, the accrued DD&A of the balance sheet will likely also be subdivided.

Long-term debt is the alter-ego to PP&E, just as accounts payable is to cash and inventories. However, debt is not always one-to-one with individual investment decisions. Debt overall reflects financial planning strategy to cover the firm's overall capital needs. Accordingly, the balance sheet may be reformatted to show assumptions for the indirect, but impacting relationship of maintenance strategy to PP&E.

Statement of cash flow

Old Daddy used to say that business is easy, "It is how much you flip out and how much you get back in." He was spot-on because cash flow is a critical indicator of a firm's ability to compete for returns. Without it an enterprise dies. A firm can have excellent returns, but be in a life threatening cash position.

The financial statement that tells the story is the "Statement of Cash Flow." Through it managers and shareholders answer some of their most burning questions. Is the business generating enough cash? What are the sources of generated cash? How is cash being used?

Cash generation or cash flow is the difference of all cash flowing in during an accounting period and all that flows out. As cash is generated from operations the firm will retain the ability to stay in business. Lack of cash, decreasing cash or over consumption of cash foretells problems. Another view is that the industry rivals with the strongest overall cash position will have a competitive upper hand on those that do not. The difference may result in the weak being devoured by the strong.

The point is clear for us practitioners. Business strategy for maintenance must explore the firm's cash case and place stress on cash management just as it does for other more obvious outcomes.

Statement of cash flow and its principles

Firms are required to report four things: where its cash came from, where it went, what was its cash flow and what is the cash balance? Cash balance is the interface between the cash statement and balance sheet. Figure 4-10 is an actual statement of cash flow.

Three things are immediately apparent. First is that the statement answers the three questions. Second is that the presentation of cash flow begins with profit and then reconciles profit to cash flow from operations. Third is that the statement goes on to identify how cash flow was affected by acquiring capital assets and the capital tapped into with which to acquire the assets.

This brings us back to a point made much earlier on. Profit in the income statement is not the same things as the cash sent to the bank. Consequently, the first section of the cash statement reconciles profit to cash. The outcome of each reconciliation line on the statement is added or subtracted from income or loss.

The starting point for the consequences of maintenance strategy is profit; the cornerstone of cash flow. From there the ramifications of maintenance strategy will be reflected in the reconciliation line items for current assets and liabilities. This effect will be seen in cash, production and maintenance inventories, DD&A and accounts receivable and payable. As the balances for cash, inventories and accounts receivable and payable move up and down; they either liberate or absorb cash.

Consolidated Statements of cash flows

	Year ended December 31		
	20X3	20X2	20X1
Cash flows from operating activities:			
Net income (loss)	$ (1,131)	$ 5,234	$ 5,463
Adjustments to reconcile net income to net cash provided by operating activities			
Depreciation and amortization expense	$ 1,476	$ 1,376	$ 1,155
Goodwill impairment loss	$ 4,069	$ -	$ -
Gain on sale of plant	$ (305)	$ -	$ -
Noncash interest expense and other income, net	$ (76)	$ (10)	$ 31
Stock-based compensation expense	$ 59	$ 100	$ 108
Deferred income tax expense (benefit)	$ 675	$ (131)	$ 290
Changes in current assets and current liabilities	$ (1,630)	$ (469)	$ (144)
Changes in deferred charges and credits and other operating activities, net	$ (145)	$ (15)	$ (263)
Net cash provided by operating activities	$ 2,992	$ 6,085	$ 6,640
Cash flows from investing activities:			
Capital expenditures	$ (2,790)	$ (2,260)	$ (3,187)
Deferred turnaround and catalyst costs	$ (408)	$ (518)	$ (569)
Proceeds from sale of refinery	$ 463	$ -	$ -
Contingent payments in connection with acquisitions	$ (25)	$ (75)	$ (101)
Proceeds from minor dispositions of property, plant and equipment	$ 25	$ 63	$ 64
Minor acquisitions	$ (144)	$ -	$ -
Other investing activities, net	$ (7)	$ (11)	$ (32)
Net cash used in investing activities	$ (2,886)	$ (2,801)	$ (3,825)
Cash flows from financing activities:			
Non-bank debt:	$ (374)	$ 1,782	$ (249)
Bank credit agreements:	$ -	$ -	$ -
Termination of interest rate swaps	$ -	$ -	$ (54)
Purchase of common stock for treasury	$ (540)	$ (4,300)	$ (2,020)
Issuance of common stock in connection with employee benefit plans	$ 16	$ 159	$ 122
Common and preferred stock dividends	$ (299)	$ (271)	$ (184)
Other financing activities	$ (4)	$ (24)	$ (9)
Net cash used in financing activities	$ (1,201)	$ (2,654)	$ (2,394)
Net increase in cash and cash equivalents	$ (1,095)	$ 630	$ 421
Cash and temporary cash investments at beginning of year	$ 1,487	$ 857	$ 436
Cash and temporary cash investments at end of year	$ 392	$ 1,487	$ 857

Figure 4-10: Example of the statements of cash flows.

This suggests that maintenance strategy will wish to reformat the cash statement to distinguish the cash flow that is related to maintenance expense in the accounting period. The practitioner will also expand the detail of current assets and liabilities: cash, maintenance inventories, and accounts receivable and payable. With the cash flow statement we can see, thus, plan and evaluate maintenance activities on cash flow.

The point here is that maintenance strategies must be formed and designed for something beyond profit, profit margin and return on investment. They must also be designed with an eye to increasing the firm's foundation cash position. In some plants and business cycles, a plant's cost structure may be such that the ability to manage maintenance cost may be the difference between experiencing negative or positive cash flow.

The second section of the statement shows how cash position has been affected by capitalized investments and costs in the business. This may include large overhauls or turnarounds if they are capitalized rather than expensed in the period they occur. The linkage of maintenance-based business strategy is obvious. Will it slow down the cash over time that will need to be invested to stay abreast of market growth? The ability to do so gives the firm strategic flexibility with respect to making the best use of its cash position.

As a point of clarification notice the gains made from the sale of a plant. Do not confuse this with the purpose of the investment section. When shown in the first section of the statement it is an accounting reconciliation to profit. The reported gain was a book rather than cash gain. Accordingly, it is backed out of profit because it did not entail cash. The cash portion of the divestiture is shown in the investment section of the cash flow statement. As maintenance strategy increases an asset's disposal value, both will be affected.

The third section of the cash statement reflects the firm's financing activities. These activities reflect the debt and equity needs of the firm. Ramifications of maintenance-based business strategy can also be traced to this section. This would be the case as overall debt and equity needs are reduced because of improved cash flow from operations and reduced investments in PP&E needed to stay abreast of market demand. The determination of cash flow ramifications of maintenance strategy must be made in light of the firm's financial management philosophies. This is compared making the determination as a one-to-one relationship to the investment in property, plant and equipment.

The result of the three sections of the cash statement is shown its southeast corner. We can see clearly the cash flow of each year and the change. The bottom line for the maintenance practitioner is how we are going to change that through business strategy for maintenance.

This chapter has explained three core financial statements. Because maintenance has been reinvested to make it an important part of business success, the practitioner must understand how business success is measured. In other words, we must understand the components parts of business success as we would a pump in the plant. If we cannot isolate and view them as a mechanism we cannot change them through maintenance strategy.

The next two chapters will build on this one. The next will explain how the details structured as components of business success by the financial statements, are put to use to form strategy and subsequently manage maintenance with the result of increasing the firm's returns. The final chapter of the two will explain how to execute the returns of strategy-driven maintenance management.

Chapter 5
Returns Sensitivity Analysis for Maintenance

The previous chapter focused on the accounting statements and principles by which all firms are judged and accordingly rewarded or penalized. Consequently, they are the structure upon which we must ultimately form business strategies that make maintenance a part of business success.

Chapter 2 explained the six stages a firm will pass through to fulfill the mission to bring maintenance to be part of business success. This chapter will introduce and explain the analysis of returns that takes place in the second stage.

The work of the second stage is to survey and understand how the firm does business as a competitive, operational and financial beast. As part of that purpose it is necessary to measure the sensitivity of the firm's returns to maintenance-based business strategy.

There is a second level of financial analysis that will take place in a later stage of the mission. It measures and confirms the returns to be expected from specific maintenance strategies that will be determined and defined during the third stage. These strategies have competitive fit, but the financial returns analysis will confirm that they have a significant impact on returns. The details of the second level analysis will also continue on to be part of executing, managing and controlling the ultimately selected strategies.

We can say this in a different way. The returns sensitivity analysis in the second stage will have clarified where the firm's returns are sensitive to business strategies for maintenance. The second level of financial analysis will evaluate the individual strategies that are later formed to tap into the quantified sensitivity. Chapter 6 describes the second level.

This progression is a fundamental departure from the historical maintenance programs to improve maintenance efficiency and equipment effectiveness. First, financial analysis is conducted to determine where there should be an action rather than justify a predefined set of best practices. Second, rather than advocate for best practices, we instead determine and design maintenance-based business strategies associated with the particular ways the firm's returns are sensitive.

This chapter will be devoted to returns sensitivity analysis. The next chapter will explain how to analyze the returns from the candidate maintenance strategies.

Business financial models

We must design, measure, execute, manage and control all maintenance strategies to move the financial statements. This is for the simple reason that they measure the firm's success and competitive position.

To guide us to that goal, we can convert the financial statements to business models. With them we can quantify and analyze business returns to be had from maintenance strategies. In a nutshell they map the "math" a layperson in accounting would follow to evaluate almost any business proposition.

There are two business models of interest to us. They are the return on investment (ROI) model and cash return on investment (CROI) model. This section will explain them.

Through the models, practitioners will trace the financial cause and effect of any maintenance strategy. Ultimately, the firm will also use them to spot, form and design, execute, and manage and control its maintenance-based business strategies. This will go so far down into the weeds that the models will likely be engaged to make choices for whether or not to approve some types of unusually impactful maintenance work requests as they arise. Furthermore, in these cases the model will be engaged to determine tactics for execution that will minimize the negative ramifications that these cases represent to short-term profit and cash flow.

The business models are a powerful tool because every component is easily and readily available from the firm's standard financial statements.

The practicality of the models as a tool is highlighted by the fact that the numbers for every element can be gathered one-to-one from the annual reports that are available by law to the public. The business models take on their greatest power as the statements are coupled with how the firm competes and operates as a business.

Return on investment model

The ROI model is shown in Figure 5-1. The first time I saw the model I was thinking like a pointy-head and missed the whole point. Cancel the boxes of the model and we have income divided by assets: hey I'm a genius, what's the big deal?

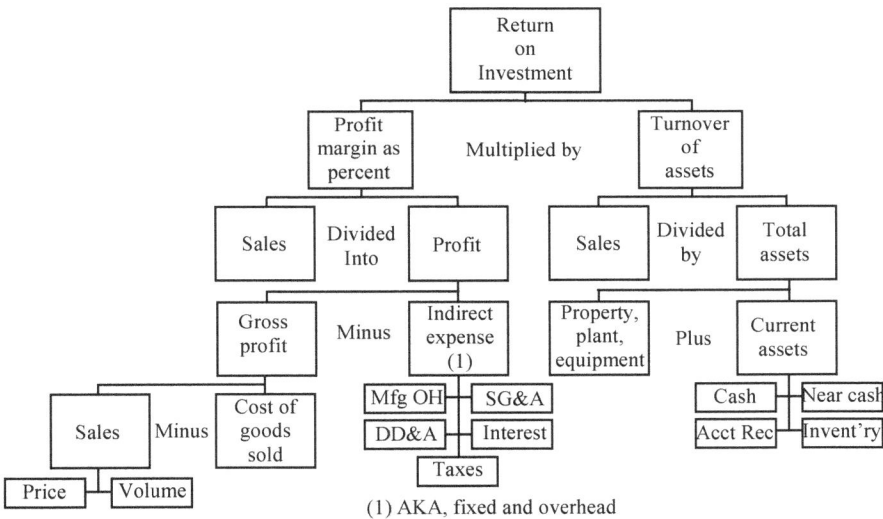

Figure 5-1: Return on investment model.

The power of the ROI model is that it makes transparent the chain of financial cause and effect for any business strategy. For one thing it links the interplay between the income statement and balance sheet. By doing so it allows the firm to confirm that a strategy for returns represents a maximum result. This is compared to maximizing the income statement or balance sheet, but suboptimizing the firm's overall profitability.

With ROI as the return at its pinnacle, the model ensures that maintenance strategy will have the maximum impact on profitability. Below ROI in the model are all other financial measures of business success and competitiveness. Through profit, the model measures how maintenance strategy will affect the size of the business. Through profit margin the model measures how maintenance strategy will affect the profitability of the firm's profit. Through turnover the model reveals how maintenance strategies will affect how well the firm uses its resources to achieve both.

As mentioned, the two sides of the model represent the income statement and balance sheet respectively. As they are, the model shows how the line items of the income statement and accounts of the balance sheet roll up to returns. Notice that the boxes of the model match one-to-one with the universal financial statements that were presented in the previous chapter.

The power and necessity of the model for forming maintenance strategy is readily apparent. It gives the firm the ability to answer fundamental questions. How can maintenance strategy generally and specifically change the boxes of the model? For each possibility, how much will the needle on the return meters move?

As the previous chapter described the three standard financial statements, it identified the generic, high-level ways that maintenance strategy can potentially affect the line items and accounts of the statements. When a firm's specific, unique cases are recognized they are applied to the boxes of the model. We are then able to clearly see how they will rollup to change the firm's returns.

This visibility is important because most strategies will simultaneously affect both sides of the model. It follows that we will be able to fully quantify how each case would increase returns.

For the income statement side of the model, a single maintenance strategy for business success can affect price, sales volume, cost of goods sold, manufacturing overhead, DD&A, SG&A, interest and taxes. On the balance sheet side, a maintenance strategy can concurrently affect actual and near cash, inventory, and property, plant and equipment.

This virtually 100 percent coverage highlights the ramifications of the mission to find the place of maintenance in the firm's business success. Unfortunately, the coverage has gone untapped. This is because programs with the mission to improve maintenance efficiency and equipment effectiveness tap into very little of that coverage.

The ROI model reflects the balance sheet; but only assets. It does not reflect the liabilities and equities sections of the balance sheet. This can be changed by structuring the right side of the model as assets less liabilities; which is actually equity. The result would be a return on equity (ROE) model.

The cash return on investment model will pick up the ramifications of maintenance strategy for liabilities. The ramifications of maintenance strategy for equity are picked up through profit as it becomes retained earnings in the equity section of the balance sheet. However, in matters of maintenance strategy we are not so much interested in ROE. This is because ROE reflects decisions concerning the mix and sources of debt and equity capital. These decisions take place separate to the issues in business that maintenance strategies can affect.

Cash return on investment model

Figure 5-2 shows the cash return on investment (CROI) model. It parallels the ROI model. However, it models what the ROI model does not; cash flow. Accordingly, the left side of the model is structured to reflect the cash flow statement of the firm's financials rather than its income statement.

The CROI model is important because it measures how well the firm is utilizing its cash to compete. For example, a firm may be generating a great deal of cash. Consequently, the cash margin is good. However, if the cash is not being applied to other purposes, the asset side will grow and drive down the turnover of assets and, thus, CROI.

Notice that the model ties together the income statement, statements of cash flow and balance sheet. If we wanted an extended model we would insert the components of the ROI model under the profit box that are common to both models. This highlights that maintenance strategy rolls up through profit and, thus, is an important part of the firm's foundation cash flow.

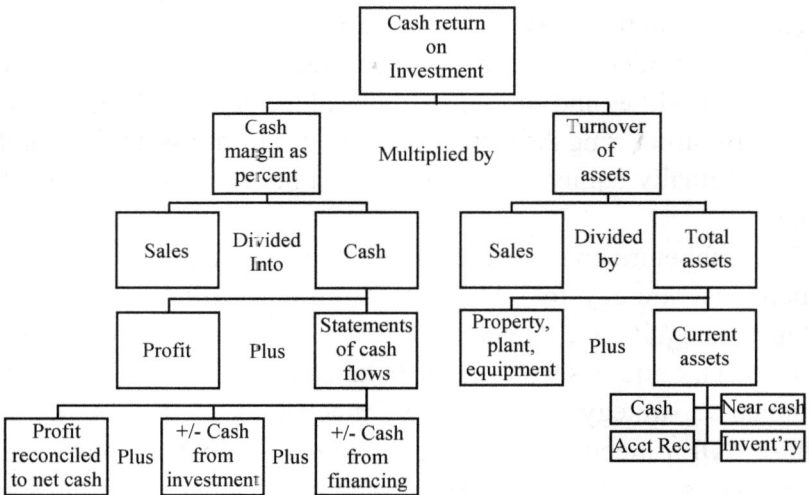

Figure 5-2: Return on cash flow model.

However, the ramifications go farther. CROI is affected by maintenance strategy in two cycles. The initial cycle of affect is through the income statement and balance sheet. In it, maintenance strategy will normally generate cash while reducing the need for cash. Some maintenance strategies will be formed specifically for cash flow outcomes.

The second cycle is to form strategies associated with the cash winnings generated by the first cycle. As maintenance strategies generate their returns, management will direct the cash with respect to two statements of cash flow shown in the CROI model: cash from investment and cash from financing. Both will reflect decisions for whether to use the generated cash to grow the business or strengthen the balance sheet.

Returns sensitivity analysis

As mentioned at the opening of the chapter there are two levels of financial analysis. Both evaluate the returns to be generated through maintenance strategy. The first is return sensitivity analysis and the subject of this chapter. As explained earlier, this is done in the context of the second stage of the mission to bring maintenance to be part of the firm's business success.

Purpose of returns sensitivity analysis

Early in the mission to make maintenance part of business success the maintenance strategist will survey the firm's competitive, operational and financial makeup. The strategist will come to understand where and how price, sales volumes, expenses, and current and capital assets can be predictably influenced by maintenance strategies.

The sensitivity analysis model allows the firm to "what-if" its possibilities. Examples are what if we could increase annual average price by 0.5 percent and sales volume by 2 percent, what if maintenance expense is excessive by 20 percent and what if we could reduce the cash needed to support the business by 1.5 percent? The list and variations are almost infinite. The earlier gathered insights will have revealed that the posed questions are legitimate to the firm.

The firm's sensitivity model is built around these what-if questions. It will give the firm the ability to determine the degree that profit, profit margin, ROI and CROI would be increased if maintenance strategies were targeted on the what-if possibilities.

Therefore, the purpose of the sensitivity model is to determine where to drill for returns. For example, a firm with a very tight gross margin will experience little effect from a relatively minor increase in sales. Alternately, small increases in the average annual realized price and the direct cost per unit may make a substantial impact on returns. Furthermore, analysis will reveal that some strategies are more significant during some business cycles than others.

Consequently, in this example the strategist would not seek maintenance strategies for increasing sales volume. The strategist would seek strategies for price and direct cost per unit; each with subdimensions upon which to further sharpen the strategic focus. Focus will also reflect the current and imminent business cycles.

The purpose of returns sensitivity analysis is somewhat akin to oil and gas exploration. The geologist and geophysist determine the hydrocarbon region and its oil and gas bearing formations. The challenge is to locate the places in the region's formations that hydrocarbons have collected in a reservoir. When we drill them we get a "commercial" well. Otherwise, we will get some oil or gas; but so little that the best business decision is to plug and cap the well and drag up. Returns sensitivity analysis for maintenance strategy will locate the "commercial" opportunities to increase the firm's business returns.

Answering some big questions

Sensitivity analysis gets to the root of a question that has less than an obvious answer for some industries. Beyond being a "necessary evil" can maintenance actually contribute significantly to business success?

The pharmaceuticals industry is a good example of where the question is important. Maintenance is typically a small expense in the overall cost structure. Meanwhile, the industry's production processes are not asset-intensive and, thus, are not critically dependant upon the effectiveness of production equipment. Therefore, why would a pharmaceuticals firm embark on a program with the mission to improve returns, maintenance efficiency or equipment effectiveness?

The second stage in the mission to develop maintenance as part of business success, ending in return sensitivity analysis, will answer the question. This could include the valuable discovery that there is no grand purpose. In business it is just as important to know what we do not have to do as it is to know what we should do.

As analysis reveals a pharmaceutical firm's true sensitivities, the mission to increase returns will define maintenance strategies with respect to what is discovered. There will be maintenance efficiency and equipment effectiveness improvements, but as subelements within parent strategies to make maintenance an important part of business success. The result would be an appropriate level of maintenance efficiency and equipment effectiveness while avoiding the typically immense cost of programs with the mission to maximize rather than optimize them.

Another example is the offshore oil and gas production industry. Maintenance expense per barrel is relatively small compared to price and DD&A per barrel. The percent of availability performance is typically into the 90s. Therefore, the question emerges once again for the firm: what counts and why? Sensitivity analysis will answer the question.

An actual case tells the story. A major oil and gas producer embarked upon a program with the mission to improve maintenance efficiency and equipment effectiveness. When the program was rolled out, it was first embraced enthusiastically by the top managers of one of the firm's largest producing regions. The program was shutdown within weeks by the same top managers, and not gently, because no answer to the question was forthcoming.

Another question before the firm is what should the staff functions for maintenance and reliability be doing for the firm; besides answering the fundamental "why-bother" question? How will they provide value to the firm and its operating units? What can the functions do for returns that cannot be done by the other units? How do we know they are working on the correct challenges? Sensitivity analysis will help reveal the answers to these questions.

Look at the problem from the perspective of successfully bringing about change. If the initiatives and actions advocated by the staff functions cannot win and sustain the advocacy of middle and frontline operations managers they are not going to succeed. It will be difficult to execute them and if executed it will be difficult to sustain them.

What-if assumptions

Figures 5-3, 5-4 and 5-5 show the dashboards of an example sensitivity model. The model is built on the financial statements of a refining and marketing firm.

It is noteworthy that the example is built on the financial statements all publicly traded firms are required by law to make available to the public. This highlights that the information needed to build a sensitivity model is basic information all firms have readily available. The point is that conducting returns sensitivity analysis is not an exotic or large undertaking; just very important.

Because the example was built from afar, it is also noteworthy that it is mundane compared to what is analyzed by a model built from an up close view of the firm as a unique competitive, operational and financial beast. For one thing, the list of assumptions on which the ability for what-if analysis is built into the model will be much richer and more extensive.

What-if assumptions may be built into the sensitivity analysis to reflect the firm's ability to influence its annual sales volume, realized average price and the ratio of direct materials to unit of product. Other what-if assumptions will reflect the firm's unique competitive advantages. Assumptions will also reflect the operational characteristics of the business, plant and its departments. All what-if assumptions are built into the model as it is reasonable to expect that maintenance strategies can actually be formed to enhance the firm's wherewithal to deal with the challenges the what-if assumptions represent for returns.

This highlights what is meant by maintenance strategy when the mission for maintenance excellence is to increase returns by making maintenance a part of business success. The strategies to influence returns will rarely be found to be the best practices such as job planning, scheduling, work management process and other now standard best practices. However, some or all of the elements of the best practices will no doubt emerge in a form molded to be part of larger business strategies to increase returns.

Sensitivity change factors

The dashboard view cf the sensitivity model in Figure 5-3 is the previously introduced ROI business model.

The dashboard presents the degree that business returns are amenable to being changed through maintenance strategies. Furthermore, the factors of change reflect the viewer's personal opinion with respect to the what-if assumptions along the bottom of the dashboard. The dashboard allows the viewer to change the assumptions and see the result for returns.
Let's look at the factors and understand their meaning. A simple example tells the whole story. If the firm's bust cycle profit were $100 million, a factor of change of 1.14 in the profit box tells us that the firm's profit could be increased $14 million by maintenance strategy.

The firm's sensitivity to the what-if assumptions will vary with the business cycle. Consequently, the model includes in its backend two sets of financial statements. They represent the firm's performance during the boom and bust cycles of its industry. The columns in the boxes of the ROI business model show both cycles.

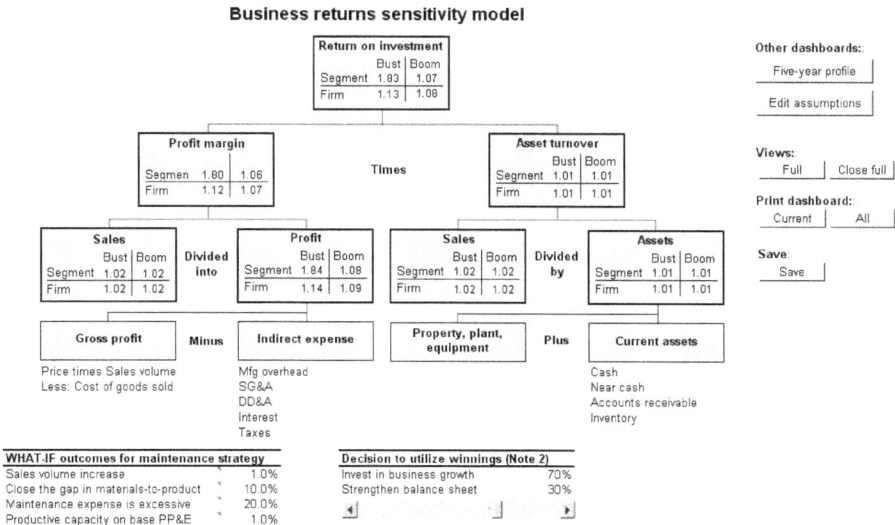

Business returns sensitivity model

Return on investment		
	Bust	Boom
Segment	1.83	1.07
Firm	1.13	1.08

Other dashboards::
Five-year profile
Edit assumptions

Times

Profit margin		
	Bust	Boom
Segmen	1.80	1.06
Firm	1.12	1.07

Asset turnover		
	Bust	Boom
Segment	1.01	1.01
Firm	1.01	1.01

Views:
Full   Close full

Print dashboard:
Current   All

Save:
Save

Sales		
	Bust	Boom
Segment	1.02	1.02
Firm	1.02	1.02

Divided into

Profit		
	Bust	Boom
Segment	1.84	1.08
Firm	1.14	1.09

Sales		
	Bust	Boom
Segment	1.02	1.02
Firm	1.02	1.02

Divided by

Assets		
	Bust	Boom
Segment	1.01	1.01
Firm	1.01	1.01

Gross profit	Minus	Indirect expense		Property, plant, equipment	Plus	Current assets

Price times Sales volume
Less: Cost of goods sold

Mfg overhead
SG&A
DD&A
Interest
Taxes

Cash
Near cash
Accounts receivable
Inventory

WHAT-IF outcomes for maintenance strategy	
Sales volume increase	1.0%
Close the gap in materials-to-product	10.0%
Maintenance expense is excessive	20.0%
Productive capacity on base PP&E	1.0%

Decision to utilize winnings (Note 2)	
Invest in business growth	70%
Strengthen balance sheet	30%

Figure 5-3: ROI model view of the returns sensitivity.

The factors in each box also make a distinction between the returns for refining as a business segment in the firm and the firm as a whole. Consequently, it serves the needs of corporate, division and frontline managers.

Management is frequently presented with propositions for which the business case seems just too good to be true. As many executives have said, "If all of these propositions were true, our stockholders would be rich and I would be an icon."

At first glance that may be the response to Figure 5-3. Does anything improve by 84 percent as is the case for the business segment's profit during its bust cycle? For that matter does anything increase by as much as 14 percent as profit does for the firm? In matters of business returns small is big; and big is questionably miraculous.

However, regarding the number as "miraculous" would be a misinterpretation of the mathematics of the message. The factors of 1.84 and 1.14 are reasonable for the subject firm in the context of the assumptions and business cycle.

A hypothetical example tells the story. A $10 million dollar increase in profit on a boom period $100 million is very different than the same $10 million increase on top of a bust period $40 million dollar profit: 10 percent and 25 percent respectively.

The case of the hypothetical $10 million occurs because some maintenance strategies create a change that then recurs year to year. Others create a benefit that varies with the business cycle. An example of the constant case is if a maintenance strategy affects a fixed expense. An example of the varying case is if a strategy affects sales revenue as the squeeze between price and cost varies with economic conditions.

Both influences can be seen for the segment in the profit box of the sensitivity model. Because of the math of relativity, change in returns drops from 1.84 in the bust to 1.08 in the boom.

Over all maintenance strategy in the subject realistic example results in a greater factor of change during the bust cycle. The purpose of sensitivity analysis is to locate where the factors will change the greatest in the context of assumptions and economic cycles.

As we look at the difference between business cycles we see that we may wish to build another view-set of factors: the weighted average over a complete business cycle. If the complete cycle were five years in a trough and two years on a peak, we could build a dashboard to show the factors calculated as a weighted average.

This type of thinking is common to firms. Firms typically form long-term expectations for price, sales volume and cost. They are used to make strategic decisions. For the same reason the sensitivity model is built on at least two sets of financial statements and may include a weighted average perspective. Alternately, the model could be built on the firm's current long-term expectation and changed when the expectations change.

Cycles of increasing returns

Sensitivity analysis delineates two cycles by which returns are increased. One is the baseline impact of maintenance strategy. It is a permanent increase in returns; recurring each year as a result of the chosen maintenance strategies.

The second cycle is the result of what the firm does with its winnings. Each year the firm's maintenance strategies generate a baseline increase to profit and cash flow. Consequently, the analysis of sensitivity to maintenance strategy must quantify the slice of benefit that will emerge as the firm puts its baseline annual winnings in play. Furthermore, the winnings will not typically be applied through a maintenance strategy, but flow to other business strategies.

There are actually two choices at the extremes of a continuum. One is to use the gains to grow the business. How will the firm increase its revenues, profits and profit margin?

An example highlights the issue of winnings used to grow the business. In some business cycles the choice for organic market-driven growth may not be available to the industry's rivals. However, the sustained and increasing competitiveness through superior returns may open the door for the firm to grow its market share during a bust cycle by acquiring other firms or their production capacity and, thus, their market share.

The choice at the other extreme of the continuum is to use the winnings to strengthen the balance sheet. Accordingly, the firm will use the annual winnings to pay off debt or buy back its stock.

Firms do not make an either-or choice. They will likely make choices somewhere in between. The lower right of the model provides a slide bar with which to look at returns as the result of a choice along the continuum.

As mentioned many times, and bears repeating, firms compete for returns above their industry's average. Figure 5-4, as a dashboard in the example sensitivity model, shows the collective contribution of maintenance-based business strategy to competitive advantage. Notice that the firm gains an initial or baseline competitive advantage. It will then grow the advantage as it puts its annual winnings in play.

The ramifications of the choice are depicted by the upper plot of Figure 5-4. The figure shows ROI for the firm during a long trough. During that time the firm's competitive cumulative change factor is growing by 3 percent per year. This is on top of the 10 percent annual "head start." By the fifth year the firm's ROI position, as a measure of competitiveness, is 27 percent greater than if maintenance had not been developed to be part of its business success. If we looked at the same charts for profit and profit margin the growth would be almost as great.[3] The shown case assumes that 70 percent of each year's winnings are used to grow the business and 30 percent used to strengthen the balance sheet.

Five years growth in return on investment

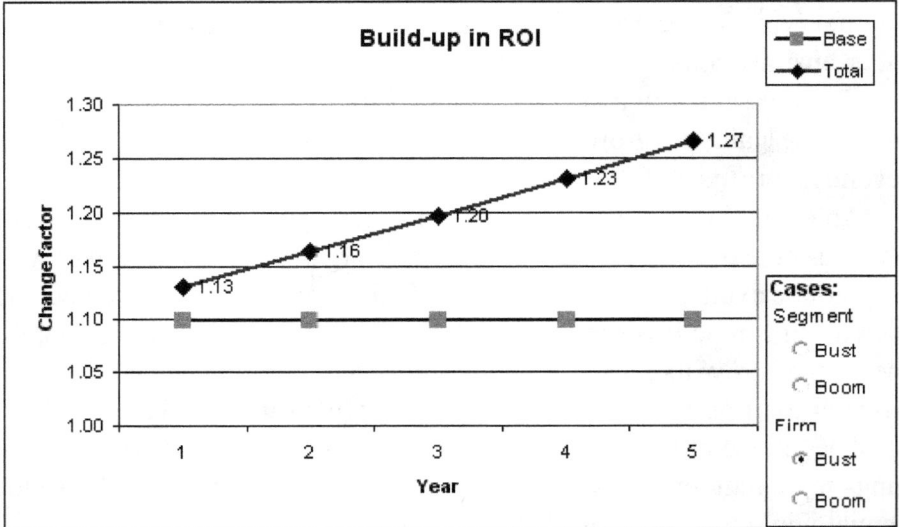

Figure 5-4: Two levels of gains.

The historical mission of maintenance programs has been limited to improving maintenance efficiency and equipment effectiveness. This is no doubt largely because, until now, we have not known how to bring maintenance to be part of business success. Instead, as firms compete for returns above the average of their industry, maintenance has continued to be an annual toll or tax cn returns. This is why we often hear it being called a "necessary evil." Figures 5-3 and 5-4 quantify the extent that the toll of maintenance on competitiveness has been the case for the firm that the model is based on.

The two figures also highlight that the toll on returns is the greatest just when the firm needs its returns to be the best they can be; during the business down cycle. This is doubly significant because the many of the

---

[3] Divide ROI by the change factor for asset turnover.

industries in which maintenance strategy is most relevant to returns are also industries that have long troughs interrupted by short peak periods.

Figure 5-5 shows the case. It compares the difference between the boom and bust for the example firm as a whole and the refining segment.

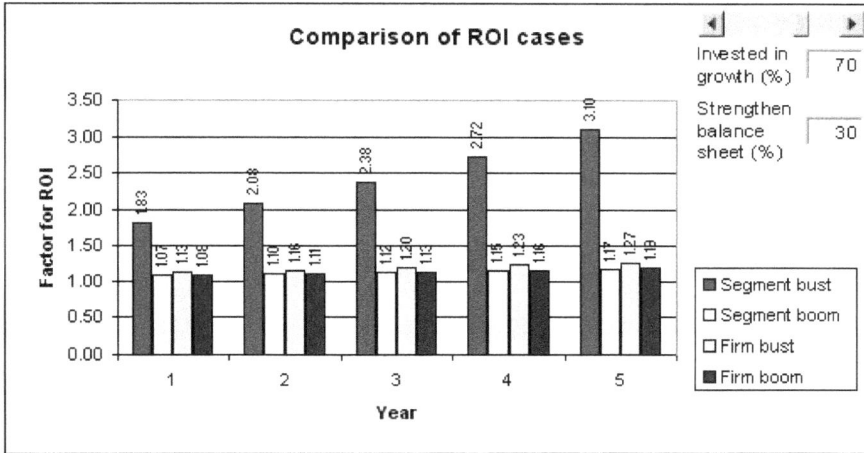

Figure 5-5: Comparison of advantage after five years.

As mentioned earlier, the dashboards of the returns sensitivity model shown in this section are based directly on the financials of an actual company. However, like its assumptions, its views are also mundane. A firm-specific model will be much more exciting and interesting. This is because it will match how the firm thinks about its competitive, operational and financial situation. By comparison, the example is almost unexciting. However, it serves the purpose of showing and explaining the nature of returns sensitivity analysis.

Envision a conference room of managers from the north, south, east and west of the enterprise. Envision the dashboards of the returns sensitivity model on a projector. Envision the managers discussing the strategic possibilities while being able to immediately see the ramifications for returns.

With this scenario, it is easy to expect that the management team will send its maintenance staff and frontline functions down a trail to increasing the firm's business success. This is especially exciting because the returns sensitivity model as a tool is easy to build. With just several weeks of effort the firm acquires the means to determine how to grow its returns and, therefore, its competitiveness for years to come.

Approach to returns sensitivity analysis

The previous three figures displayed representative dashboards for returns sensitivity analysis. The chapter actually reveals that all manufacturing firms have an important task to be done. It is to measure if its firm's returns can be improved through a mission to make maintenance a part of business success.

This is an immensely important organizational task. A firm needs to know and understand all of its possibilities if it is to make the best choices amongst them. An awareness of the possibilities through maintenance strategy has not historically been on the table. This is because, until now, we have not known how to manage maintenance to grow business returns. This section will describe the steps to accomplish the task; one that will most likely require several weeks.

Let's first get our bearings for where we are in the context of the overall mission to make maintenance a part of business success. The strategist has already formed and documented an understanding of the firm as a competitive, operational and financial beast. Consequently, the strategist understands the many ways that the firm's returns can be influenced. It follows that the strategist has also developed a good sense for whether or not maintenance strategies can actually be devised to predictably influence the returns.

This opens the gate for the strategist to build the firm's returns sensitivity analysis model. However, weighing the hog does not make it heavier. When the sensitivity analysis is completed the next stage in the mission to increase returns will define the specific maintenance strategies to do so. The strategies will be directed at actually tapping into returns that the sensitivity model has found to be there ready to drill and produce through maintenance strategy.

The steps to build and utilize the returns sensitivity model are as follows:

1. Establish the representative accounting periods and adjustments.

2. Establish agreement for what can be predicted and influenced by strategy.
3. Establish the what-if assumptions of the returns sensitivity model.
4. Build, sanity-check and refine the sensitivity model.
5. Support management as they use the model to reach strategic decisions.

As mentioned earlier, management's decisions flow through to the next stage which is to develop specific maintenance strategies. As they are developed a more rigorous model will evaluate and confirm their individual financial significance. The strategy returns analysis model is the subject of the next chapter.

Step 1: Establish the representative accounting periods and adjustments. The chapter's sensitivity model distinguished two accounting periods that represented the polar opposite business cycles.

Therefore, the first step is to select the accounting periods that represent the extremes. The strategist may want to include other cases such as an accounting period somewhere between the extremes. The accounting periods to be incorporated in the model should be established with management.

This step will also identify adjustments to the selected financial statements for unusual accounting events that would distort the picture. For example the financial statements behind the example returns sensitivity model report a large write down of goodwill. Since it was not recurring, the transaction was reversed in the period's three financial statements.

Step 2: Establish agreement for what can be predicted and influenced by strategy. Before building the model it is good to spend time to ensure that it will reflect possibilities that management regards as credible and feasible.

For example, the strategist could embark upon a path of building a model that includes a what-if element for increasing sales volume. The work to survey and understand the firm will have suggested the possibility. However, does management envision that is it actually possible to change sales volume?

Accordingly, the strategist should list which of the line items and accounts of the financial statements could change and, in turn, would be sensitive to maintenance strategy. The strategist will then confirm the list with management. There is nothing to be gained by analyzing something for which there is minimal credibility.

Step 3: Establish the what-if assumptions of the sensitivity model. The strategist, from his understanding of the firm as a competitive, operational and financial beast will list the what-if assumptions to be built into the model. There is no limitation and the list will be worded uniquely to reflect the firm as a unique enterprise.

The strategist is essentially doing the heavy lifting on behalf of the people across the enterprise that will use the model. Accordingly, the strategist should list the firm's characteristic what-if assumptions and establish with the model's users that the list is feasible and covers everyone's issues of interest.

Step 4: Build, sanity-check and refine the sensitivity model. The next step is to actually build the model. The strategist has settled the details across the firm such that all are comfortable that the model is fully correlated with the firm's business success.

The model will be built as a set of dashboards. The dashboard views of the model will reflect the representative accounting periods, how the financials can be influenced and the what-if assumptions. Consequently, through them management will be able to look at the possibilities to increase returns in a Rubic's-cube-like fashion.

There will be discoveries as the model is built. They may cause the builder to revisit the steps prior to this one.

The builder will sanity-check the model with people across the firm who are regarded as the sage relative to elements in the model. This action will likely cause the model to be refined.

Step 5: Support management as they use the model. The purpose of the returns sensitivity model is to understand the extent and means that maintenance can be a contributor to business success rather than take a toll or tax on success. It follows that the model fulfils its purpose as management gains the wherewithal to make strategic decisions.

Thus, the strategist will support management in their decision-analysis and decision-making process. This may involve a range of tasks. For example, the strategist may be asked to pull up additional information as new questions arise. Another may be to build additional dashboard views to support current, on going and periodic decision-analysis and decision-making.

At this point the firm will have confirmed that a mission to make maintenance a part of business success makes good business sense. The next stage is to form the business-type strategies for maintenance.

An interesting phenomenon is the rule of five. The rule is that solutions rarely exceed five distinctive branches at any given level and fewer than five is usually the case. The rule seems to prove itself when strategies are formed. Accordingly, we can expect up to five core strategies to emerge; each with up to five substrategies and so on. The next stage will define them.

The stage after strategy definition is to measure the return impact of each core strategy. The objective is to confirm and quantify how each will significantly affect returns and then execute the returns. That is the subject of the next two chapters.

Chapter 6
Measurement and Interface Measures

The previous chapter presented and explained business models. They converted the financial statements that were explained in Chapter 4 to cause-and-effect-type models of business returns. With them, we can trace the impact of maintenance strategies, actions and outcomes to the firm's returns.

Chapter 5 showed how business models are used to evaluate where and how the firm's returns are sensitive to maintenance strategy. Every firm's financial structure is different in character such that we cannot safely assume that any given strategy will actually have a noticeable impact on its returns. The models to conduct returns sensitivity analysis determine exactly where the firm's financial profit, profit margin, return on investment and cash return on investment are sensitive to the touch. It follows that the goal of reinvented maintenance is to touch them.

In this chapter, three abilities will emerge that the firm must develop with which to routinely manage maintenance as a part of its business success. First, we need to be able to measure all proposed maintenance strategies and important tactical decisions. Both can only be measured if we can clearly see their many cause-and-effect relationships up to returns. This ability is called upon during the firm's periodic strategic planning cycle and when action decisions arise in the day-to-day maintenance operation.

Second, we need to form the detail with which we can effectively execute the strategies as measured by actually realized, sustained returns. The way that most ensures success is to execute returns rather than strategies. This ability will be called upon each time the firm's strategies change in response to changing business environment. Executing returns is the subject of the next chapter, but utilizes the interface measures developed in this chapter.

Third, we need a workload-based maintenance budget and means built upon it to control and forecast variance. The budget is actually built as the engine to the financial-statements-based model.

To do this, the chapter will explain how the business models are extended to what this book calls "interface measures." The explanation will explain nonfinancial measures as compared to financial measures. The chapter will then provide examples of interface measures which are based on the concept of nonfinancial measures. However, the chapter's purpose is to demonstrate the method of forming the measures rather than prescribe a set of measures. Finally, the chapter will describe the process for building the interface-measures-based financial model.

Nonfinancial measures

It sounds stupid, but the financial statements are financial measurement. This is because their objective is to measure the firm's business performance. This begs the question, "what else is there?" The answer sounds even more stupid; nonfinancial measures.

To manage maintenance to be part of business success, we must make a distinction between financial and nonfinancial measures. There is a huge difference. The relationship is that all dollars reported in financials and the returns calculated from them are the outcome of nonfinancial drivers.

The point is that we evaluate the firm per its financials; but its financial outcomes are the convergence of many nonfinancial drivers. An example is maintenance expense; a financial measure. It is partially driven by jobs per year per tradeperson; a nonfinancial measure. When the ratio changes, maintenance expense changes. What is noteworthy is that the variables of the nonfinancial measure are measureable and controllable. We select and implement strategies to do exactly that.

We can extend the nonfinancial measures in the numerator and denominator to job types and how trades are engaged directly and indirectly in the plant. It follows that we must plan, direct and measure maintenance at the level of its nonfinancial measures. Accordingly, the firm can subdivide how hours are engaged and act to change and steer the driver of engagement.

Even though we cannot manage with financial measures, they have a critical place in the grand scheme of things. They tie the diverse wide ranging nonfinancial drivers of success together in a single business system. Without the systems view, we can see very little of the full ramifications and outcomes of maintenance as part of the firm's business success.

In fact, this was the fatal flaw of maintenance management principles and practices before the field was reinvented. Programs before this reinvention focused on improving a short list of nonfinancial drivers without making the linkage to the business system.

The concept of nonfinancial measures is the platform on which we ultimately succeed in increasing a firm's returns through the management of its maintenance. The book calls them interface measures because they reside like meat in a sandwich between the traditional financial statements and all maintenance strategies, actions and controls. As we consider an action we do so through to the interface measures they touch. We can quantify the change to the variables of each affected interface measure and roll that up to the firm's financial statements and returns. In other words, for an action to be taken or maintenance results delivered, what will the firm's financial statements and returns look like?

Interface measures

With the reinvention of maintenance comes the principle of interface measures. This chapter will attach them as extensions of the business return on investment and cash return on investment models that were explained in the previous chapter. Consequently, this book will explain interface measures as downward off the bottom of the models.

The explanation is subdivided financially. The subdivisions are gross profit, manufacturing overhead expense, assets and cash flow. They will be further subdivided by their primary categories. An example is gross profit with its subdivisions of sales revenues less cost of goods sold. Sales, in turn, is subdivided by price times sales volume.

The returns sensitivity analysis of the previous chapter has revealed where maintenance strategies and actions matter for returns. The insight reveals where we need interface measures to link maintenance action to sensitivity. As we drill down to specific nonfinancial measures, we do driven by our understanding of what, were and why the returns are sensitive to the touch.

As we identify and define the interface measures we will concurrently reach back into the firm's database and mine its data: something that is relatively easy to do. We will quantify what has been the case and then quantify what the measure should become.

As we deal with the measures and associated data we may find the need to put "data traps" in place; something that is also easy to do. They allow us to quantify interface measures for which necessary data is currently limited or not being captured. Often times only several weeks of newly captured data can start the show.

This is a good occasion to make an important point. Firms now typically have huge amounts of data in its databases; waiting to be put to good use. When there is no data for a specific point of interest, it is easy to begin collecting data by automated means. Although the principles and means to do so are now easy to put into play without an IT program, the understanding of the tools has not caught up with the general population. The point is that as the chapter explains interface measures; please do not assume that there is any significant difficulty that prevents us from doing almost everything we would wish to do: you will be wrong.

The development of the firm's interface measures is influenced by and built on everything that has been explained by previous chapters. They were the industry's platform strategy, five competitive forces, understanding the firm as a competitive, operational and financial beast, sensitivity of returns to maintenance strategy, and defined maintenance strategies.

In conjunction with measuring how a maintenance strategy will affect returns it is easy to visualize the place of interface measures. As we look at each strategy we ask ourselves what nonfinancial interface measures must be formed to reflect their impact on returns and will the measure be changed significantly by the strategy.

Before the reinvention of maintenance, the "strategies" of our field were largely an automatic conclusion. They were to install the standard best practices for maintenance excellence and equipment effectiveness. They lacked guidance though interface measures. Instead, the focus was inward to the best practice rather than outward to returns. Strategic analysis did not ask, for example, how exactly would work order scheduling change the outcome of various interface measures and, therefore, what must we design the firm's scheduling method to do? The answer would have rarely looked like the standard best practice for scheduling. In fact, the best practice would have rarely emerged as strategies in themselves.

Without the interface measures the firm's strategic and technical maintenance actions will float and be pushed about by the breeze of the moment. To quote an old joke, "The problem with loafing is that we never know when we are finished."

This chapter will present interface measures for the categories of gross profit, manufacturing overhead, balance sheet assets and cash flow sections of the financial statements. However, we cannot in this book offer a prescriptive set. Interface measures are always built on the firm as a unique competitive, operational and financial beast. Therefore, the chapter will demonstrate the method based on the obvious. In real life, a firm's measures would have some similarity to this chapter, but will be much more fascinating. Truth is always stranger than fiction.

Interface measures for maintenance expense

Rather than start at the north end of the income statement, as has been the book's pattern, for the purpose of explanation it may be more effective to first sink our teeth into interface measures for maintenance as a manufacturing overhead expense. The discussion is most common to all readers' experience.

Chapter 6

Inherent, achievable, actual and target

Figure 6-3 presents an example set of interface measures to maintenance expense. Before jumping into them we need to set some definitions. They include the definition of inherent, achievable, actual and target that appear in the interface measures for maintenance expense.

Almost all maintenance expense is founded on the core active hands-on maintenance tasks to maintain the subject equipment, facilities and grounds. The **inherent** steps and hours to conduct a maintenance job include them. Inherent work does not account for the associated administrative and logistic steps and time before, during and after the inherent work.

An example of administrative activity and time is to acquire a work permit. Another example is steps spent to write and deliver feedback on the work plan. An example of logistic steps and time is getting people, parts and tools to the work and into action. Therefore, inherent represents the technical design of the jobs. Inherent steps and time define the work to be done. On it we define all associated administrative and logistic action to do the steps.

Achievable includes the entire operational and managerial context of doing a maintenance job. Consequently, on top of the inherent work it includes all administrative and logistic activities and time. However, achievable reflects that all steps will be conducted with 100 percent productivity. This means that all avoidable setbacks are in fact foreseen and avoided. As a point of reference, a job plan represents the achievable case for direct work.

Achievable reaches farther then the direct work. It includes all indirect requirements as part to the overall makeup of the maintenance function.

Actual and **target** play together. Actual refers to the resources engaged and consumed to conduct the period's collective workload and maintenance functioning. Target refers to the line set which the plant will try to meet or exceed. At its extreme, target would be set to match achievable.

Figure 6-1 depicts the definitions and their interrelationship. Achievable represents the upper limit that, through total maintenance expense, we can improve profit and profit margin. It is also the limit that the cash utilized to support direct work, thus, needed to run the business can be reduced.

Very few firms can quantify what the achievable is for their firm. Consequently, they experience continued loops of creeping actuals pushing up the target to creeping actuals; and so on. Maintenance as reinvented puts this problem in the past.

Target in Figure 6-1 is actually a managerial decision. It is a decision for the degree that the firm will strive to improve its profit, profit margin and utilize cash. It is important to make this decision rather than let plant operational dynamics

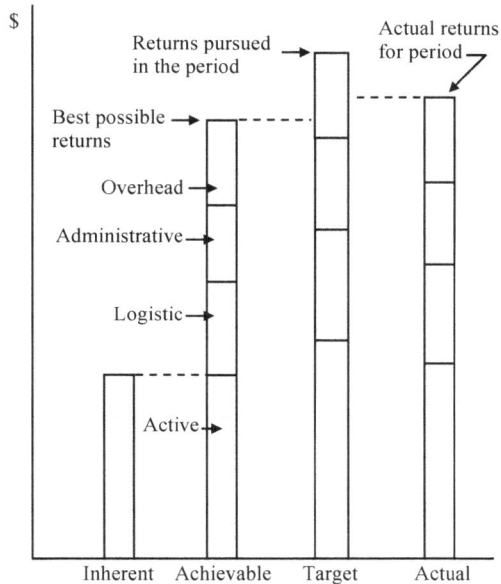

Figure 6-1: Inherent, achievable, actual and target for maintenance work.

make it for the firm: as has almost always been the case before maintenance was reinvented.

Actual in the figure is the actual outcome for profit, profit margin and utilized cash. This, against a target set built upon a workload-based budget, is managed through controlling and forecasting variance. With them the firm is able to report the gap between target and actual with respect to the firm's financial statements, returns and engaged cash. Budget and variance is the subject of later chapters.

Equivalent jobs and workload design

A firm's total maintenance workload is typically comprised of jobs of with a wide range of trade hours. The range is driven by asset, work and trade type. For example, proactive work usually entails substantially fewer average hours per job than corrective work. Some types of corrective work have a size distinctively different than another; especially with respect to types of equipment or facility. Work that is classified as mechanical often entails more hours on average than electrical.

Furthermore, some work types displace others with respect to actual occurrence and time between occurrences. This is especially the case for proactive jobs. They are expected to reduce the number of corrective jobs per accounting period. This is doubly important because proactive jobs typically require substantially less time and materials than corrective jobs.

Without "equivalent jobs" as an equalizer we would get an incorrect reading of the possibilities and outcome of maintenance strategies. Figure 6-2 shows the problem hypothetically. A preventive maintenance job is shown to require on average in the plant two hours compared to ten hours for corrective work. Consequently, a PM as an equivalent to the corrective work type is one fifth of a job.

If workload design were to add three PMs to the full set of maintenance jobs occurring over the year, the result would be one less corrective job to do. This may be the result of no longer occurring or because the interval between occurrences has been extended for some of the corrective jobs.

Type	Average hours	Equivalent jobs
PM	2	0.2
Corrective	10	1.0

Type	Before	After
PM	0	3
Corrective	10	9
Total jobs	10	12

Change by	Number	Percent
Count	2	20%
Equivalent	-0.4	-4%

Figure 6-2: Principle of equivalent jobs.

If we measured the change in maintenance expense through the number of jobs without the principle of equivalent jobs, the firm's workload would appear to increase by 20 percent: appearing to reduce rather than increase returns. However, on the basis of equivalent jobs, we would rightly report an increase in profit and profit margin because we are doing 4 percent less direct maintenance work to sustain the same level of business success.

Equivalent jobs will be based on recognizing distinctions such as assets, job and trade types. For each the workload is determined by mining historical data and arriving at a conclusion. As time passes, the firm will become increasingly accurate in its ability to predict the direct hours for each category. Ultimately, these details will roll up to equivalent jobs and the plant's ability to measure and steer its maintenance-driven returns will become increasingly effective.

Why is the principle of equivalent jobs an important issue? The answer is because a firm has a degree of control over the plant's workload. However, this is not to be confused with deciding to not do work that needs to be done. That is contrary to the principle of making maintenance a part of business success.

The control is that we can design maintenance jobs to be applied to equipment, facilities and site. This is compared to what is needed as it arises. Through various methods the workload engineer determines optimal set of work types and trades to sustain performance and condition of the equipment, site and facility.

The calculation of Figure 6-2 highlights why we are concerned with workload design. Accordingly, some maintenance strategies for making maintenance a part of business success may be directed to workload reduction. This will roll up to profit, profit margin and engaged cash for the simple reason is that it will reduce manufacturing overhead and reduced cash.

With respect to Figure 6-1, the inherent column would shrink. We would also expect the logistic, administrative and overhead components of the achievable column to shrink. This would be the case as proactive work reduces the intensity of logistic and administrative activity in the work and the overhead function to support them.

We already spoke of developing the details of equivalent jobs with respect to asset, work and trade type. These are the foundation details to building the workload-based budget. Strategies to change workload would change their profile. With time, a firm will see a trend in equivalent jobs. The firm will track the trend in returns through the interface measures that are constructed for the firm. As the trend progresses until reaching its sustained optimal, business returns will increase and cash engaged will decrease.

Nonworking and total tradedays

Ultimately, maintenance payroll is largely driven by tradedays engaged in work plus tradedays on the payroll but not in the position to do work. This includes starts, quits and breaks. It may include transportation to get to and from the start and quit points. It will also include tradedays for training, vacation, holidays and sick days.

These tradedays are a different management problem than those engaged in actual work. Rather than set targets, management sets policies and ensures that they are complied with. If compliance is complete the outcome for maintenance expense and, in turn, returns is preordained. In other words, returns are recognized through policy, but compliance determines whether they realized.

However, interface measures must be present that segregate the tradedays with respect to doing work and tradedays not available to do work. The measures will also reflect the need to deal with the possible gap between policy and compliance.

Figure 6-3 shows that there are considerable possibilities for interface measures to move maintenance expense. We do not have to be very imaginative to think of them. In fact, those of the figure lack the breadth, imagination and subdivisions we would expect to see in an actual case. However, they are adequate to demonstrate the principle of interface measures. Furthermore, the book is constrained by its policy of confidentiality from being more imaginative.

Interface measures

For each strategy or real-time action we can quantify an impact on one or more interface measures and, in turn, what the financial statements and returns will look like after the action. Also notice that the interface measures include targets. In these cases the target case is set by management's decisions and is included in the interface measures.

The firm's map of interface measures may begin with a measure comparing maintenance expense to all other overhead expenses. It is conceivable that this comparison may be made with specific types of overhead, i.e., operator labor.

However, we need to know that the ratio is improving driven by maintenance expense rather than increases in the other overhead expenses. We may also need to pull some overhead expenses out of the calculation because they are actually direct expense to production volumes, but reported as an overhead.

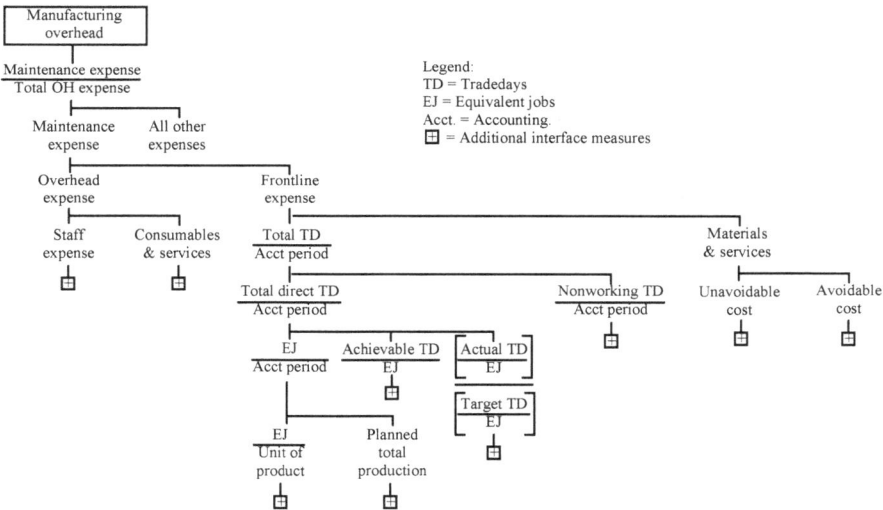

Figure 6-3: Representative interface measures for maintenance expense.

Moving downward we will need to further segregate the expense interface measures so that we can find our way to its many nonfinancial drivers. We will want to segregate subexpenses according to our ability to predict and control outcomes. Therefore, the practitioner will likely place a branch in the map for maintenance overhead and frontline expense.

The overhead expenses include maintenance staff costs such as management, supervisors, planners, schedulers, engineers and corporate roles. It also includes overhead materials and supplies, and services that are not related to individual maintenance jobs. If we want to evaluate changes such as an additional planner we would use this path to assess the consequences for returns.

Frontline expense spans all tradedays that must be engaged because of the firm's maintenance workload. It also includes the materials and parts, and services associated with the workload. This is the first subdivision under frontline expense.

Typically, materials and services are a substantial expense. However, they are largely uncontrollable except at the periphery. By controllable it is meant that different decisions can cause a different outcome. The most obvious controllable possibilities are rush order expense, material specification and vendor.

However, most maintenance jobs will largely require what they require. Consequently, we would likely have a limited amount of interface measures for materials and services than for other more controllable parts of the total maintenance expense. At the least, these measures would serve the purpose of giving the firm the ability to accurately budget the year's total maintenance expense and forecast the remaining year.

Accordingly, the branch for maintenance materials and parts in the figure does not depict as many opportunities to influence the firm's returns. However, interface measures could segregate the unavoidable expense of parts and materials and those that could be avoided. Each avoidable case may be represented by an interface measure at the next level down

By comparison the tradedays branch of the map has a high degree of controllability and we can influence it a great deal. Total tradedays engaged determine a large part of the overall maintenance expense, thus, a significant part of manufacturing overhead.

However, control or influence should not to be confused with the trivial action of arbitrarily cutting tradepeople. What is meant by control and influence is distinctive. It is that the plant can manage and steer the drivers that determine the number of tradedays that need be and are actually engaged to sustain sales, cost of goods sold, expense, balance sheet assets and plant condition.

The tradedays branch begins with total tradedays per accounting period. It then branches off to the direct and nonworking tradedays per accounting period. By this branch we measure and deal with two different types of management problems. The total direct branch is a matter of managing the efficiency and effectiveness of maintenance work. The nonworking tradedays branch segregates the administration of policies associated with human resources management such as preparing for the day and going home, breaks, vacation, training, etc.

In both cases, there are additional subdivisions to reflect all drivers to the interface measures. At the levels denoted by the "+" box these interface measures are further developed downward to their entirety.

In the figure, there may be three basic issues to measure under the total direct tradedays branch of interface measures. The first, equivalent jobs per accounting period, reflects workload design. As described above, the assortment of maintenance tasks selected to sustain equipment effectiveness and plant condition decide how much work must actually be done. An optimal scheme for equipment, facilities and site will reduce the plant's annual workload and, thus, tradedays needed to maintain the plant.

As the workload is reengineered, we would see that the achievable average tradedays per equivalent job will decline. This will occur as we determine those places where lower labor intensive proactive work displaces higher intensity corrective maintenance during the accounting period. This will also affect materials and services and be reflected accordingly in their branches.

Firms would love to know what the maintenance expense should be, and steer to it pulled by planned production for the accounting year. Possible interface measures associated with maintenance strategy for that purpose are shown on this trail. The first interface measure under equivalent jobs per accounting period is equivalent jobs per unit of production. The other shoe to the interface measure is planned total production and its profile for the accounting period.

The next interface measure in the branch measures the feasible best possible (achievable) performance with respect to tradedays per equivalent job. This is the work to conduct all work associated with a maintenance job and includes administrative, logistic and administrative steps to do the work. It also assumes no unforeseen surprises.

The third branch deals with management decisions for spending and whether or not the plant meets the plan for spending. Going into the accounting period, management will establish a target for direct tradedays relative to the achievable tradedays measure: essentially a target for measurable, influenceable business returns. The other part of the branch reflects the plant's success at meeting the target.

Therefore, the third path under direct tradedays engaged per accounting period sets the returns we expect to generate compared to what could be generated. Whereas, one interface measure sets the line for what is achievable, another sets the line for what will be accomplished. Consequently, we see interface measures of actual tradedays per equivalent jobs compared to the target for the measure. It follows that with the plant's data this is the level at which we set the level of expected, feasible performance and, therefore, expectations for returns.

Let's think ahead of the book here. Chapter 8 is concerned with budgeting, and variance reporting and forecasting. The system will be built partially on the gap as a variance between direct and target TD per EJ. Furthermore, the budget and variance system will be built with job and trade type data rather than equivalent jobs. Equivalent jobs will be the rollup of the detail. These would, as data-based details, be interface measures subordinate to those shown in Figure 6-3. On top of the actual and target we would apply nonworking tradedays as a factor to bulk up to total salary cost of the workload conducted.

When the budget is developed it would reflect the relationship of achievable versus target for work and trade types. They will have been rolled up from the inherent case to include administration, logistics and active time to do work and nonworking time. Consequently, the figure of interface measures shows total tradedays per equivalent jobs. However, if in the figure we had mapped all measures we would have seen measures emerge that are specific to operational units, and asset, work and trade types.

Once again it is a good idea to stress the point of data. The interface measures are built and work with data. The data exists in all modern-day manufacturing firms. It comes from its many management systems and their databases. If exactly what we need for some measures is not immediately available, it is easy to set up new data traps such that in several weeks we all have everything we need to put the ball in play. Somewhere in between is data with quality weaknesses. Once again we would take immediate measures to accumulate data for which the quality issue has been eliminated.

One thing is not addressed, but an important outcome driven by decisions to close the gap between actual and achievable. It is the impact on working capital; specifically cash needed to run the business. This will be reflected in the interface measures for balance sheet assets.

Business model and workload-based budget

How interface measures work to make maintenance a part of business success is apparent as we look at the interface measures map of Figure 6-3. We would develop them "underneath" the return on investment and cash return on investment business models (Figures 5-1 and 5-2) that returns sensitivity analysis has found to be sensitive to the touch of maintenance strategy.

As maintenance strategies move various interface measures at the lowest levels in the map they will move the measures shown in the figure. As the measures move so does manufacturing overhead. As manufacturing overhead moves there is a chain reaction up through the business models, of the firm's financial statements, to profit, profit margin and engaged cash.

Therefore, mapping interface measures links our actions to the firm's returns. These may be strategic plans or current-day actions. Going the other way, once we have set targets for the contribution of maintenance to returns, we will go downward to the lowest-level interface measures to control our day-to-day actions and, thus, assuring that the planned returns will be realized.

As mentioned before, the "+" boxes denote additional levels of interface measures. However, where are they, what are they? In the case of maintenance expense, once formed, they are the details of the plant's production-driven workload-based budget. In other words, the business model and budget are essentially a single system. The budget is the engine under the hood.

Within the "budget," as the engine to the business model the interface measures shown in Figure 6-3 are mapped all the way down to completely reflect the production and maintenance nature of the plant and parent firm. For example, all measures may be subdivided by groups such as responsibility and equipment centers, facilities and site. Equivalent jobs will be subdivided by work and trade type. They may also be subdivided if the nature of managing the work of maintenance is distinctive. The work types may be further subdivided by trade type as it reflects organizational responsibility and structure. In other words, the details will have many dimensions reflective of the firm as a competitive, operational and financial beast.

As these details are set up, the system as an integrated business model and budget is built such that its elements can be varied for whatever reason. The ability built into the model to vary drivers will reflect changes in the firm's business environment and the firm's response to them. This makes the budget a decision-support tool through its ability to be a business model; and vice versa. The business ramifications for returns will be one of the front-end reports in the tool.

The budget with its details, reflecting management decisions, can also be used real-time to evaluate the results of important decisions for occurring maintenance actions. Its interface measures are the foundation on which to build the variance reporting, control and forecasting system. The point here is that interface measures are central to managing maintenance as part of business success. The budget and variance system are the subject of Chapter 8.

Interface measures for gross profit

We started the discussion of interface measures with maintenance expense. We could conjure up, from afar, measures that are reasonably universal in nature. Having set the example, we can now continue the concept for gross profit. For gross profit, we cannot so easily conjure up generally universal interface measures. Cases vary too much from firm to firm.

Before maintenance was reinvented, we practitioners tended to regard availability performance as the core issue for gross profit: percent of time the plant performs at a target level productive capacity or quality. Our attentions driven by the perspective was overall equipment effectiveness (OEE) and its ramifications for availability, quality, scrap, etc. In contrast, maintenance, as reinvented, has the purpose of affecting returns via price, sales volume and cost of the sold goods.

Figure 6-4 shows the gross profit model. Recall that it is the bottom layer of the return on investment business model (Figure 5-1). Attached to it are the interface measures for price and volume. The measures for cost of goods sold are the subject of Figure 6-5.

Sales: price and volume

Business strategy for maintenance can affect price. That it can is especially important to returns if the firm has a normally tight gross profit margin. A very small improvement in price can be a significant increase. This is because an increase in price does not carry an associated cost of sales. Instead, the price increase goes straight to the gross profit and profit lines of the income statement.

Figure 6-4 points to average price per accounting period as a possible primary interface measure. However, the book will not attempt to extend the interface measures to its lower levels. This is because

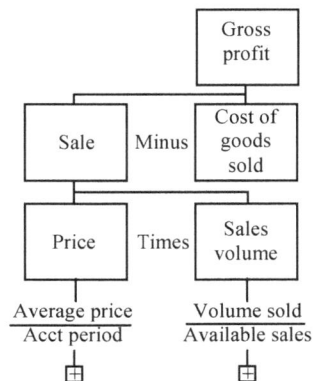

Figure 6-4: The top-level interface measures of gross

they are very unique from firm to firm and fact is always stranger than fiction.

These measures will reflect issues such as price linked to quality and service. They could relate to the firm's ability to respond, survive and recover from unforeseen short, peak periods in which there are price spikes due to a production disruption in the industry. The same type of strategy could be aligned to avoid the firm's need to go to spot-type markets or competitors to meet sale commitments.

The point is that are many possibilities. The first step of a program to make maintenance a part of business success begins by coming to understand the firm as a competitive, operational and financial beast. Defining and mapping interface measures for price and volume absolutely depends upon it.

Sales volume is also potentially sensitive to maintenance strategy. However, not so much in the manner we practitioners have viewed it in the past. A firm is of course concerned with productive capacity. However, the issue for gross profit and return on investment is the volume of sold product and inventory balances relative to sales. In other words, when we wax poetic about availability performance we may be reciting to empty seats. We should be speaking to being able to meet all possible sales opportunities and the goods inventory to support it.

Sales volume strategies will also be especially impactful if the gross profit margin is not naturally or normally tight. In that case speaking to sales volume and inventory aligned to sales rather than availability performance will be the attention grabber. The issue for availability is inventory aligned to volume rather than the more-is-better view of the past.

The concern for volume and inventory must be especially so when the plant already has high availability performance; something that is not unusual in some industries. When a plant already has a percentage well into the 90s, how reasonable is it to expect that we can tap even a relatively small fraction of the gap? If we can, would the skills and cost to reach and sustain it be feasible?

The point is that maintenance strategies must be part of allowing the firm to meet its every opportunity to make profitable sales. Accordingly, what is described as availability performance has to be aligned to what drives sales volume and price.

Therefore, the interface measures of Figure 6-4 may be mapped to reflect sales volume as a percent of the sales volume that was available to be made. Below it, there would be interface measures tied to bringing the percentage as close as possible to 100 percent. What the strategic possibilities and their interface measures are will also be a case of fact trumps fiction. Accordingly, the figure stops at the top most interface measure.

Cost of goods sold

At this point in the gross profit model we will have built interface measures for the firm's topmost line. The other shoe to drop is the cost of goods sold.

Some maintenance strategies will affect sales price and volume. However, reducing the cost of goods sold (COGS) is also a possibility through maintenance strategy. The difference is that the maintenance strategy is directed at the aspects of the production system that, if they perform more consistently, will affect cost of goods. Examples are to produce less scrap or off-spec product.

In chemicals and refining there are formulas that set the line and measure the relationship between feedstock and the units of product extracted. If we explored them and the plant as a production system, we may find maintenance strategies that would help operations hold performance in its power zone.

Accordingly, we need to take an accounting-based perspective of maintenance strategy. Figure 6-5 show the perspective to be the ratio of direct resources engaged and consumed by the production process to produce the units of goods finished.

The business model of cost of goods sold is reflected by the integration of inventory, cost of goods sold and production. Accordingly, maintenance strategy would affect COGS back through inventory as production achieves and sustains the best ratio of cost to unit produced.

Figure 6-5 shows the business model and interface measures for COGS. Let's reiterate the basic equation of inventory as a resource cost that flows through to be goods and, thus, COGS. The inventory available to the firm for sales is the combination of additions to inventory plus beginning inventory. The inventory withdrawn is the inventory available during the accounting period less the ending inventory. In some businesses the amount withdrawn to make sales may be measured directly; one-on-one.

Another view is to evaluate the ramifications of

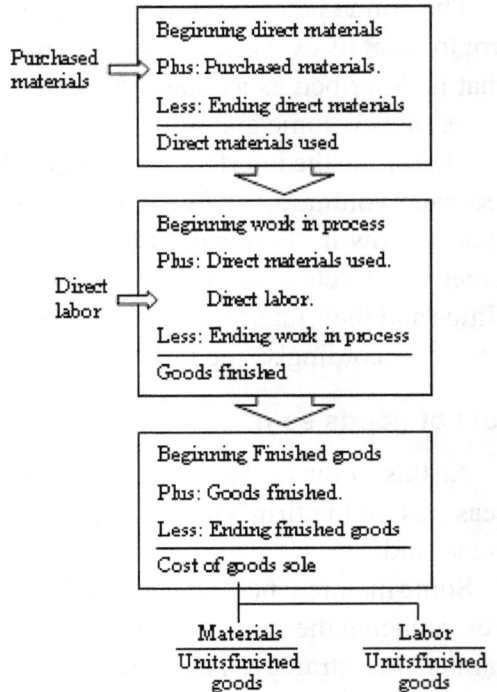

Figure 6-5: Business model for cost of goods sold.

maintenance-based business strategies for COGS back though inventory. The ramifications will appear in the return on investment and cash return on investment models. Targets set relative to the strategies are reflected in the budget, and variance report and forecast system.

This is shown in the cost of inventory and COGS model presented by Figure 6-5. Materials are acquired, inventoried and transferred to work in process. The rate that they are is reflected in the ratio of product units to direct materials and labor. The relationship will be reflected in the "goods finished" of the work in progress inventory. As the relationship or ratio match the best possible outcomes of the finished goods; inventory will reflect it.

A plant will always have one direct cost; materials. Labor may also be a direct cost that varies with the number of units produced. If so the same concern for the ratio of labor to product arises.

Accordingly, there may be two fundamental interface measures coming off the COGS model. Both reflect the degree that maintenance strategy can be developed to hold these relationships to a target. Because they are unique to every plant, mapping a full set of interface measures is not attempted in the figure.

The term "units of finished goods" in the interface measure requires some explanation. Along with the goods that were finished during the period, it includes "equivalent finished units of goods."

The term "equivalent" is an expression of output in term of work and material applied. This is compared to output in terms of physical units. At some point firms classify work in process as equivalent to finished units of goods.

Cash flow ramifications

The gross profit model and interface measures of course drive profit. They also influence cash flow. As the firm excels at the gross profit model, if significant, three working capital accounts they will be affected. As they are, they will either generate or use cash.

More specifically, gross profit performance will affect inventory levels, cash balance, and accounts receivable and payable. They are driven by decisions and performance for matching production to available sales and to maximize the ratio of direct resources per unit of finished goods. This will be reflected in the cash flow model.

Interface measures for balance sheet assets

Current assets, and property, plant and equipment (PP&E), have a significant affect on the firm's return on investment and cash return on investment. It is, therefore, important that there is always a possibility that maintenance strategies can affect returns through both types of assets. This section will look at some representative interface measures for both.

Chapter 6

An asset-driven business strategy for maintenance can affect accrual and cash-basis returns along multiple paths. While affecting assets, a strategy can concurrently affect sales, COGS, expense, DD&A, interest, and cash flow.

Current assets

The view of assets in the return on investment business model (Figure 5-1) will immediately reach a first fork in the road: current assets and PP&E. Let's first take the fork to current assets. Figure 6-6, the interface measures map for current assets, shows the case.

The primary thrust of strategies for current assets is to reduce the average balance over the accounting period. If accomplished, the ratio of sales revenue to assets increase. In turn, return on investment and cash return on investment increase by the amount of the increase; all other things being equal.

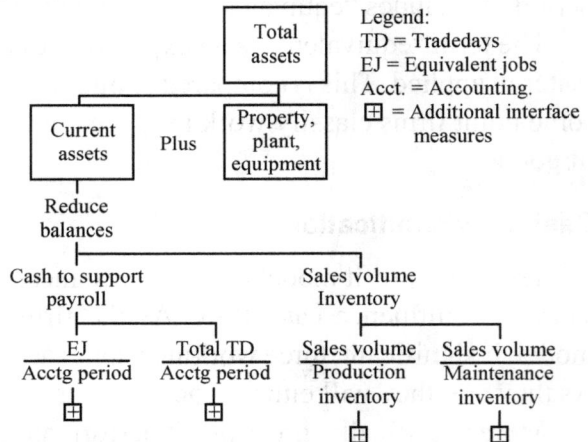

Figure 6-6: Interface measures for current assets.

As it is possible, the changed balances will flow to cash. In turn, cash will flow to other places in the business or out of it. The case may be mixed in decisions for investments or financing. Alternately, cash may be used to retire debt or reacquire outstanding shares. If a firm did not take such actions it would eventually produce a quick ratio (current assets divided by current liabilities) that analysts would consider as reflecting the poor use of the firm's assets.

There are two paths to reducing asset balances. One is to reduce the need for cash to run the business. For maintenance this may include reducing the workload for the accounting period or tradedays per workload. The former is a work redesign strategy. The latter is a productivity strategy. Both cases appeared under the interface measures to manage maintenance expense.

The second path of maintenance strategy is to reduce inventories as a ratio of sales. There are two cases: production and maintenance inventories. It is an important distinction because they are different problems with different ramifications for returns.

Production inventory is typically a substantial portion of the firm's asset base. Therefore, any reductions in the average would affect the turnover of assets. It could also produce a one time blast of freed cash and then permanently reduce the cash needed to manage the business. A few years ago a business writer made a name for himself by pointing to the 'hidden factory" and that firms use a large part of their cash resources to fund it.

Therefore, we should examine the possibility of maintenance-based business strategies in the context of reducing production inventory. The most obvious possibility would be strategies tied to sales volume and COGS. As maintenance strategies help the plant better manage the uncertainties of production performance, can the plant carry lower production inventories?

This is a good time to make a point about what constitutes effective business strategy for maintenance. There are always good looking strategies that may actually only exist in a perfect, transparent, measurable and accurate world. In such a world, a maintenance strategy could be highly consistent with competitiveness.

However, we must always ask ourselves if the envisioned outcome could actually be managed and, if so, would it make a difference? In other words, is an outcome reasonable within the normal noise and chaos of the business operation? Before maintenance was reinvented, we practitioners tended to not question whether practical reality matched the theory behind the justification for maintenance best practices.

Chapter 6

Property, plant and equipment

For property, plant and equipment (PP&E) the thrust is to reduce the rate of growth in assets relative to the rate of growth of market share. Figure 6-7, the interface measures map for PP&E, shows that there are two dimensions for which maintenance strategy may present itself. Once again, the possible maintenance strategies, thus, interface measures are varied, many and unique. The book will not attempt to imagine a representative set beyond several possible high level measures. Those shown are not offered as always the case. They are offered here as a demonstration of method.

The first dimension is strategy developed to reduce the magnitude of investment. In other words, increase the capacity or value of PP&E per dollar of investment.

The other aspect is to find strategies that allow capacity or value to be acquired in smaller increments. One aspect of the value of such strategies is that the firm will be better able to match its business strategies to the long-term uncertainties the firm must deal with in its industry.

Another value of maintenance-based business strategy directed at incremental increases has been mentioned before in the book. As firms acquire capacity, they drive down price, thus, reduce their industry's price as they attempt to utilize all of their capacity. In other words, the larger the necessary incremental capacity the greater the self-inflicted damage on revenues.

An actual example demonstrates the implications of maintenance-based business strategy for PP&E. An oil and gas production firm was preparing to make a substantial expenditure for a subsystem on an oil process platform. The capital to be invested was $100 million. An availability analysis study was conducted to confirm that it would perform as required by contract. Accordingly, for the first time in the design of the system the frame of reference was availability rather than purely the production process.

The team recognized that small changes in valving and piping as maintainability improvements substantially increased the productive capacity of the system. Consequently, both choices for PP&E shown as

142

interface measures in Figure 6-7 were open to the firm; and choice in business is valuable. One could be to reduce the magnitude of the capital expenditure. Alternately, the firm could expect to push back the time until capacity must be added in the future.

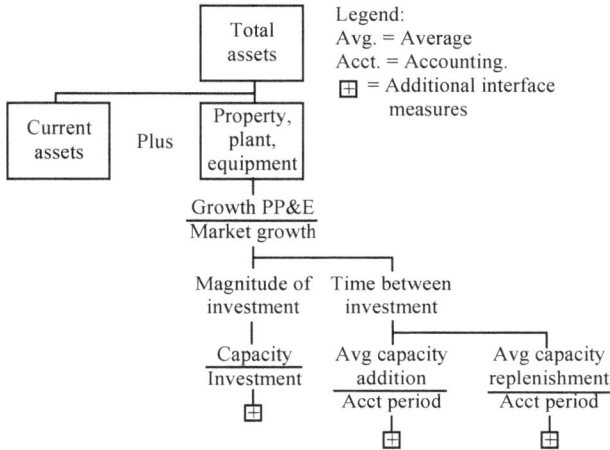

Figure 6-7: Interface measures for property, plant and equipment.

The focus of maintenance strategy will be to extend the time until investment is required, in turn, the average investment over several accounting periods. These strategies will largely reflect the ability to get more units of production per asset base, thus, extending the time until actual performance runs up against the capacity of the asset to deliver it. Strategies that do this will increase return on investment through the ratio of sales to balance sheet total assets.

This may or may not be the case for replenishment of capacity or value; i.e., turnarounds and overhauls. This would be the case especially if a better ratio results in less expenditure of capacity for unit produced.

Interface measures for cash flow

Cash and cash flow is the blood of life; drain it and die. Therefore, the final set of necessary interface measures is associated with the cash return on investment (CROI) model shown in Figure 6-8.

There may not be a distinctive set of maintenance strategies for CROI. Instead, the model reflects the strategies that are built or defined for gross profit, maintenance expense and balance sheet assets. Consequently, to form the interface measures for the CROI model we look at the model with respect to the strategies with origins in the other models. These are summarized in the figure as four different performance areas.

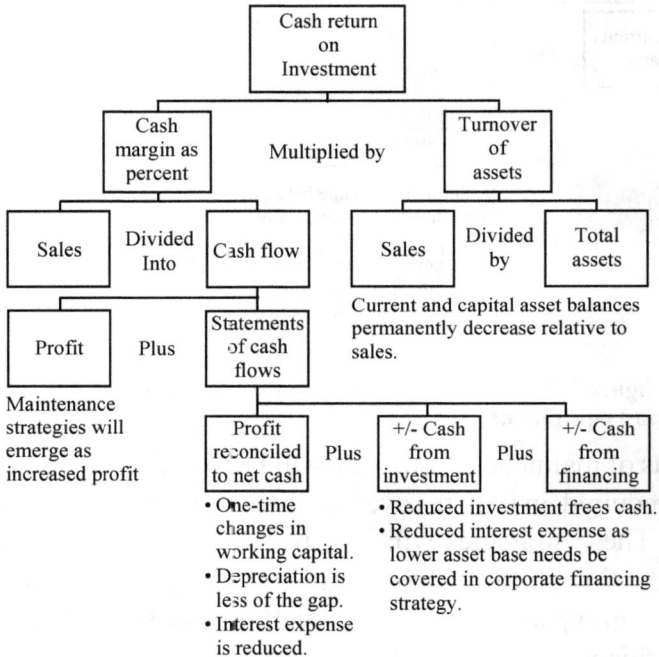

Figure 6-8: Cash flow model and areas of strategy.

For the performance areas, interface measures are placed on the model driven from two directions. The first direction is to be an extension to the interface measures formed for gross profit, maintenance expense and balance sheet assets. The interface measures for CROI would take their lead from them, but reflect their ramifications for cash. It is as if we are identifying the remaining interface measures to individual strategies tied to other models.

The second direction begins with the summaries of the four cash driving areas of the figure. Management may have formed specific cash strategies, and target flow and balance. In turn, the maintenance strategist would develop interface measures to reflect them.

Approach to Interface-measures-based financial analysis

This and the previous two chapters have dug deeply into the principles and methods of finance, accounting and modeling. The previous chapter explained how to build a model for returns sensitivity analysis and utilize its output as part of developing the firm's set of maintenance strategies.

We are now in position to build the financial-statements-based analysis model to rigorously evaluate the returns that candidate business strategies for maintenance will generate for the firm. That is the subject of this section. The purpose of the procedure is to determine exactly how the strategies will increase the firm's returns and, at the same time, see what the firm's financial statements will look like. With the findings, management will make its final decision for which maintenance strategies to accept or discard.

Something else will emerge at this juncture. The model's engine will become the firm's workload-based maintenance budget. This is an important and fortunate outcome of modeling because the resulting budget is required to execute and then manage the firm's maintenance strategies.

Schematic of financial analysis

It may be helpful to take a high level view of the financial-statements-based analysis process and where the budget as its engine emerges in the process. Figure 6-9 provides such a view; revealing a loop that actually becomes a business planning cycle to the firm.

The financial model will be three related frontend views. With them we will see the financial outcome that is possible when maintenance is made an integral part of business success.

The first view is the business models of return on investment and cash return on investment. They allow us to see how the business returns will be changed by the maintenance strategies being evaluated. The second frontend view is the firm's financial statements. Through the view we will see what the statements will look like as a result of the strategies. The third frontend view is the maintenance budget which is also the engine to the model. Through the frontend views the model will eventually become part of the routine strategic and daily management of maintenance.

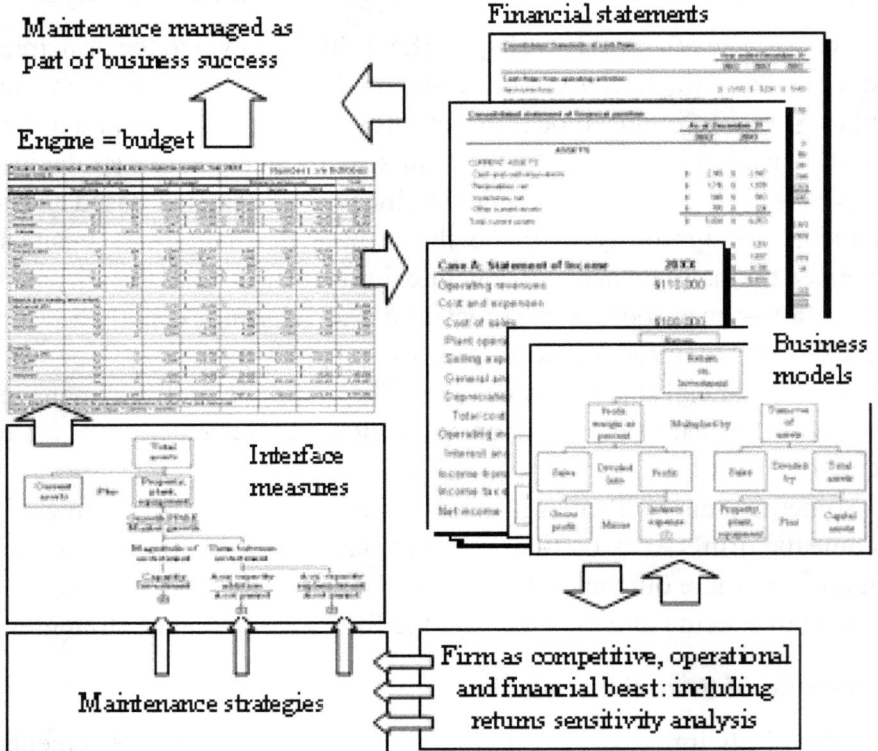

Figure 6-9: Overview of financial analysis.

The three interrelated frontend views of returns, financial statements and budget depict the firm as a competitive, operational and financial beast. The understanding was built into the loop when the firm set out on the mission to make maintenance a part of the firm's business success. Out of the quest for understanding and returns sensitivity analysis, as part of the quest, we formed a set of business strategies for maintenance.

For the strategies we map a system of interface measures. They allow us to quantify and measure the elements of the strategies. They then flow into the engine of the business model.

Approach steps

As we move into the financial analysis, we have two things in hand from the steps leading up to this point. First, we have a set of maintenance strategies. We are ensured that the strategies have two characteristics. One is that they fit the firm competitively. The other is that they are directed at the ways and places that the firm's returns are sensitive to strategies; including maintenance.

Second, we have the returns sensitivity analysis model. Building the model has given us the foundation from which we will now map downward to the interface measures. We will now continue on where the sensitivity model stopped. Consequently, some decisions that affect the financial analysis have already been settled. An example is the representative accounting periods that were selected to base the returns sensitivity model upon.

We are now ready for rigorous interface-measures-based financial analysis. The steps are as follows:

1. Map all interface measures as indicated by the candidate strategies.
2. Establish the what-if and sensitivity variables to be built into the financial model.
3. Establish the frontend views to the model.
4. Build and sanity-check the engine calculation: budget.
5. Support management as they make strategic and tactical decisions.

Step 1: Map all interface measures per the candidate strategies. As mentioned earlier, we have a set of candidate maintenance strategies in hand. The first step is to form a complete map of interface measures.

In this step we would begin at the bottommost level of the return on investment and cash returns on investment models and map the interface measures downward from them. However, we would form them as a direct reflection of the collective set of strategies. The step would map the interface measures down to the lowest level necessary to quantify, control and influence the affect of the strategies will have on the firm's returns and financials.

Step 2: Establish the what-if and sensitivity variables to be built into the financial model. Into the returns sensitivity analysis model (Chapter 5) we built assumptions with which we also built mechanisms to allow what-if and sensitivity analysis. Now we will evaluate the set of candidate strategies to identify the set of what-if and sensitivity issues we want to build into the model to test the range of possibilities, consequences of actions and make strategic and tactical decisions. They will reflect how the firm's business situation changes with time and how the firm would respond to them. They also reflect how people across the firm foresee themselves routinely using the model to support the strategic and tactical aspects of managing maintenance.

Step 3: Establish the frontend views to the model. The final model of returns and financial statements is not a "do it and put it away" piece of work. The model with its frontend views will be a standing decision-analysis and decision-making tool.

The purpose of this step is to ensure that we are building a model headed in the direction of being a full powered decision-analysis and decision-making tool for strategies and day to day operations. This requires that we confirm that the people who utilize the system will be given the frontend views and the drilldown, rollup and slice-dice capability that will allow them to manage their responsibilities. This and the previous step will occur concurrently.

Step 4: Build and sanity-check the engine calculation: budget. The lower level interface measures are actually variables in the calculation of higher level measures. Therefore, this step will actually build the system of interrelated calculations. The finished work is presented as a budget, that rolls up to the firm's returns and financial statements.

It is always a good idea to stop and sanity-check the calculation with others across the firm; numbers in a tough business. They tend, with fresh eyes, to be able to spot thing that do not smell right. They also tend to improve the calculation with fresh ideas.

Step 5: Support management as they make strategic and tactical decisions. The purpose of financial analysis is more than just to quantify the extent and means that maintenance strategy can be part of business success rather than take a toll or tax on success. It follows that the model is a gift that keeps on giving because management gains the wherewithal to make strategic and tactical decisions.

Thus, the analyst will support management in their decision-analysis and decision-making processes. This may involve a range of tasks. For example, the analyst may be asked to pull up additional information as new questions arise and possibly upgrade the model to incorporate the ability to regularly deal with the issues behind the question. Another may be to build additional dashboard views to support current, on going and periodic decision-analysis and decision-making.

The end result of the initial financial analysis for strategic planning is to leave us with a set of maintenance-based business strategies that will enhance the firm's business success; competitively, operationally and financially. Another end result is a tool that will live on to support all sorts of purposes.

We now have our strategies in hand and some powerful decision-analysis and decision-making tools. Just as exciting we have "inadvertently" built a useful budget with which we eventually build a variance control and forecasting system.

What comes next is to implement the strategies that have passed the test of financial confirmation. However, as introduced in earlier chapters we execute returns rather than strategies. This draws heavily on the interface measures and requires a break from the traditional approach of project management. What comes next is to explain how to execute returns; because that is what the firm wants.

Chapter 7
Execute Returns

This book explains how maintenance has been reinvented with the result that firm's maintenance can now be made an important part of its overall business success rather than only a necessary evil. Accordingly, let's ask ourselves again the three questions with which management tests all grand and glorious propositions to advance business success. Does it make good business sense? Can it be measured? When will we get our money?

As the book explained how to seek out competitively and financially significant strategies, through which maintenance can increase returns, it was immediately clear that reinvented maintenance makes good business sense. As the book continued on to explain the financials-statements-based method to connect strategy to returns it was clear that the proposition can be measured in ways that are visibly effective and practical.

Therefore, maintenance, as reinvented, passes management's first two tests with flying colors. Before reinvention, claiming to pass these tests would have been stretching the blanket.

This chapter will test reinvented maintenance with the third question: when will we get our money? The answer is that the measurable flow of money will begin within 100 days or less of beginning to execute specific returns.

To pass the test of the third question the chapter will clearly prove the 100-day claim. The best form of proof is to explain the general "project" approach to executing returns. In the process of reinventing maintenance, the traditional project management approach was also reinvented to match the concept of executing returns.

However, we must deal with the 600 pound guerilla in the room that is the unspoken concern expressed by management's third question. The third question is not all about "when," but "if." All business initiatives face a large risk of failure. The risk is that a given initiative will not generate returns of significant magnitude; or at all. In fact, data shows that more business initiatives fail than not. In the field of maintenance and reliability this is just as true.

The foundation principle presented in this chapter is to execute results rather than tasks. In the vernacular of reinvented maintenance, the principle of result-versus-task means that we will execute business returns rather than strategies. Before reinvention, firm's executed maintenance best practices and then tried to find the financial result.

The collective set of maintenance strategies formed to this point will increase the firm's competitiveness because they increase returns. However, we go for returns, as the jugular, rather than strategies. This is because executing individual strategies rarely ensures returns.

An example demonstrates why. One set of strategies may have the business purpose to reduce the firm's annual and shorter-term total maintenance workload. However, when executed all that has been accomplished by the strategies is that the "required" maintenance will have been reduced.

Meanwhile, another set of strategies may have the business purpose to steer maintenance to its current optimal annual and shorter-term average expense. Unless, the elements of both strategies converge on the interrelated elements that both reduce the required expense and guide the firm to spend less as it is has become possible, the actual returns from reducing the maintenance workload will not occur anytime soon; if at all.

To counter this risk, we execute returns rather than the strategies. As we do, we will pull in the synergistic elements across both sets of strategies. We would likely further subdivide the entire synergistic collection of elements into slices of incrementally increased returns, thus, shortening the time until the firm gets its money.

The chapter will explain the execution of returns at two levels. First, it will introduce and explain the principles on which the method to execute returns is built. Second, it will introduce and describe the methods and tools for planning and managing the execution of returns.

Principles for executing returns

We have made a bodacious claim. The firm "will get its money" sooner rather than later. However, as we do, we have to realize that management may be listening politely but is thinking, "Why did I know they were going to say that?" As an executive said, "If we adopted every proposition we would be rich and I would be an icon."

We need to offer details that can be inspected, such that the manager can audit and confirm intuitively that our confidence in the promise is earned. To meet this requirement, we will first give proof through principles: this section. We will then give proof in the form of process, method and tools: the next section. The next section is the working details of this section.

The principles that give proof of the validity of the promise are as follows:

- Real-work trumps goal-work.
- Focus one result at a time
- Lead abilities, and lead and lag measures.
- What is success, are we succeeding.
- Accountability for execution.
- Project management reinvented.
- Reduce the need to manage change.

Real-work trumps goal-work.

General Patton is alleged to have said, "During war, all other human endeavors shrink to insignificance." A university's athletic director made the distinction between a championship year and a championship program. Successful firms are the latter if they reach and sustain the position of making returns above their industry's average. In other words, they cannot let Patton's rule apply permanently.

Instead, successful firm's have two dimensions of focus. One is getting its work done as a going business: the "real work." If not done, the consequences will be immediate and not good. We will call this "mandatory" activity.

The second is to do the work of taking the firm's game to the next level. If the firm is a competitive leader, it is the work of staying ahead of the posse. If this type of work is not done, there will eventually be a price to pay. We will call this "goal" activity.

The outcome processes of successful, meaningful goal-work will join the firm's mandatory real work. However, until then mandatory activity will always trump goal activity. On any given day mandatory activity, as real work, is urgent; goal activity is only important. Give anybody one of each to do and guess which will be done and which might not.

There are several messages here for successful execution. First, for the outcomes of goal-work to eventually become real-work, it must be accepted by the firm's people as a worthwhile addition to real-work. If it is not obvious that goal-work will result in real-work that improves or sustains the firm's competitiveness the firm will very likely fail to reach its goal. If it does pass through the gauntlet of execution, whatever has been executed will probably be killed off as soon as its executors move on to other things. The chapters prior to this one described the approach to develop maintenance strategy that overcomes this threat for the very reason that it is clearly linked to competitiveness.

The second message is that the real-work takes up almost all available space and attention. Trying to bring goal-work into the firm is akin to being the youngest child in a family of ten siblings. To get a piece of the action the youngest has to slip around the crash, bang and turf of the big kids. In other words, the challenge of execution is not just achieving it. It is how to achieve it in the midst of everything else that is going on and will never go away or even slow down.

The step-by-step approach to execution must recognize these two fundamental messages. The remaining principles go straight at that absolute necessity. If we do not, we are doomed.

Analyses by entities that measure this sort of thing have found that less than half of all business projects actually succeed. Some people go through their entire career and never participate in a successful business project. If we are brutally objective and honest with ourselves we would admit that, before reinvented, few maintenance programs would be judged as successfully reaching beyond maintenance as a necessary evil.

Focus one result at a time

In the movie classic MASH, a field hospital trauma surgeon was being pressured to do several surgeries at a time. His response was, "I do one thing, do it well and move on."

If we were a firm's management, we would be glad for such a philosophy. This is especially so if we said, "We increase returns one incremental slice at a time, lock it in and move on to the next."

Why? The reason is that the more the increments of return we pursue at one time, the less it is likely that the firm will experience increments at all. Rather than one bridge serving the community we have multiple costly, half built bridges of no value.

Maintenance has been reinvented to be able to put a circle around specific increases in returns. When we focus on one or just a few increments at a time, the firm will most assuredly gain competitive advantage. The work to sustain the advantage will be absorbed into the firm's "real work." If we focus on many or all possibilities; the gained total returns will be minimal or none at all.

Let's look at goal-work in the context of real-work. Real-work is not going to move aside and make room for goal-work. Therefore, a principle of focus is to continuously hold the level of ongoing goal work to a small percentage of the firm's total work. As we land the outcomes of a body of goal-work to be a routine normal part of real-work, we bring on another increment of returns for execution.

What is the magnitude or measure of focus? The stages to develop competitive and financially significant strategies have formed strategies as goal activities that matter. They matter because they contribute to the firm's absolute long-term need to generate returns above their industry's average.

Rather than execute them, we now resort to packages of integrated actions that will produce an incremental increase in one or more returns. These packages are the "unit" of focus.

This brings up the question, what is focus? We can answer it in measurable terms. A person or a team takes on only one to three incremental increases at a time until executed. At the firm level, focus is controlled by the individuals or teams available to take on initiatives.

"Executed" by this metric has its own measure. The measure of executed is that the set of abilities to generate the return have become a normal part of the firm's real-work. They have become mandatory for the simple reason that no person in the firm as a team would ever advocate taking points off the score board or to not run the plays that we all now know will put more points on the board. That is why real-work remains as real-work.

The importance of focus in monetary terms is highlighted by Figure 7-1. The magnitude of profit, profit margin, return on investment (ROI) and cash return on investment (CROI) produced by the returns-execution approach is substantially greater then the traditional project approach to implement strategies, practices and processes rather than returns. Each step on the build up of returns is called a return execution initiative (REI) and is the "unit" of focused execution.

One ramification of focus on returns is that the time to reach the first increase in profit, profit margin, ROI and CROI is moved forward. Hand in hand with time to first returns is that the time to reach full payoff is accelerated. The build-up of returns is further increased because the time between each step up in return is shortened by avoiding blanket actions and, instead, targeting specific drivers to returns through REIs. The total affect is that focus causes returns to stack sooner, faster and higher.

Focus has another ramification as shown in Figure 7-1. Focus and its delivering REIs include all necessary foundations to sustain gains once they are reached. The returns-execution approach ensures that gains are sustained because the elements across strategies that would act to sustain the returns are pulled into the REI. In other words, each REI to execute incremental returns is comprehensive in its ability to both reach and than permanently protect a return.

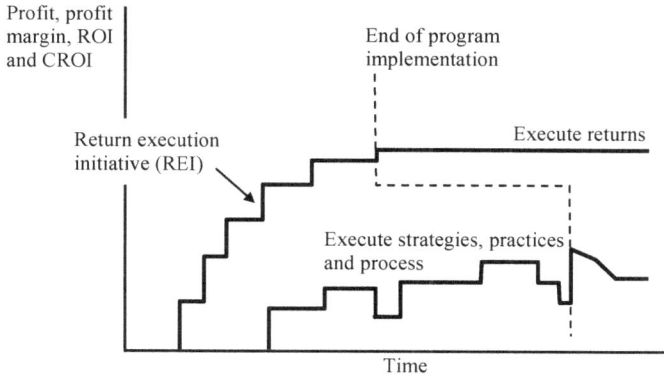

Figure 7-1: Comparison of payoff profiles of the returns execution versus strategy execution approach

Everything done to this point makes focus possible, actually surgical. The foundations have already been laid and management can visibly see them. Accordingly, when management has its typical skeptical silent thought, "Why did I know they were going to say that," the practitioner is in a position to show that the claim for returns to begin soon and assuredly is justified. In doing so, we have reduced to minimal the risk of failing to get the returns.

Lead abilities, and lead and lag measures

We have all heard sermons on lead and lag measures. The reader may be thinking, "Here we go again." But wait, there is more. We have actually been chewing on the principle all along in the book.

However, the book takes the principle further than lead-lag measures. For maintenance, the primary lag measures must be returns: profit, profit margin, return on investment and cash return on investment. The lead measures for maintenance are the interface measures demonstrated in Chapter 6. We will now add "lead abilities" to the line up.

The returns are the mathematical outcome of the interface measures as they respond directly and quantifiably to lead abilities. For example, if we have the ability to deal with elements of tradeday productivity, then the interface measures between the ability and overhead maintenance expense in the income statement will roll up through the financial statement to drive the calculation of profit and profit margin. Consequently, there is a chain of cause and effect from specific real-work as an organizational ability to a quantifiable slice of returns.

Along the chain of lead abilities and lead and lag measures we must also keep our eye firmly on another principle. The chain must have predictable outcomes and we must be able to influence those things that cause the outcomes.

We must ask ourselves if a subject outcome for returns is both predictable and influenceable. An example is repair parts. We can easily predict the cost of parts on manufacturing expense, thus, returns. However, the firm cannot much influence the expense through the firm's organizational ability to manage its maintenance parts inventory. We would have to look to lead abilities elsewhere in the firm such as those that design workload and specify materials.

The thrust of executing returns incrementally as the basis of focus recognizes and makes hay through the principles of lead to lag, and predictable and influenceable. We trace back from returns, through interface measures to lead abilities whose routine function will cause a predictable and influenceable outcome for returns. Just as important we influence returns through our ability to control the abilities.

These cause and effect chains are packaged as REIs. REIs as packages are the "unit" of focus in execution. We keep them tight so that most will increase returns beginning within 100 days.

Let's look at an example in our common experience: weight management. The lag measure is scale weight. The highest level interface measure is calories consumed versus expended. Below it are interface measures that roll up to calories consumed and expended. The relationship of the match or difference between calories consumed and expended has a completely predicable outcome on scale weight. Furthermore, the measure is both predictable and influenceable.

However, these lead and lag measures are not good enough to get the job done: they do not actually do work. We must put in place lead abilities and work them routinely before the lag measure will move to were we want it to be and stay there.

One set of abilities is to be able to measure accurately and continuously the calories being consumed. Through them we can control calories into the system. Another ability is to know what the calorie consuming pounds of our body are (muscle, bones and organs). Along with that is the ability to compute what this fat free body mass is consuming with respect to our level and events of activity on any given day. Another set of required abilities will be able to "design" meal plans tied to the measurement of calories in and out of our body, and thereby prevent the over and under consumption of calories.

The abilities are the deliverable of goal-work and become "real work" as part of our daily life. If we ask a person with these abilities in place they can tell us that today their fat pounds remained steady or changed by X pounds.

Lag measures are always the center of attention. This is because they are the measures on which the firm is judged. Without digging into the details of the firm, lag measures tell the shareholders, bankers and competitors whether or not the firm has the lead abilities to be successful. How the lag measures go, so goes everyone's world: summer camp for the kids, college education, job security, etc.

Returns as the lag measure are also easy to get, thus, creating an additional fixation. However, as lag measures they do not tell the whole story. Just as for scale weight, returns are driven by the phenomena across the entire business system that we can neither predict nor control. For example, a person's scale weight can and does inexplicably swing by multiple pounds over 24 hours. Consequently, it is important that the firm will be able to report how each return has been increased during the accounting period by measuring the actual performance of the lead abilities.

Furthermore, if we cannot report how returns changed during the accounting period, as management reviews returns it cannot know if the firm's returns will get better, are starting to get better or have already gotten better. And if so, when and by how much? Therefore, it is immensely significant that maintenance, as reinvented, has reinvented the traditional project management approach to deal directly with the chain of cause and effect from predictable, controllable lead abilities to returns. We could say that executing returns is synonymous with executing cause-and-effect chains. An REI is one or more of such chains.

What is success; are we succeeding

We will move returns A and B from X to Y by the date of Z. Each focal incremental return for execution as an REI will come with such a measure of success. In fact, we will have made this determination before we make the declaration. As done, we will have stated how the firm will know if it is successful. Just as important, we have set the yardstick against which the firm will be able to know if it is succeeding.

What is success and is the firm succeeding is the basis on which accountability during execution is built and managed. It is also the basis that accountability continues once execution is successful. Just as important, it is the basis that accountability is willingly accepted. This is because on any given day as individuals we know that what we are doing is needed to put points on the board. We care because when we do the well being of our families, fellow workers and communities are better off for it.

As all of us driveway basketball stars know, we have to keep our head in the game; and keeping score does that. When we do, our athleticism is actually greater.

However, in the execution of returns it is a mistake to only keep the score with respect to execution. We should begin keeping score for permanently occurring performance.

The ultimate score of all maintenance strategy is the returns. We as individuals must be able to see that our actions to build the individual organizational abilities matter for returns.

Therefore, we will need scoreboards that drive us through to an executed return. Accordingly, we defined an executed incremental return as one for which its driving abilities are fully functional and a normal part of the firm's real-work. As we monitor actions during execution we can put a dates on the time at which the subject incremental returns will increase. More specifically, we can place a date that the change in returns will begin to increase. We can establish the month that the change will first appear in the firm's financial statements. And at the time of the first and all subsequent statements; we can report how the returns are greater than they would have been without the executed ability in place.

Accountability for execution

Many of us have seen documentaries on the United State's Navy's Blue Angels precision flying team. During their post-show debriefing they go around the table. Each aviator (Navy does not have pilots) talks about what was not executed as well as it should have been and then declares, "I will fix it." They also report on what they "fixed" before the last show and if it worked.

Successful execution requires that same sense of urgency, self accountability and self commitment to both. Executing returns through REIs keeps clearly in front of us the ramifications of not "fixing it" with respect to what returns "could have been, but will not be" in the reporting period for which they were scheduled to first appear.

We strengthen self commitment to execution through the method to report progress tied to returns. An effective means is to conduct a regular meeting of teams or individuals responsible for executing specific abilities. Their progress determines if returns A and B will actually move from X to Y by date Z.

The meeting, as a short process, in what ever form taken, has a particular characteristic. First, it is focused on abilities that will directly and visibly affect the execution of specific returns. Second, it is focused on how teams and individuals are bringing the firm closer to being able to generate and report a change in its returns.

The format is first to report what did I do last week that brought the firm closer to being able to report an increase in the targeted incremental returns. Then I declare one to three things will I do this week to bring the firm closer.

With the collective declarations by all accountable individuals, we can project whether the returns will appear in the financial statements and returns as scheduled. How many of us have ever have the happy opportunity to make a commitment to something the CEO finds important and our fellow employees depend upon for the quality of their lives.

Notice something important here. The process to monitor execution does not speak to what I did and will do that is important. As we mentioned before, what is "important" has a high probability of getting eaten by mandatory "real-work." If we focus on "important," our execution meetings will be a continuous discussion of what is still not done. The road to hell is paved with good intentions.

Focusing on what was done last week that got the firm closer to the prize returns and what will be done this week causes accountable teams and individuals to make a personal commitment to taking action this week. Furthermore, they know that the firm is counting on them to stand and deliver for reasons that matter.

Like the Navy aviator each team and individual also has a very personnel reason for commitment and the goal is to keep it on the surface for all to see and appreciate. What I, as the aviator, fixed before the last show and will fix before the next show has consequences. If I do not commit I will continue to endanger myself and others. Worse, I will have it on my conscience if something bad happens.

Project management reinvented

Another aspect of visible proof that management will get its money soon and the risk of not is greatly reduced is that reinventing maintenance also resulted in a departure from traditional project management. The traditional approach is enticing because it gives us a false sense of the precision for which we can foresee every task needed to be successful. Its tools cause us to believe we can be accurate in an inaccurate world. Want to hear a belly laugh, tell God your plans.

The problem that reinvention had to overcome is that traditional project management only deals effectively with one of three risks to success: task risk. The unserved remaining two risks are white-paper and integration risks. Furthermore, task risk is the least potentially fatal of the three.

Task risk is the possibility that a designated task will not be carried out properly. In other words, tasks will not be delivered in budget and on time. Consequently, project management is centered on identifying tasks and their milestones, resources and cost. These details are orchestrated with planning tools that generate snapshots of the project as shown in Figure 7-2.

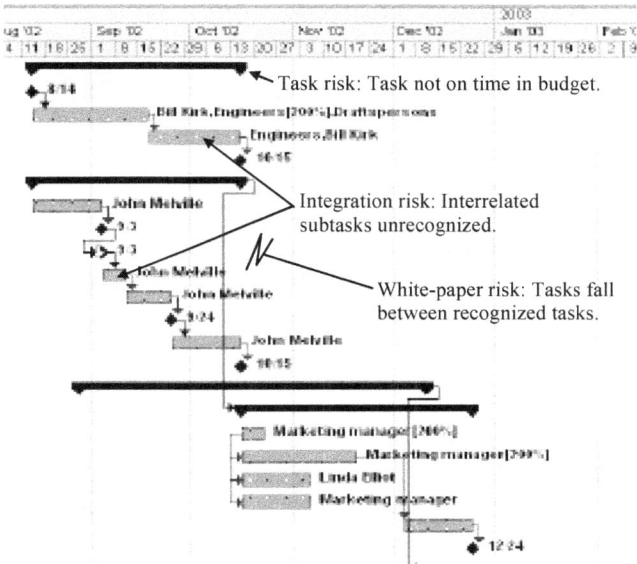

Figure 7-2: The risks inherent to traditional project execution.

To the Gantt bars of such tools all task details are attached except for one: returns resulting from the task. The biggest reason is that the connection is impossible due to the way projects are planned. Rarely, can any one task or group of tasks be been plotted back from explicit incremental returns. Furthermore, only after all planned tasks are done, will the project leaders be able to see if there is a payoff. Even then, the firm may not have a way of actually spotting, measuring and reporting the benefits promised from the project.

Figure 7-2, as the embodiment of classic project management, does not deal with the remaining two risks to a successful outcome: white-paper and integration. These are the reasons there may not be an actual return or the magnitude of return that was hoped for after all tasks have been executed as planned on time and in budget.

White-paper risk is defined as overlooking tasks between the Gantt chart bars. These tasks are lost in the white paper of the chart. Worse is that there is nothing natural to executing Gantted tasks on time and in budget that would cause the project team to find what was overlooked in a timely manner rather than by post mortem; if at all.

The other risk is integration risk. This too is fatal because the final payoff of a project is the outcome synergism between the tasks. Individually, most tasks have no affect. Furthermore, if we do not tackle individual tasks in the context of their interrelations to other tasks they will lack the mutual molding that makes them work together as they must to generate the benefits promised for the project.

The damage from white-paper and integration risk is potentially fatal. This is because they do not emerge until all tasks are done. Only then can we determine if we are successful; which may also be an impossible distinction. Worse, there is a high probability that results will fall far short of the promise and the firm cannot determine what is missing without almost completely reexecuting the project in the style explained in the next section. The ship has sailed and the firm must learn to be happy with what they did get: possibly only a moral victory.

The solution is a "returns execution initiative" (REI). We call it an REI because what is being executed are returns not the tasks of implementing a maintenance strategy. In other words, we are executing results. Everything done is directed and tied to the result, or we do not do it.

We plan an REI by working backward from the returns through the interface measures that were mapped and built into the financial-statements-based analysis of maintenance strategies.

Through the interface measures, the REI planner maps back to the abilities and subabilities that will drive the returns through the interface measures; once the abilities are up and running. In essence a REI is a package of abilities tied to a slice of new returns for the firm. The slice is quantified starting upward from the results of the abilities which are, in turn, quantified per the interface measures. Consequently, REIs are formed by putting a boundary around a least-size group of abilities able to measurably cause a return to increase.

Because we package the REI in this manner we are able to form bite-size packages of work for execution. We are easily able to get our arms and minds wrapped around each and engage firm personnel in helping the executor pull them off. Bite-size REIs are also the basis that we can expect returns to change within 100 days or possibly weeks from go. Furthermore, we will have set the "units" of action we can effectively slip into and around the ongoing, never ceasing real-work that demands everyone's attention.

When executed by the earlier definition of "executed," the abilities are an integral and well accepted part of the firm's ongoing, routine real-work. In other words, they are not likely to be killed off once the executor leaves the building.

Figure 7-3 shows that REIs are essentially vertical, whereas, the traditional project approach is horizontal; as has been maintenance best practices programs before maintenance was reinvented. The difference is the two fatal risks are almost eliminated by the vertical approach. Meanwhile, planning tasks to be on schedule and in budget is still done for activities in the vertical REI. However, these practices can be limited to subexecutions within the REI for which traditional project planning and management is important to keeping them on track.

REIs put in place new abilities intended specifically to roll up to returns through interface measures. However, until now the book has not defined exactly what an ability is. Let's do that now.

A firm acquires organizational abilities as it becomes increasingly competitive and profitable, and a more attractive place to work. An ability is reached when a firm knows the following:

- What tasks and processes must be performed.
- Which people best perform the tasks and processes.
- What information the people need to perform.
- How to measure and ensure sustained performance.
- How to structure and reinforce the effort.

We can see from the definition and elements of an ability why an REI has a high probability of success. These are elements of being effective and efficient with respect to organizational performance. Accordingly, it is not surprising that they are an integral part of a REI. This is because abilities are what is being built to execute returns. Before we do, we determine how returns will be changed and exactly what the abilities to do so must smell, look and sound like to drive the return.

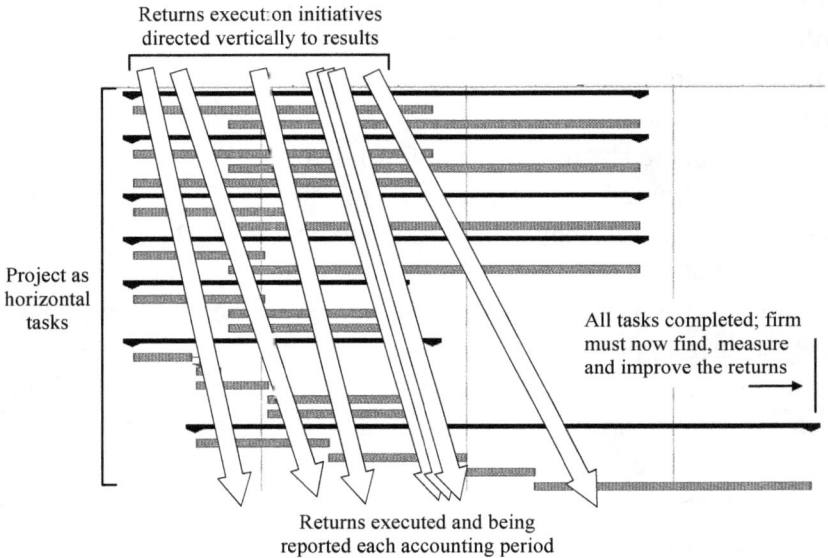

Figure 7-3: Vertical execution of returns cutting across traditional horizontal project execution.

Reduce the need to manage change

The final principle is not so much a "do" as it is a consequence of the previous principles aligned to executing returns. A central issue for predicting the potential for success is how well change is managed. We could also say that that the issue is how well we plan each REI such that the headwinds against success are reduced to an easily manageable level or to be largely a nonevent.

We can judge qualitatively the degree that we have reduced the difficulty of managing change through executing returns along three dimensions of change management: sponsorship challenge and readiness.

Sponsorship is the visible actions of advocates to build coalitions for change, communicate why the change is needed and support activities to bring about the subject change. Challenge is the size and difficulty of the change itself. Readiness is the degree that the firm can absorb and adopt the change.

The first dimension for managing change is sponsorship. Sponsorship takes place at three levels: executive, middle and frontline. The sponsors at these levels should be more than just managers. When wide managerial and nonmanagerial sponsorship exist the difficulty of managing change will be greatly reduced.

The execute-returns approach pulls strong sponsorship because, one way or another, everyone is either accountable for returns or feels the consequences. Furthermore, it is surely human nature to want to do something of importance for the well being of others beside just ourselves. Execution working back from returns asks people at all levels to be sponsors for measurable returns they can influence through their initial and continuing activities. If strong sponsorship is not natural to the REI we must reconsider what we are proposing to execute.

There is another aspect of executing returns that pulls sponsorship that the book calls the five agreements. The agreements are important because everyone wants to know they are betting their energies through sponsor-ship on a winning horse. REIs push us to reach the agreements with every move we make toward building the abilities to drive the returns. With all firm personnel that we depend upon to make the returns a reality we must have their agreement that the REI is solving the correct problem, is going about it in the correct way, has developed a good solution, recognizes all obstacles to the solution and has designed solutions to the obstacles into the overall solution.

Along the dimension of challenge there are four characteristics by which risk from challenge is typically measured by change professionals. They are as follows:

- Extent that the entities across the firm will be engaged in reach-ing and sustaining the targeted change.
- Number of people who are touched by the change or will be en-gaged in the change once it is in place.

- Type of change ranging from a rule or policy to a major strategy.
- Magnitude of change from small and uneventful to major and dramatic.

Along the dimension of challenge, because of our focus on executing returns incrementally, we reduce substantially the entities and people engaged in each packaged REI. Each REI has strategic significance. However, many times the involved change is policy in nature and realigning existing practices and process. Now processes and practices are changed surgically rather than wide ranging. Since all changes are focused on the precise drivers, REIs are typically small and uneventful.

The third dimension of evaluation is how well the firm matches up against the challenge at hand. Some would call this the firm's readiness for change. The characteristics of readiness are as follows:

- The firm's inherent capacity to adapt.
- Nature of top to bottom leadership in the firm.
- Current amount of change taking place in the firm.
- The firm's track record with change.

Along the dimension of readiness, REIs reduce the extent that readiness is an issue. This reduces the degree that the firm's current inherent readiness will be put under pressure as REIs are executed.

The principles presented to this point in the chapter, packaged to execute incremental returns, positions each REI at the lower end of difficulty of change as shown in Figure 7-4. For each REI, the probability of success is normally strong in the face of natural headwinds to change. This is because an REI allows us to work around these headwinds rather than manage them. Consequently, any actions for change management will be greatly reduced in difficulty and magnitude. This is doubly important because change management is an aspect of execution that is still more an art than science.

Planning to execute returns

Let's start the explanation of the "planning" for executing returns by taking inventory of what we have in hand at this juncture. We have an

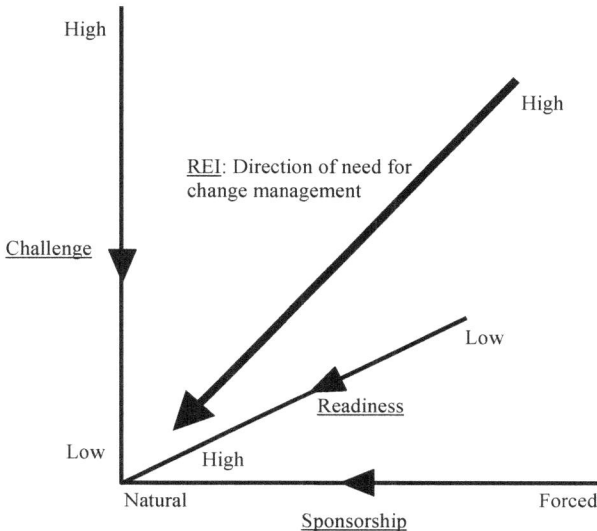

**Figure 7-4: Dimensions predicting the probability
of successful change.**

accepted set of maintenance strategies designed to a reasonable degree of detail. Recall that one principle of naturally downsizing a program with the mission to make maintenance a part of business success is to not spend time designing more about a strategy than what can be accurately de-signed. This is the principle of matching the degree of specification to the degree that something is specifiable.

At this point the firm is also comfortable that its accepted set of strate-gies fit the firm as a competitive, operational and financial beast. Further-more, that the result will be significant to the firm's returns as compared to gains lost in the rounding.

We have a rigorous financial model with which we tested the strate-gies before the final managerial decisions were made to accept them. Just as important, the engine to the financial-statements-based model is actually a budget that will play many roles as each incremental slice of returns is executed and sustained. Just as key is how the model and its budget-based engine were built upon the set of interface measures that connect returns to the abilities that will increase them.

169

Now we will set off on a trail along which are the following steps.

1. Update our bearings and set a course.
2. Circle the interface measures on the map for individual REIs.
3. Map the abilities downward from the circled interface measures.
4. Assign abilities for execution.
5. Prepare an assignee-based lane chart for executing abilities.
6. Set the timeline for reportable returns.
7. Quantify the incremental returns.
8. Meet periodically to keep score and adjust the execution plan.

Step 1: Update our bearings and set course. As we work our way down the path to reinvent the firm's maintenance to be a part of its business success, life goes on. Therefore, at the time of setting initial and updated execution plans we should review what is going on around the firm that may suggest that we should revise any currently standing intentions, plans and expectations. Examples would be a shift in the firm's business environment or business-level competitive strategies.

During the overall process of execution we will occasionally return to this step. When we do, we may find that some of the REIs underway should be redirected. Since by design REIs are bite-size in nature, the firm is able to be flexible and agile. This is because the firm is not over-committed to any particular path. If it wishes, the firm can even stub off a current REI, take the winnings and reset the course to capture a different prize.

Step 2: Circle interface measures on the map for individual REIs. Now it is time to begin delineating REIs amongst the many possibilities. The process is actually a decision process.

The step places the firm's entire interface measures map on the table and literally circles clusters of interface measures. Circling is shown by Figure 7-5 with respect to an interface measuring map presented by the previous chapter. The firm has decided to tackle specific returns increasing by the act of circling a set of related interface measures. The REI will ultimately be defined and managed with respect to abilities downward from the lowest interface measures in the circled sets.

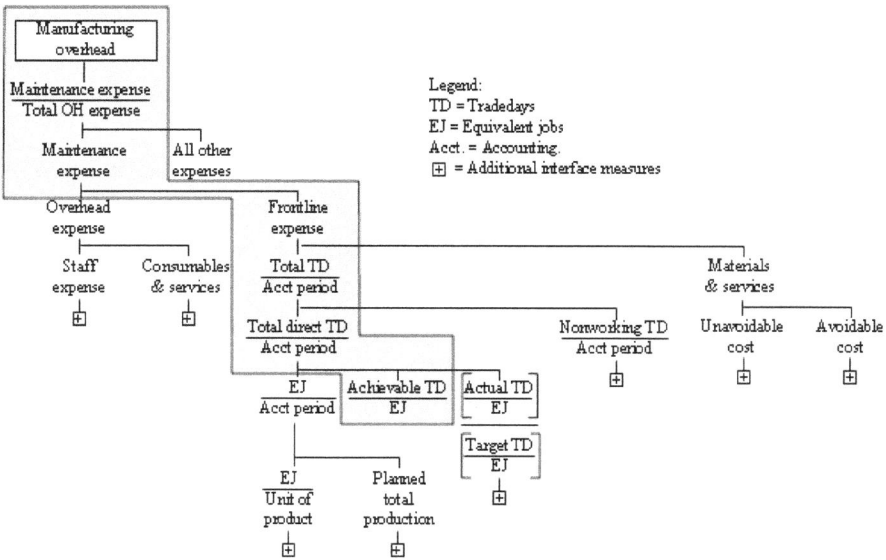

Figure 7-5: The concept of setting REI around interface measures.

The circling process distinguishes "And" and "Or" relationships at the branches of the interface measures map. In the figure we can see the case of "Or" in many places. What this means is that the firm does not have to include all branches in the subject measure to the same REI. This is because they are additive. If we circled both, the executed incremental return would be greater. If we circle less than all branches the firm will pick up the remaining part of the total possible incremental return as part of another REI.

An "And" case is one which requires that all branches at a junction must be circled as within the same REI. If not, returns will not increase regardless of the effort expended. The map in Figure 7-5 does not go down far enough for the "Or" case to appear.

An example may be that abilities under one branch improve some aspect of performance. Meanwhile, the abilities under another branch actually harvest the improvement such that the firm's returns actually move. This is a very common case across maintenance.

Step 3: Map the abilities downward from the circled interface measures. Now that we have circled sets of interface measures, we map the system of distinctive abilities that, when in place, will move them. The abilities are extracted or "written" from the details of the various strategies whose elements are relevant to predicting and influencing the subject interface measures.

From the bottommost interface measures we would begin mapping abilities as shown in Figure 7-6. An interface measure is shown above the broken line; although there may be more than one. The measure is moved by the two abilities directly linked to it. Then the map defines the subabilities that must function in good form before the topmost two abilities will be able to affect the interface measure.

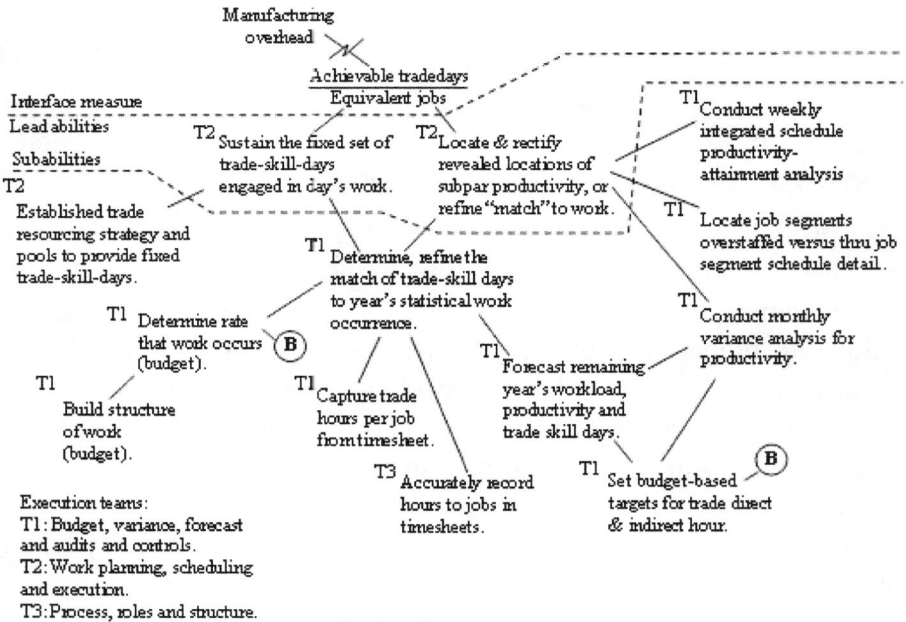

Figure 7-6: Abilities mapped and assigned to teams.

The resulting map is a system of organizational abilities. They will not only predictably move the measures, but through them the firm can actually influence the measures.

Wording is everything as we map the abilities. One reason is that it sharpens our focus on the incremental return being executed. Wording tells us what to leave in, what to leave out. If another REI leads back to the same ability, its wording from that direction will reveal the exact refinements that must be made to the common ability.

The map looks as if a great deal of work is being planned; however, that is not usually the case. The objective is to identify abilities that can be assigned to teams and individuals as single accountable achievements. Consequently, many of the subabilities may be assignments requiring as little as hours; upward to days. A few may require more than a week. However, as a set they will generally require less than 100 days. In fact, this goal affects the firm's decisions for what its individual REIs will include for execution

When the executor sets out to execute an assigned ability, the unforeseen will reveal itself and be taken into the execution or passed off to the execution of another REI. This is an important principle because few of us are prescient, although traditional project management is essentially based on the belief that we are. Consequently, we have to rely on activities to execute a challenge to reveal to us what we were not able to foresee.

An important intent of the REI approach to execution is to define what we do know to expect, get out and make it happen while looking to discover what we did not know that we did not know. Through such a plan-by-doing philosophy we virtually eliminate the earlier mentioned white-paper and integration risk that makes high the risk of failure in classic project management.

Step 4: Assign abilities for execution. One rule of execution is that no person or team shall execute more than three of the mapped abilities at a time. Sequencing the execution of subabilities will somewhat automatically regulate the rate that abilities are taken on with respect to a group of abilities mapped to an REI. Otherwise, the program manager must make sure that executors are not violating the principle across multiple REIs.

The process of assigning executors is demonstrated in Figure 7-6. Notice the coding given to teams: T1, T2 and T3. Therefore, this step will view the mapped abilities and decide the person or team who could best take on each ability. The map is annotated accordingly and becomes an execution management document.

Step 5: Prepare an assignee-based lane chart for executing abilities. Earlier in the chapter white-paper and integration risk were identified as a big reason that traditional project planning practices have a considerable chance of project failure; defined as the failure to generate significant benefit as planned. The biggest reason is that we do not know what we do not know.

We can take away a message from recognizing the two risks. We should not spend a great deal of time with project planning. Instead, we want to establish what we should be doing, where to get started and how to reach the end outcome.

Figure 7-7 shows the scheduling method for the REI approach to execution that meets the criteria to plan, without over-planning. All plans have a rate of decay. When decay has progressed such that the lane chart of Figure 7-7 no longer tells the tale, it is quickly reworked.

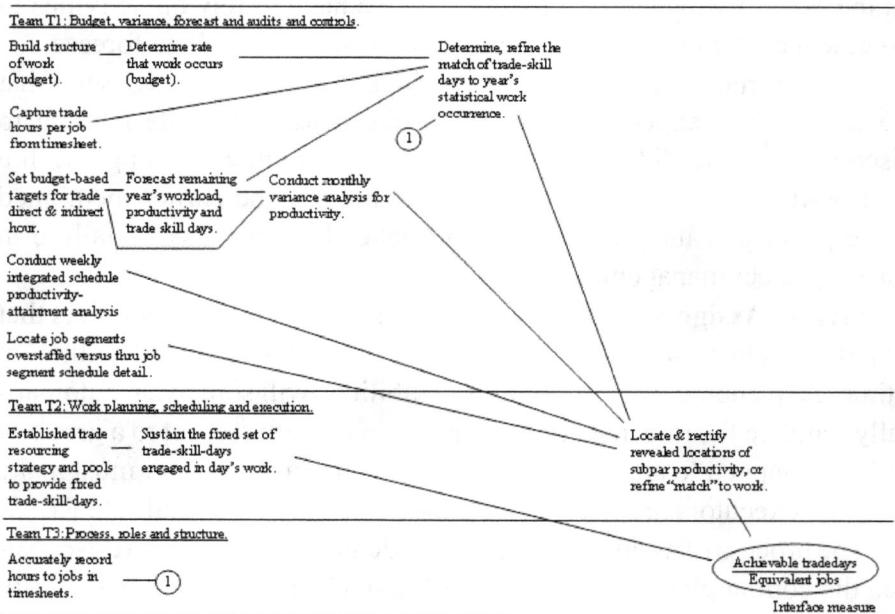

Figure 7-7: Lane chart for executing abilities up to an interface measure.

Notice four principles at work in the chart. First, the items are taken from the abilities map. Second, they are placed in lanes with respect to the teams identified on the lead activities map.

Third, the activities are placed in their lanes based on "general" sequence. This is "general" because the team may elect to do some in parallel according to the one-to-three rule of activity. Progressing from left to right, a team executes one or more abilities at a time. As one is pushed across the finish line, another along the lane is pulled in for action. The number of subabilities taken on at any one time is left to the executor to decide.

Fourth, sequence is also reflected across the lanes. The charts shows each team in what cases it cannot make some moves until another team makes it move. Accordingly, teams will collaborate in the process of making their individual decisions to act.

Step 6: Set timeline to reportable returns. If we were management we would want to know when the firm can begin to report that "Our returns are greater than they would have been by X." Setting the date that the statement will be possible is the purpose of this task.

The lane chart serves a purpose. It allows us to estimate when the systems of abilities that will drive returns through the interface measures will be in place and working their magic. Extrapolating from them we can mark the calendar for when the abilities will start putting points on the board. Thence, it is a matter pointing to the first financial reporting period that the results will appear in the returns and financial statements.

One thing is notable about executing returns through REIs. It is that the timeline we are most interested in is when returns will begin to increase. We are only interested in the timeline for abilities because they decide the timeline to increased returns. As we mention later, we report our activities as the degree that the firm has moved closer to triggering returns.

Step 7: Quantify the incremental returns. The abilities roll up through interface measures to increase returns by a measurable increment. At the end of each reporting period we will be able to measure the chain of cause-and-effect for returns. With it the firm will be able to know that its returns were greater by an amount or percent greater than they would have been if the abilities had not been part of the firm's "real-work."

Now that we have identified and mapped the abilities and charted them sequentially for execution, we can quantify the incremental returns.

Therefore, this step is to quantify the "from X to Y" portion of setting returns goals from the result of making maintenance part of the firm's business success. The "when" portion of the goal will have been set by the previous step.

Step 8: Meet periodically to keep score and adjust the execution plan. How implementation is measured and controlled is also a departure from traditional project management. The focus is the result, thus, were we are with respect to the abilities we have set out to put in place and make fully operational.

Consequently, the program needs to be reported and controlled to that end. The thrust is to make the right moves with respect to each ability. Therefore, control should assess primarily what is the next envisioned several moves to be made and why are they essential to reaching the targeted ability. There are two levels of control.

First is to assess what was done last week and why it was necessary to get closer to increasing the targeted incremental returns. More impor-tantly, at the time of the project meeting what several activities will the team tackle this week and how are they essential to getting the firm closer to increasing the targeted returns. This view may be extended a week or two further out but should be allowed to change without the pressure of "but you said." Too often projects fail to succeed because they are so committed to a conclusion for action that they cannot respond to opportu-nistically take advantage of what has been learned while taking action. The firm may be well served to prepare a weekly report that captures these simple requirements.

The second level is to review and refine the abilities map and lane charts based on water under the bridge. The road to payoff passes through many new insights. Consequently, it is important to stop and revisit and refine the charts based on the travels. As they are, the charts will be extended to new lead abilities.

To this point the book has described how to reinvent maintenance to be an important part of the firm's business success. The chapters have explained the process to determine, evaluate and design the maintenance strategies that would directly and significantly increase profit, profit margin, return on investment and cash return on investment. The progression was capped off with explaining how to implement the strategies by executing their returns.

Just as maintenance has been reinvented, new disciplines must be brought to the management of maintenance. The remainder of the book will present and explain them. It is not feasible to expect maintenance to be a part of business success if the firm cannot budget the year and then control and forecast variance. Nor is it a feasible expectation without organizational structure for both the strategic and tactical work of maintenance, audit and control systems to confirm the continuing integrity of process and organization, the best practices of the past molded to maintenance strategy and the information technology tools that make all things possible.

Chapter 8
Workload-Based Budget and Variance

We immediately think of cost control, cutting or saving at the mention of budgeting, and reporting and forecasting variance. However, that is far from the business purpose. In a few words, budgeting and variance reporting and forecasting is about managing maintenance as a part of the business rather than only managing maintenance and equipment. The budget and variance report and forecast are collectively the mandatory body of actionable information a firm must have to do that.

Of course, an unavoidable, but beneficial, outcome of budgeting and variance reporting and forecasting is that overall maintenance cost is under control. However, what is actually being managed, according to a budget as a business plan, are the drivers that decide cost.

Because they thread throughout the explanation, the chapter will introduce the two strategic dimensions a budget and variance system deals with. It will then explain why the approach of traditional accounting to budget and reporting variance is so little help in the management of maintenance and equipment; let alone allow the firm to manage maintenance as part of a business. We must understand this before it is possible to understand what does work and how to build it.

The chapter will then explain how workload-based budgeting and variance reporting and forecasting works by explaining what both entail. Finally, the chapter will layout the steps to build a budget and variance system.

One thing will quickly become apparent as the chapter unfolds. It is hard to envision any program for maintenance and reliability being as successful as it could be without the body of information that is described in this chapter. It is fascinating to imagine how the programs we have all seen would have been different.

Before kicking off the explanation, it is important to make a point. The solution to budgeting and variance reporting and forecasting for maintenance is not intended to interfere, change or replace the traditional accounting system and its budget and variance. As a parallel system, it serves the nature of managing maintenance as part of the business that the traditional system cannot. Consequently, the system increases the power of the traditional system by giving the firm the means to explain its content with granular and transparent details.

Two strategic dimensions of budget and variance

Budgets and variance reports and forecasts, as a body of information, are actually the convergence of two strategic dimensions: workload and resources. The workload dimension deals with the work that will be required to conduct the business strategies the firm has chosen for the year. This is not limited to direct maintenance work. It includes every type of work to effectively operate the overall maintenance function as part of the business.

The budget derives and defines work down from the firm's business strategies. As it does, all work is made granular and transparent with clearly established accountability. The variance report tests our expectations for the year's workload, confirms that work is being executed and allows us to forecast if the year's work will vary from plan.

The second strategic dimension is strategy for the resources associated with the direct and indirect workload for managing maintenance as part of the business. Whereas, workload is largely dictated by what work will be necessary for the firm to succeed at its business strategies, workload does not dictate strategy for acquiring the resources to execute it. In fact, a firm has a range of possible strategies; including continuing the status quo.

Accordingly, the budget allows management to form and test different strategies for resources and make final decisions for which road to take. The resulting granularity, transparency and accountability become the foundation upon which the variance report and forecast will provide the information needed to confirm and reevaluate the resources strategies and take timely action as the year unfolds.

What works, what does not

Traditional accounting books dollar outlays and inflows from producing products and services. Its overarching purpose is to measure, track and report business results and financial position. The problem that has haunted us for years is that traditional accounting does not give management the wherewithal to manage maintenance as part of business success.

Why? A primary reason is how information is structured by the traditional accounting system. It is not structured as it must be to manage maintenance as part of the business.

Contrast in structure

The structure of the traditional accounting system is two dimensional. The first dimension is responsibility center. The second is accounts. At this point in the chapter, we will contrast what works and does not by looking at the accounts dimension of the structure. The responsibility dimension will be a topic later on in the chapter.

The accounts structure of traditional accounting is shown in the simplified budget and variance of Figure 8-1 for the maintenance function. Each line item of the traditional budget and variance report is an account in the accounting system. Every transaction for each responsibility center is recorded to one or more accounts in the firm's "Chart of Accounts." The line items of the firm's financial statements are the results of the closing process by which all accounts are brought together to report income, expenses and final balances.

Upon the line items, as accounts, the budget forecasts what is expected to be spent. As the year unfolds, the variance report reveals what was spent with respect to each account and compares it with what was forecasted by the budget to be spent.

That is what the traditional budget and variance report tell us. Unfortunately, there are many more important things it does not tell us. This gap leaves the firm unable to manage maintenance as part of the business.

Area Variance Report Month X, Year 20X2							
			Month			Year to date	
GL	Account	Actual	Budget	Variance	Actual	Budget	Variance
61900 Mater							
61801 Contr							
61802 Maint							
Area total ma							

Area Budget: Year 20X2						
GL	Account	20X1	20X2	Jan	Feb	Mar
61900 Material issues						
61801 Contract services	← Accounts from firm's chart of accounts					
61802 Maintenance labor						
Area total maintenance						

Figure 8-1: The accounts structure of the traditional accounting system.

There are two reasons the firm is hogtied. First, because spending is reported as accounts, we cannot see the results or outcomes that the resources engaged by the business have brought about. Consequently, resources are engaged without any real means to measure what is appropriate according to a legitimate plan. Second, we cannot see the interrelationships of the engaged resources to a common result or outcome. Consequently, the firm does not have any real means to know the true total resources that should be expected and engaged directly and indirectly to do the work of the period.

The alternative to the traditional system is to structure the budget and variance on workload tied back to the firm's business strategies. Resource strategies are set and then reflected in each workload line of the structure. More important, experience has shown that almost any type of information is possible with such a structure.

The budget and variance approach that is normal to large jobs is often consistent with a workload type structure. Unfortunately, the method does not work for all other types of maintenance. Consequently, the ability to budget and analyze variance has always been limited to large jobs. All other maintenance work is quantified and tracked in the context of the accounts of the traditional accounting system. This undermines the firm's ability to manage maintenance as part of it overall business success. This is because so little is know about the largest part of its annual running maintenance work.

The budget for a large majority of the firm's annual running maintenance work is the previous year's spending bumped up by a percentage. In many cases, the previous year's actual spending is almost regarded as a "scientific" measure of a true norm for spending. For payroll, the budget is essentially set by counting noses and possibly attempting to justify the need for additional staffing. Ultimately, the budget is settled by negotiation between firm, plant and maintenance management because there is so little in the budget that is evidence-based.

A children's medical advice column printed a letter asking the doctor when a toddler could be potty trained. The doctor wrote, "When the child can sit still for two minutes." When can a firm manage maintenance as part of its business success? When the firm can do workload-based budgeting and variance reporting and forecasting.

Contrast in budget

Figure 8-2 contrasts the traditional accounts-based budget for maintenance with a workload-based budget. Both pertain to the direct maintenance work for the same production area and its direct and indirect resources. Both show the same total four numbers for payroll, materials, services and total. However, what is the "information" of the traditional system is a merely a rollup of much greater information provided by the workload-based budget.

Consequently, a whole host of differences are immediately apparent. First, the number of jobs for each workload line has been determined and shown by working back from the firm's business strategy-based plans for the year. Second, accountability for work and resources is very clear because the budget has structured workload on dimensions, many which reflect accountability. Third, we can see clearly the resources that will be engaged by each workload line. Fourth, the interrelationship of resources converges on each workload line, thus, fully revealing the full true direct and indirect resources that each engages as a consequence of the firm's resource strategies. Fifth, and not shown, behind each "number" of the table are the layers of background drivers to each line through which management can drill-down to confirm and understand why the numbers are what they are.

The contrast is profound for managing maintenance as part of the business rather than only managing maintenance. Firms have typically known very little about their maintenance work as distinctive workload lines. What was known is exponentially less with respect to the connection of work and its resources to business strategies.

Workload-based budget format

Process maintenance: Workload-based budget for direct work, Year 20X2								
Process Area A								
	Number of jobs		Labor		Material & service			Total
Work type & class	Month Avg	Year	Hours	Payroll	Material	Service	M&S	expense
Corrective								
Mechanical-MW	100.0	1,200	33,663	$ 1,277,629	$ 960,000	$ 144,000	$ 1,104,000	$ 2,381,629
Piping-PF	43	516	14,475	$ 549,380	$ 412,800	$ 61,920	$ 474,720	$ 1,024,100
Electrical	67.0	804	6,151	$ 233,458	$ 40,200	$ 8,040	$ 48,240	$ 281,698
Instrument	13.0	156	2,947	$ 111,846	$ 117,000	$ 1,560	$ 118,560	$ 230,406
Subtotal	223.0	2,676.0	57,236.4	2,172,312.2	1,530,000.0	215,520.0	1,745,520.0	3,917,832.2
Proactive								
Preventive-MW	67	804	6,049	$ 229,567	$ 9,648	$ 1,206	$ 10,854	$ 240,421
MAG	7	81	1,645	$ 62,441	$ 1,048	$ 161	$ 1,210	$ 63,651
RBI	4	46	940	$ 35,681	$ 599	$ 92	$ 691	$ 36,372
Electrical	120	144	2,938	$ 111,502	$ 1,872	$ 288	$ 2,160	$ 113,662
Instrument	75.0	900	4,250	$ 161,316	$ 35,100	$ 2,700	$ 37,800	$ 199,116
Subtotal	165	1,975	15,822	600,507	48,267	4,447	52,715	653,222
Dispatch (per standing work orders)								
Mechanical-MW	NA	9	2,210	$ 83,884	$ -	$ -	$ -	$ 83,884
Piping-PF	NA	6	995	$ 995	$ 995	$ 995	$ 995	$ 2,984
Electrical	NA	3	862	$ 862	$ 862	$ 862	$ 862	$ 2,586
Instrument	NA	4	2,498	$ 2,498	$ 2,498	$ 2,498	$ 2,498	$ 7,493
	NA	22	6,564	$ 88,239	$ 4,354	$ 4,354	$ 4,354	$ 96,947
Projects								
Mechanical-MW	NA	10	13,247	$ 502,769	$ 80,000	$ 434,500	$ 514,500	$ 1,017,269
Piping-PF	NA	12	15,896	$ 603,323	$ 96,000	$ 521,400	$ 617,400	$ 1,220,723
Electrical	NA	-	-	$ -	$ -	$ -	$ -	
Instrument	NA	2	1,889	$ 71,696	$ 29,000	$ -	$ 29,000	$ 100,696
	NA	24	31,033	$ 1,177,787	$ 205,000	$ 955,900	$ 1,160,900	$ 2,338,687
Area total	388	4,675	110,655	$ 4,038,845	$ 1,787,621	$ 1,180,222	$ 2,963,489	$ 7,006,698

Area Budget: Year 20X2						
GL	Account	20X1	20X2	Jan	Feb	Mar
61900	Material issues	1,733,992	1,787,621	148,968	148,968	148,968
61801	Contract services	1,144,815	1,180,222	98,352	98,352	98,352
61801	Maintenance labor	3,917,680	4,038,845	336,570	336,570	336,570
Area total maintenance		6,796,487	7,006,688	583,891	583,891	583,891

Traditional budget format

Figure 8-2: Full information is the information gap between the traditional and workload based budgets.

The firm now has information it has not had in the past. It can now ask and answer powerful, impactful questions of itself it never could before. It follows that the annual budget process is transformed from negotiating a "number" to collaborative decision-analysis and decision-making.

Contrast in variance reporting and forecasting

The contrast is even greater between traditional and workload-based variance reports. The problematic contrasts between the workload-based and traditional budgets are also the case for variance reports. However, the contrasts that can be seen in Figure 8-3 are additionally profound.

Workload-based variance format per workload line

Process maintenance: Month's variance: Month XX, 20XX							
Corrective: Mechanical-MW							
		Activity			Budget cost		
		Jobs	Dir hrs	Payroll	Material	Service	Total
Budget	Total	110	2,753	119,724	125,000	600	245,324
	Per job		25	1,088	1,136	5	2,230
Actual	Total	100	2,375	106,423	80,000	12,000	198,423
	Per job		24	1,064	800	120	1,984
Subvariance per workload line	Total variance			13,302	45,000	(11,400)	46,902
	Due to jobs			10,642	8,000	1,200	19,842
	Due to resources			6,297	37,000	(12,600)	30,697
	Due to overtime			(3,638)			(3,638)

Versus

Area Variance Report Month X, Year 20X2							
			Month			Year to date	
GL	Account	Actual	Budget	Variance	Actual	Budget	Variance
61900	Material issues	201,674	189,560	(12,114)	611,072	568,679	(42,393)
61801	Contract services	23,931	32,505	8,573	72,512	97,514	25,002
61801	Maintenance labor	362,357	361,826	(531)	1,097,942	1,085,479	(12,463)
Area total maintenance		587,962	583,891	(4,072)	1,781,526	1,751,672	(29,854)

Traditional variance format per total production area

Figure 8-3: "What really happened" is the information gap between the traditional and workload based variance reports.

The traditional variance report gives only total variances for the production area. In contrast the workload-based variance report provides variance for each workload line. Consequently, the first profound contrast is that the traditional system does not show what really happened variance wise. It only shows total, thus, net variance.

The reality is that the total as net variance is made up of many offsetting variances throughout the workload lines shown in the budget of Figure 8-2; some important, some not. This is shown in Figure 8-3. The workload line experienced a $13,302 underrun for labor while the reported total variance for labor is a $531 overrun. Obviously, much more is happening than a $531 overrun.

Worse, the firm will not know this because the traditional variance report hides it. Cases will remain hidden variances that, if dealt with and learned from, would have changed the firm's fortunes. They are like gold coins strewn about in the tall weeds.

The ramifications of the contrast can be heard in senior managements' typical lament about the traditional variance report, "Each month we have big questions, but can't get an answer. If we get an answer we know it is not a good one." The other side of the lament is the remark frequently made by staff people who are regularly tormented for an answer, "Every month they ask me what caused the variance. I don't know and don't have time to research it. I just give them something."

In contrast, the workload-based variance report provides the variance for each workload line in the budget; information management has not had before. However, to completely eliminate hidden variances, variances must be reported more deeply than just total variance for each workload line. This is the second profound contrast with the traditional system.

Accordingly, the workload-based report identifies the subvariances for each resource of each line item. The example of Figure 8-3 shows a variance report designed with three subvariances for each workload line of Figure 8-2. Although not limited to the three, the shown subvariances are jobs per workload line, variance in resources per job and variance in overtime. The matrix will be explained later in the chapter.

These subvariance matrixes are a powerful demonstration that almost any type of information is possible when we structure the body of information to match what is needed to manage maintenance as part of the business. Another demonstration is the conspicuous absence of another topic.

There is no reference to contrasting abilities to forecast the variance for the remaining and total year as the year unfolds. This is because the traditional system cannot produce forecast based information that would be anything but misinformation. The workload-based system can because its structure, budget workload lines, and subvariance matrix are the platform on which the ability to forecast variance rests. This is a third profound contrast. Forecasting will be explained in a later section of the chapter.

Building the workload-based budget

The budget is built generally as sections relative to the concentric circles shown in Figure 8-4. The center is the direct work done by trades. The outer circle does the strategic-level work that is required to enable the firm to manage maintenance to be an important part of its business success. The circle between the center and outer circles does the work that plans, organizes and controls the direct work and the associated resources.

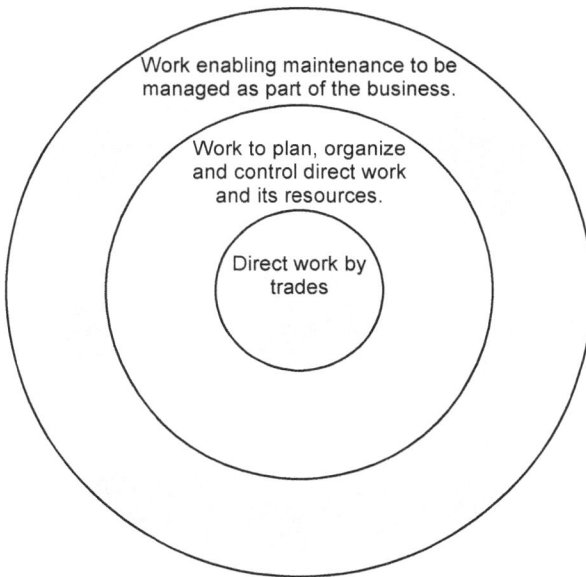

Work enabling maintenance to be managed as part of the business.

Work to plan, organize and control direct work and its resources.

Direct work by trades

Figure 8-4: The budget sections as concentric work.

The sections of the budget are built for all three circles. The circles do not imply an organizational hierarchy for the overall maintenance function. In fact, there are many possible variations driven by unique combinations of issues for the firm. However, the workload-based structure will typically reflect the concentric roles.

Set the budget workload structure

We have already explained one departure from the structure upon which transactions are presented by the traditional budget. We connect resources to workload lines that were derived top-down as necessary to implement the firm's business strategies. As resources are engaged, they are recorded in the accounts as transactions linked to the workload line.

We make another departure from the traditional structure. As mentioned previously, the structure has two dimensions: accounts and responsibility center. Revenues and costs, as accounts, are attached to the responsibility centers as shown by Figure 8-5. Upon the centers, the traditional system budgets cost and revenues top-down and records actual costs and revenues bottom-up.

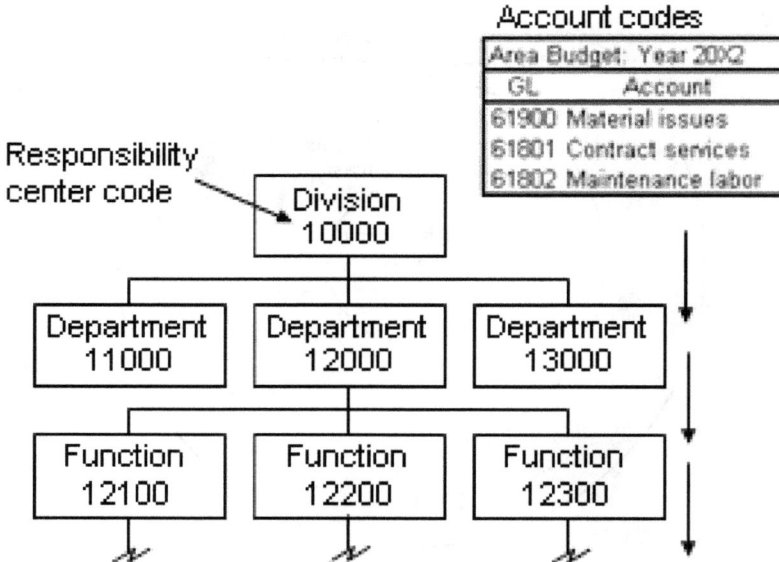

Figure 8-5: Responsibility centers and accounts in traditional accounting.

Just as accounts, centers are generally chiseled in stone. If how we will manage maintenance as part of business success requires us to change the centers and accounts structure we will, like Don Quixote, waste our life away fighting windmills.

We get around this absolutely necessary inflexibility of the traditional system by building the workload-based system to operate in parallel to it; giving us the information the traditional system cannot. In the workload-based system we layout a structure that works for managing maintenance as part of the business. Figure 8-6 is a page from the budget section for direct work: the inner circle of Figure 8-4. The workload structure is the leftmost column. A structure would also be set that suites the nature of the middle and outer circles of the figure.

Notice that responsibility still appears in the structure. However, responsibility goes beyond the centers at the traditional system and is many dimensional. Although work types, tied back to business strategy, dominate the structure we can see dimensions of responsibility in the form of department, work type, and trade. Crew is also implicit in the example as it is related to a specific work type, trade type or area. However, crew could have been shown explicitly or by another structure in another section.

Structure for budget and variance based on workload as line items.

Outcome of firm's resource strategies tied to each workload line item.

Process maintenance: Workload-based budget for direct work Year 20X2

Process Area A

Work type & class	Number of jobs		Labor		Material & service			Total
	Month Avg	Year	Hours	Payroll	Material	Service	M&S	expense
Corrective								
Mechanical-MW	100.0	1,200	33,663 $ 1,277,629	$ 960,000	$ 144,000	$ 1,104,000	$ 2,381,629	
Piping-PF	43	516	14,475 $ 549,380	$ 412,800	$ 61,920	$ 474,720	$ 1,024,100	
Electrical	67.0	804	6,151 $ 233,458	$ 40,200	$ 8,040	$ 48,240	$ 281,698	
Instrument	13.0	156	2,947 $ 111,846	$ 117,000	$ 1,560	$ 118,560	$ 230,406	
Subtotal	223.0	2,676.0	57,236.4 2,172,312.2	1,530,000.0	215,520.0	1,745,520.0	3,917,832.2	
Proactive								
Preventive-MW	67	804	6,049 $ 229,567	$ 9,648	$ 1,206	$ 10,854	$ 240,421	
MAG	7	81	1,645 $ 62,441	$ 1,048	$ 161	$ 1,210	$ 63,651	
RBI	4	46	940 $ 35,681	$ 599	$ 92	$ 691	$ 36,372	
Electrical	12.0	144	2,938 $ 111,502	$ 1,872	$ 288	$ 2,160	$ 113,662	
Instrument	75.0	900	4,250 $ 161,316	$ 35,100	$ 2,700	$ 37,800	$ 199,116	
Subtotal	165	1,975	15,822 600,507	48,267	4,447	52,715	653,222	
Dispatch (per standing work orders)								
Mechanical-MW	NA	9	2,210 $ 83,884	$ -	$ -	$ -	$ 83,884	
Piping-PF	NA	6	995 $ 995	$ 995	$ 995	$ 995	$ 2,984	
Electrical	NA	3	862 $ 862	$ 862	$ 862	$ 862	$ 2,586	
Instrument	NA	4	2,498 $ 2,498	$ 2,498	$ 2,498	$ 2,498	$ 7,493	
	NA	22	6,564 $ 88,239	$ 4,354	$ 4,354	$ 4,354	$ 96,947	
Projects								
Mechanical-MW	NA	10	13,247 $ 502,769	$ 80,000	$ 434,500	$ 514,500	$ 1,017,269	
Piping-PF	NA	12	15,896 $ 603,323	$ 96,000	$ 521,400	$ 617,400	$ 1,220,723	
Electrical	NA	-	- $ -	$ -	$ -	$ -	$ -	
Instrument	NA	2	1,889 $ 71,696	$ 29,000	$ -	$ 29,000	$ 100,696	
	NA	24	31,033 $ 1,177,787	$ 205,000	$ 955,900	$ 1,160,900	$ 2,338,687	
Area total	388	4,675	110,655 $ 4,038,845	$ 1,787,621	$ 1,180,222	$ 2,963,489	$ 7,006,688	

Workload determined for each workload line item.

Figure 8-6: Budget for direct work structured on work.

Many factors influence the structure. The structure could reflect how a group of work must be managed or relative size. Another possibility is to reflect specific business strategies. There may be multiple structures serving different roles and business purposes. Furthermore, we will typically pull and combine elements of multiple information systems into single structures for the workload-based system. The possibilities, variations and permutations are almost endless. The point is that the structure is not dominated, decided or constrained by the centers and accounts of the traditional system.

The structure is also greatly influenced by what the firm understands about its work in the context of the firm's business success. As the budget is built and goes operational through its mirroring variance report, the firm will deepen its understanding. Accordingly, the structure will likely be refined and expanded in its earliest budget cycles. It can also change with time as the firm's business strategies for maintenance change.

The point is that the workload-based structure is molded, and easily so, to match the firm's competitive, operational and financial characteristics and how maintenance can be managed as part of the business. Because we are doing the analysis outside the traditional system, the structure is completely flexible. The flexibility opens a whole new world because without the ability to work from an appropriate structure it is not possible to manage maintenance as part of the business.

Therefore, the first step to building the budget is to set the workload-based structure. The designer should draft the structure for cross-firm review and finalization. The front-end work to understand the firm as a competitive, operational and financial beast will have prepared the designer to draft a good initially proposed structure for consideration across the firm; north-south, east-west.

Set the workload profile for direct work

The next step to building the budget is to determine the profile for each workload line. The profile is the rate and timing that work is expected to occur as the year unfolds. Each profile will reflect the drivers such as annual demand and production cycles, seasons and their weather, events such as turnarounds and overhauls, etc. The workload lines in the budget view (Figure 8-6) for direct work are the 12-month rollup of the profiles.

Once the profiles have been established, the firm has in hand the budget of work that must be served by the firm's final resource strategies. As they are established, the firm is gaining new insight into the firm's workload; one line at a time. Beside their role in building the budget, the profiles will no doubt be put to use in all sorts of business planning, forecasting and decisions.

The concept of forming the workload profiles is obvious, but where does the data come from? The greatest single source is, of course, the EAM/CMMS. This is because it captures so many details for each work order. This leaves us with a huge amount of detail to make something of. The data is generated as work is requested, approved, prepared, managed and executed, and closed. If the EAM/CMMS is not capturing everything we need, it is usually because it is not being captured rather than cannot be easily captured.

Why and how data is available is immediately apparent when we view the typical boxes of a window in EAM/CMMS (Figure 8-7). Each time, throughout its life as a work request and order, that new information about a job is entered and updated in a box, the entered information flows to database tables located on the firm's overall information system (SAP, Oracle, etc.).

In turn, it is easy to use off-the-shelf data mining tools to reach into the database and extract the data we need to analyze and form each workload line. It is important to make the distinction that we are not working though the EAM/CMMS when we do. We are capitalizing on its data.

The previous section explained the budget's workload-based structure. The data fields in the tables of the EAM/CMMS are of such that it is easy to build the workload lines in accordance with the structure. An inspection of the window shown in Figure 8-7 quickly reveals that there are many elements of categorization that make the structure and its many permutations possible. They are evident in the window and just as they would be for the windows represented by the tabs at the top of the active window. It follows that it is easy to link together all of the fields needed to form the workload line profiles and then develop the full details for each workload line.

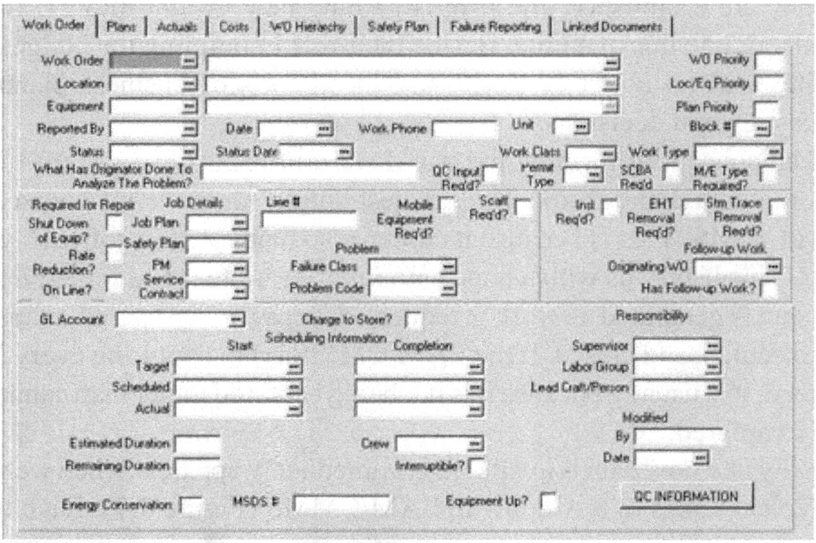

Figure 8-7: Window view of a CMMS.

The data available to build the budget is not limited to the EAM/CMMS. Data that is not available through the EAM/CMMS is almost always available from the databases of the firm's other systems. These other systems will also offer details on which the workload-based structure can be given additional distinctions. This is an important point because off-the-shelf data mining tools allow us to easily join together data from different systems resulting in data as if there were a single system.

If there is not an existing system to generate a necessary piece of data, ERP-type technology allows us to easily build the supplemental, typically small, systems making the data available. These are most often built to support a specialized process associated with the operation of a business strategy for maintenance. As the process functions, it generates the data.

There is another important point being revealed here. The EAM/CMMS collects much of the data we need to make maintenance a much greater part of the firm's business success. However, it cannot effectively serve most of the processes that are required to fulfill the goal; including budgeting and variance reporting and forecasting.

This is because the EAM/CMMS has its own narrow purpose; as most systems do. It is to manage and administer the conduct of field work in the plant and capture equipment history. This is an important distinction because misplaced, overstretched expectations have long held maintenance back from reaching its importance to overall business success.

The rate and timing that work occurs for each workload line is largely determined statistically from the database tables. The exception is the large jobs which are identified in advance and budgeted individually before management makes a final decision to include them in the year's budget. The profile of their associated workload line is shaped by when the firm plans to do them.

The statistical determination is adjusted based on expectations for the plant's situation as it varies from year to year. It is also adjusted as the firm progressively learns more about its work.

For some workload lines, analysis is not limited to forming profiles based statistical counts and timing. Instead, they may be built upon the statistical relationship of competitive, operational and financial characteristics as drivers of work. For example, some workload lines will be tied to the statistical relationships between work and the firm's planned aggregate production profile. Another example is to relate to the workload impact of using feedstock of varying assay and quality. The possible list is endless and a new role for reliability engineering: forecasting maintenance work back from business strategy through its impact on equipment.

The data, as statistics-based information, will be discussed, brainstormed and validated with personnel across the firm who are close to the work and its drivers. After the first budget cycle, the previous year's monthly variance reports will be an important contributor to the annual budget process because they look so deeply at what actually happened.

Ultimately, the budget analyst should establish a consensus for the final figures. This is especially so for the initial budget cycle. The analyst will find that the individual views of the workload line profiles are all over the map and the discussion will cause them to converge. This is an important discovery and outcome. Until the divergence of expectation is eliminated, maintenance and equipment will continue to be managed with divergent game plans; each competing against the others.

When opinion is replaced with fact, built on data, most firms immediately begin to operate differently as its daily conversations and actions are being influenced by new and better information. This affect will emerge long before the final budget is available and making its full contribution to business success. In fact, that has already started even before reaching this point of building the budget.

Set hours and payroll on workload lines

The next step to building the workload-based budget is to determine the trade hours for each workload line as a result of the firm's resource strategies for engaging trades in the business. One important outcome of this part of the budget is that it gives the firm's the ability to deeply understand trade hours relative to workload which is, in return, connected to business strategy and returns. This is important because a firm will never have full control of its business success and destiny until it has the insight and information it needs to make fact-based strategic decisions for its trade resources.

The strategic and tactical decisions that management must be able to make for trade hours are wide ranging and reflect the firm as a competitive, operational and financial beast in its current and future business environments. Even the "change-nothing" decision as a trade resource strategy requires that the firm deeply understand the nature of trade hours needed to execute the firm's workload lines.

The ability to understand trade hours connected to workload has huge and many ramifications. What the ramifications are for the firm will appear as time passes and the challenges change that confront the firm. What ever they are, the firm will only have the option and opportunity to fully act upon them if it already has in hand the ability to relate trade hours to workload. Building the columns related to trade hours of the direct work section of the budget (Figure 8-6) puts the ability in place. As an ability, it will be ready to respond to changing circumstances while the firm's competitors are caught competitively dead in the water.

The hours of interest for the firm's direct workload lines are direct and overhead trade hours. Accordingly, the firm will need to distinguish between them in the budget. This is because they are different management problems, subject to different resource strategies and have different accountability.

Ultimately payroll is hours for which their full dollar cost per hour is driven by rates, benefits and taxes. This suggests that the firm will need to build the budget to distinguish between the cost drivers that are largely set by negotiation or uncontrollable and those the firm can control in the shorter-term.

Accordingly, the hours and payroll columns shown in the budget page of Figure 8-6 are a rollup of these four dimensions from background sections that present the details related to determining them and their full dollar cost.

Managements' three questions. When the workload lines are structured in the budget and then profiled; the firm will know and understand the details of its workload in the context of the firm's the business success. Now management's question is, "What is it going to take to do the work?" Actually the question is three questions. What will it take? What need it take at its best? What will our strategy-driven targets be for the budget period?

The answers to the first two questions lead to answering the third. The final answer appears as the hours and payroll columns of the budget (Figure 8-6). If the firm has not learned to answer the second and third questions, the columns will reflect the answer to the first question. And the answer is, "It will take what it takes."

Until the workload-based budget and variance method was invented, the "take what it takes" answer to the first question has been the only answer across industry because it was the only answer possible. Worse, as Figure 8-2 demonstrated, the answer is delivered by the traditional budget as a single number without transparency or granularity.

Answers to the second and third questions have always been based on each individual's "sense" of the answer or by counting noses as the "fact-based" answer. The firm that can legitimately answer the question has an immediate competitive advantage. This is because the firm will be able to quickly reshape its resources strategies each time the business and resources environment shifts. When it does, the firm will gain an immediate advantage in returns over those competitors that will be months slower to respond; if they have any ability to legitimately adjust their strategies at all.

Direct hours. To answer the three questions we begin at the core of the matter; trade direct hours for each workload line. Around this core we build the trade overhead hours associated with the direct work. Around both, we give dollar value to the hours.

Before continuing, let's define what is budgeted as trade direct hours. Trade direct hours are the hours engaged to do all of the tasks to execute an individual job. This includes the time needed to conduct all administrative, logistic and active tasks from the point of assignment to the point when the trades' roles in executing the job are complete.

With the definition, we can set a point of reference to managements' three questions. One job at a time, the planners' traditional job is to identify all possibly foreseeable administrative, logistic and active work steps and time a competent tradeperson would take to conduct them. As a group of jobs matching a workload line, the planners' work is collectively the baseline information to answering the question, "What is the best the trade hours can be?" The question is answered by adding factors to the planners' aggregate baseline to reflect the average unavoidable, unforeseeable time to do a workload line.

This suggests another point of contrast to be made between maintenance as reinvented and the long standing maintenance best practices. Managing maintenance as part of business success is done with respect to groups of jobs: workload lines. Best practices for maintenance management are concerned with individual jobs. In one case we manage maintenance as part of the business in the other we manage individual work orders. Management has often been frustrated when the distinction has not been made. It has expected to get the returns of managing maintenance as part of business, but do not because the plant is actually managing maintenance.

Determining the direct hours to be budgeted per workload lines will draw heavily on data captured through the EAM/CMMS. Each workload line will entail a type-specific use of the data to arrive at the answer to the second question: what is the best the hours per workload line can be.

Depending on how the firm captures data that is pertinent to the analysis, we may also need to reach into the databases of the payroll system. This will be the case if the supervisory staff records hours by timesheets which are later entered into the accounting system rather than EAM/CMMS. This is likely the case because the timesheet hours are the substance with which the firm manages payroll, employment taxes and benefits and, therefore, must be rigorously protected.

Through ERP-type systems, hours as data are pulled into the EAM/CMMS from the accounting system when maintenance personnel call up and review individual work orders. In the case of contract maintenance, it is very likely that the tables will be located in the contractor's accounting database system. Whatever the actual case, it is never a significant technological restriction to making data available.

There is a difference in the meaning of the data available to quantify the workload profile and the data available to quantify the best-it-can-be case for trade direct hours. This is because the answer to all three of managements' questions is approximately the same for each workload profile. The incurrence of work is driven by the outcome of the firm's competitive, operational and financial decisions. The firm may elect not to do occurring work, but nobody enters imaginary work in the EAM/CMMS or does work that does not occur. Therefore, what has been the actual case is reasonably equivalent to the best-it-can-be and target cases for a given workload line.

By comparison, trade direct hours to do direct work are mostly decided by many influences that are external to the workload. Of course, the most obvious influence is how many trades are permanently and flexibly engaged in the plant. Another example is the degree that policies increase the percentage that total payroll hours are available to do direct work. Others are the mix of trade types in the plant and centralization or decentralization of crews and facilities.

Therefore, the challenge for budgeting workload line hours is to answer the second question: which is the best-it-can-be. The fullest potential to improve business returns through trade resource strategy is the gap between the first and second questions: will-be compared to best-it-can-be. Thence, the third question is what is the trade profile that the firm will engage to execute the workload line: the target question. The answer to all three makes up the resources strategy for trade engagement.

The ability to answer the three questions in each budget cycle will improve rapidly beginning with the first budget cycle. In the first cycle, resources engineering looms large. It is helped along with the data mined from the firm's databases.

After the initial budget cycle, the previous years' monthly variance reports will be a heavy contributor to budgeting direct hours. Furthermore, as the previous year progressed, it hours-type data came to reflect the firm's target case, rather than will-be-what-it-will-be case. The variance system will provide an immense amount of measurement and analysis. As it does, the firm will make new discoveries abut its workload profiles while concurrently learning more about the trades and hours it takes to get it done.

When the firm can increasingly better answer the best-it-can-be question, it can better answer the next question which is a primary purpose of resources strategy; where to set the target. More important the target will be set without the fear that comes with setting largely negotiated or arbitrary targets.

With the ability to set smart targets relative to the baseline of best-it-can-be, the firm will be able to conduct all sorts of resources analyses. For example, what is the profile of trades needed to accomplish the firm's workload with the highest productivity? In our current profile, what trades are bottlenecks to productivity and what are the strategies we can take to remove the bottleneck by optimizing the profile?

Payroll hours. To reach payroll hours, the budget process layers overhead hours on top of the direct trade hours. These are the trade hours the firm must pay for, but are not engaged direct work. They include start-quit time, break, vacation and sick time, training, special projects and others. By choices made for structuring the hours in the budget, they could also include other aspects such as hours lost to transportation. Overhead hours, and their relationship to direct hours, are largely driven by management's policies, rules and decisions.

The development of total hours is a process of nonfinancial measurement as explained in Chapter 6. Hours, trade and workload lines are nonfinancial. This is an important distinction because most decisions in business are made on the nonfinancial level and then converted to financial information.

The plant's hours for each workload line are converted to financial information by applying the cost of an hour to them. These include rates, benefits, taxes, etc.

The result of attaching indirect hours and dollars is highlighted in Figure 8-6 as payroll and its hours. Just as important, it is accompanied by sections in the budget with which the firm can understand and remember why the budget is what it is.

When the "dollar" layer is applied, the result of workload lines and the resource strategies will flow up along various paths through the income statement, balance sheet and statement of cash flow to emerge as profit, profit margin, return on investment and cash return on investment. Just as important, we are not just predicting the outcome for returns. We have broken the budget into the types of information the firm needs to control both the workload and trade resources as drivers of the returns.

Set parts, materials and services on workload lines

The final task to build the budget for direct work is to attach maintenance parts, materials and contract services to each workload line. Contract services are defined as services associated with the jobs of the workload lines. It is not contract maintenance. Contract maintenance is budgeted in accordance with the previous explanation of how to quantify the outcomes of strategies for trade hours.

Budgeting parts, materials and services is a different challenge than workload profiles and hours. One difference is that there is normally substantially less required analysis. The analysis is done by mining data from the EAM/CMMS database. In some cases, it may be necessary to reach into the databases of inventory, purchasing and services management systems. As mentioned before, ERP-type information technology makes it easy to reach in and join data from separate databases.

The process for budgeting maintenance parts, materials and services is straight forward. For each workload line we sort parts, materials and service data captured in the EAM/CMMS and match it to the budget's workload-based structure. Once sorted, the results are converted to factors or measures of usage. The analyst may develop the factors to serve special interests to the firm. The factors are adjusted if the underlying resource strategies have been changed for the budget year and would cause them to change.

Finally the budget workload lines are extended to include maintenance parts, materials and services. Most typically the activity level of each workload line profile is multiplied by the factors. The result is shown in Figure 8-6 as materials and services columns.

There may be specialize background cases of interest. For example, the involvement of a category of resources may be presented by workload lines. The purpose may be to get a complete insight for exactly where and the rate that resources are consumed and engaged. It also allows the analyst to seek all sorts of comparative relationships between workload lines.

The nature of parts, materials and services is such that they are not highly controllable. A firm can predict usage, but be limited in its opportunity to influence usage. As there is both the option to predict and influence versus only predict may lead to building different sections in the budget. This puts in place the ability to test resource strategies for their ramifications to the financial statements and returns.

In Figure 8-6 we can see another power of building budgets outside of and parallel to the traditional accounting system. The accounting system may classify parts, materials and services in many different accounts. However, the granularity of the accounting system may not be relevant to managing maintenance as part of the business. Accordingly, the budget would group the accounts to be accounts of importance to roles across the overall maintenance function. Accounts may also be split and regrouped as part of the grouping scheme. The final grouping scheme will influence what sections will be built in the budget.

Maintenance overhead and programs

To this point we have formed the budget for the sharp point of the spear: direct work by trades. As shown in Figure 8-4, this is the center circle of the budget. To manage maintenance as a part of a business, the budget must now be extended to include the two outermost circles of the figure.

Along with other matters, organizational design affects these circles. Organization design is the subject of Chapter 11. This is because organizational design determines the full set of roles needed to manage maintenance as part of a business and how the integrity of the roles will be protected. Roles are important because we can very specifically define and quantify work against them.

The two outer circles are respectively tactical and strategic in nature. Tactical is concerned with managing and supporting the direct work at the frontline. The roles being budgeted make real-time and short-term decisions with respect to planning, organizing and controlling field work.

Strategic is concerned with determining and reshaping the firm's workload linked to its business strategy. It is also concerned with the resource strategies to execute the workload lines. Strategic develops the data, information, processes and systems to manage maintenance as part of the business. Finally, strategic is concerned with protecting the integrity of the data, information, processes and practices that make the firm effective at each circle of the figure.

The budget will build sections for both circles. This is because the firm needs to plan at these levels to ensure that maintenance can and, thus, will be managed to be an important part of its success.

Middle-circle budget. The middle circle of the budget will account for the roles and resources to plan, organize and control the direct workload lines of the center circle. Since the center circle is connected to executing the firm's business and resources strategies the importance of the middle circle is clear.

The budget includes maintenance managers and the supervisory hierarchy, roles and numbers that report to them. This is done by evaluating the line-by-line profiles for direct workload. With that, management can decide the staffing profile with which the firm can be ensured that the budgeted workload lines, as a business plan, will be effectively and efficiently executed.

The budget process will also draw upon the workload profiles to determine the types and numbers of planners and schedulers needed to stay abreast of all job planning, organizing and control needs as the year unfolds. The budget for staffing both these practice areas will reflect how the firm has uniquely molded and aligned its planning and scheduling practices to support the firm's business and resources strategies. For the planners' role, budgeting must include staffing to support annual budget development.

Finally, most, if not all, clerical positions will be budgeted in the middle-circle section of the budget. These may be decided by the needs of all circles. Examples of clerical support are to capture data and information, and generate and distribute reports. Utilizing ERP-type technologies to automate the processes of maintenance and expand the geographic reach of a single clerk position will greatly decide the necessary staffing.

Maintenance usually requires overhead supplies and services to support the overall maintenance operation. They are included here. Training is also typical to this section of the budget. These are budgeted so that management will have a complete picture of maintenance as part of the business.

Outer-circle budget. The outer-circle section of the budget determines and budgets the strategic roles and their work and resources that make it possible to manage maintenance as part of the business. Without the work of the outer circle, the firm is limited to managing maintenance work and equipment effectiveness. In fact, that was the normal case until maintenance was reinvented. Many corporate departments have fallen on hard times because this distinction was not made; allowing the strategic roles to go largely unrecognized.

The roles of the outer circle as an issue in organizational design are explained in Chapter 10. However, to explain the nature of what is being budgeted, we need to touch on the subject here.

At the highest level, executive management views the large picture and makes decisions that affect the entire firm. At each level down, management will do the same with respect to their domain. Consequently, it follows that a specialized role of management at all levels is to develop strategy for their respective domain. The catch is that these managers do not have the time and specialized expertise to do so for maintenance.

What is budgeted in the outer circle are the roles to do the strategic planning work as an extension and on behalf of the domain managers. However, the roles do not set or own the final strategies. They conduct strategy analysis and design, but do not make strategic decisions. The managers make the final strategic decision once they have collaborated with the specialized strategic planner in forming the candidate strategies.

The role points to two others. One is to implement the strategies ultimately decided upon by the managers who are accountable for them. The other is to audit and protect the integrity of the parts and pieces that the strategies have caused to be put in place. These roles are also conducted on behalf of the managers that own and are accountable for the strategies.

Therefore, the budgeting processes for the outer circle determines the roles, skills and headcount to do the work of these roles and others. The skills include strategic planning, finance and accounting, budgeting and variance reporting and forecasting, automated audit and control, organization design, systems integration, and reliability and maintenance practices.

If outside resources are to make up the skill set, they are included in this circle of the budget.

Frontend to the budget

Obviously, the resulting budget is not the delivered budget document of the past followed by negotiating a number. The firm now has an inclusive budget for managing maintenance as part of the business: a business plan for maintenance. Its purpose is to provide management with the information they will need to make the decisions needed to run maintenance as part of the business.

Accordingly, we must now think about the frontend section to the budget and its subsections. Of course, the fundamental frontend is a summary of the final budget. However, the frontend is especially important because the budget is a body of information that is powerful, wide and deep. The easy functionality of modern ERP-type technologies makes the information possible. However, if management must "work the pages" of the budget to arrive at conclusions and see the results, the power of the information is diminished.

The frontend will include subsections through which analysts and managers can do what-if analysis. To give the firm the maximally powerful ability to do what-if, the frontend subsections must make it possible to rollup, drilldown and slice-dice the many-layered details of the budget. Hand in hand with these abilities, it must be possible to see the impact on the firm's financial statements and returns. This is done by embedding a business model in the budget.

Figure 8-8 shows an example of an interactive dashboard that can be built into the budget as a frontend subsection including elements of an embedded business model. Through such tools, analysts and management can evaluate and make decisions in the context of a business model. An example demonstrates why this is so important.

A dollar change in maintenance, as manufacturing overhead expense, will not just affect profit through expense. The dollar may concurrently affect profit margin (profit divided by sales) though the aspects that affect sales. At the same time, the dollar may affect return on investment (profit divided by total assets) beyond just change in profit. This would be the case as the dollar changes return on investment through working capital, including cash, and property, plant and equipment.

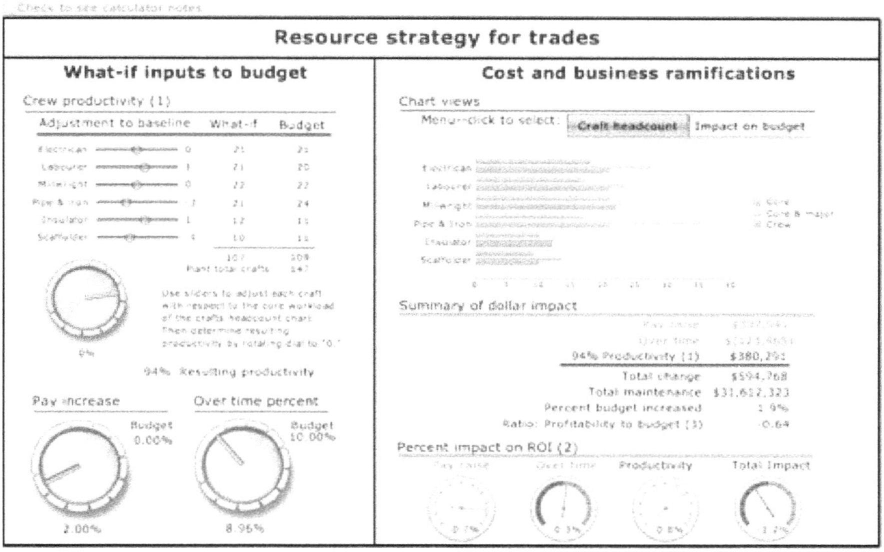

Figure 8-8: Interactive dashboard built into the budget.

Without a business model in the budget, management will be forced to make decisions based on incomplete information. This is doubly unnecessary because the workload-based budget and dashboard technology makes full information an easy accomplishment.

The example dashboard is designed to evaluate and settle on a multi-dimensional resource strategy for trades. What the book is not able to show is that the dashboard of Figure 8-8 is that it has what is called, "dynamic visibility." This means that, on-click, the user can move amongst all sorts of views and interact with them. The views match strategic topics, user roles, etc. Through them the firm can make its final decisions by making settings on the dashboard and then sending them back into the final budget; itself subject to changing decisions as the budget cycle progresses.

As a point of reference, a role belonging to the outer circle covered in the budget is to build the budget and its variance reporting and forecasting system. In the role, the builder will poll all stakeholders in the system to determine what frontend subsections must be built in the budget to serve their diverse needs. Once the budget is built and passes through the annual budget cycle, the builder may be called upon to modify and upgrade the frontend.

Variance report and forecast

A budget has been put in place that was built in the context of the year's business plan for maintenance as integral part of the firm's overall business plan. Now the firm needs a body of information that allows it to know whether it is successfully implementing the plan; and if not, where and why not. Furthermore, the firm needs to be able to forecast how variance to date and changing surrounding circumstances will affect the remaining and total year. Both types of information must arrive in the managers' and analysts' inbox soon enough that the firm has time to deliberate and take action that is the correct solution to the right problem.

The good news is that the budget has positioned the firm to deliver and work with this life-blood-type of information. This is because the variance report and forecast are an extension of the budget. This section will explain them.

Variance reporting

The firm must be able to do variance analysis for each direct and overhead workload line of the budget. However, the necessity and nature of some variances are such that analysis and reporting need only be basic. That is normally the case for the second and third circles of Figure 8-4 because they are largely staff roles.

Workload line variance. The greatest necessity and challenge for variance reporting and forecasting to generate actionable information is at the center circle of the budget: direct work. Therefore, the explanation of variance as a body of information will focus on the direct work section of the variance report.

The most basic information is to report the variance for each workload line of the budget's workload-based structure. The basic information is shown in Figure 8-9.

Process maintenance: Workload-based budget for direct work, Year 20X2
Process Area A

Work type & class	Number of jobs		Labor		Material & service			Total
	Month Avg	Year	Hours	Payroll	Material	Service	M&S	expense
Corrective								
Mechanical-MW	100.0	1,200	33,663	$ 1,277,629	$ 960,000	$ 144,000	$ 1,104,000	$ 2,381,629
Piping-PF	43	516	14,475	$ 549,380	$ 412,800	$ 61,920	$ 474,720	$ 1,024,100
Electrical	47.0	60.4	6,151	233,659	40,300	6,040	10,340	201,600
Instrument								
Subtotal								
Proactive								
Preventive-MW								
MAG								

Process maintenance: Month's variance: Month XX, 20X2

Corrective: Mechanical-MW

		Activity		Budget cost			
		Jobs	Dir hrs	Payroll	Material	Service	Total
Budget	Total	110	2,753	$ 119,724	$125,000	$ 600	$ 245,324
Actual	Total	100	2,375	$ 106,423	$ 80,000	$ 12,000	$ 198,423
		Total variance		$ 13,302	$ 45,000	$(11,400)	$ 46,902

Figure 8-9: Total variance reported by workload line item is new information.

In the example, total variance for the workload line is an underrun of $46,902. A further inspection reveals that the drivers of the underrun for the work line were payroll and materials. The total underrun was diminished by $11,400 for services.

The figure shows variance for the accounting month. However, variance is reported for year to date using the same format. A third type of variance report is to show months as trends over a rolling period of time. Besides showing change, trends are also the bridge between the month and year-to-date variance reports.

What is noteworthy is that the example is information the firm has not had in the past. Figure 8-3 showed that the traditional information for variance is a single line total for a production area as a responsibility center. Nothing is provided that is workload-based.

As pointed out earlier in the chapter, the traditional area-level variance report would have caused management to be reasonably happy with the month's variance: an overrun of only $4,072. However, the underrun of $46,902 reported for the workload line tells management there is much more going on; possibly a substantial overrun or more being masked by the underrun for the workload line and others. With a variance report based on workload lines, the firm would have been able to immediately locate all significant overruns and underruns for workload lines. Both may have presented the firm with opportunities to learn how to increase its returns.

Subvariance at the workload line. However, this is still not good enough. Important variances are still hidden from view. To find all important variances, we need to be able to search for variances below rather than along the workload line. This is because important variance can still be hidden at the workload line.

To solve the problem, the total variance for each workload line is extended to subvariances as shown in Figure 8-10. Now we can see variances with respect to the amount of work done, and the resources and overtime to do the work.

		Activity		Budget cost			
		Jobs	Dir hrs	Payroll	Material	Service	Total
Budget	Total	110	2,753	$ 119,724	$125,000	$ 600	$ 245,324
	Per job		25	$ 1,088	$ 1,136	$ 5	$ 2,230
Actual	Total	100	2,375	$ 106,423	$ 80,000	$ 12,000	$ 198,423
	Per job		24	$ 1,064	$ 800	$ 120	$ 1,984
	Total variance			$ 13,302	$ 45,000	$(11,400)	$ 46,902
	Due to jobs			$ 10,642	$ 8,000	$ 1,200	$ 19,842
	Due to resources			$ 6,297	$ 37,000	$(12,600)	$ 30,697
	Due to overtime			$ (3,638)			$ (3,638)

Process maintenance: Month's variance: Month XX, 20X2
Corrective: Mechanical-MW

Figure 8-10: Subvariance to total variance tells management what really happened.

Let's look at the figure's subvariances matrix. The "due to jobs" line reports what part of the total workload line variance is due to more or less jobs being completed than was expected for the period. The "due to resources" line reports the degree that resource to do the period's work varied from the resources expected to do the type of jobs that took place. The "due to overtime" line shows if overtime was greater or less than the overtime budgeted for the jobs of the workload line. The columns of the subvariance matrix reveal the role that payroll, materials and services play in each line of subvariance.

It is readily apparent why the subvariance matrix is important. Without it, it is easily possible that variances along a single workload line could be reported as minor even though there are actually large offsetting variances along the subvariance lines. To prevent this, the firm must be able to search for variances at the subvariance level.

The variance matrix in the figure is not limited the three subvariances. The matrix is generated through a set of algorithms that are automated to pull data from the databases of other systems and into the backend of the variance report. The sets are engineered to deliver subvariances of interest to the firm with respect to its business and resources strategies.

The best measure of information is the degree that it guides us to the questions we should ask rather than require us to think of them. A variance report with subvariance matrixes easily passes the test. This is demonstrated by the figure's matrix. With only a quick glance and without must thought, all of us can immediately see questions needing answers. Furthermore, the system is built such that we can easily drill down to the root cause to get our answers.

Audit and control. The variance for "due to jobs" opens another topic not immediately visible, but resting behind the variance reporting system. As analysts and managers are viewing the subvariance they must be ensured that that information means what it is meant to mean. An example is the variance for work done. Was there less work to do or was there work left undone that should have been done?

This is an example of a case for which the variance system must be backed by automated audit and control. Its purpose is to ensure that the integrity of work processes and rules allowing the firm to manage maintenance as part of the business are being sustained and protected.

For example, as analysts and managers look at the number of jobs done in the case of preventive maintenance, they must be able to trust that automated audit and control has routinely confirmed that each week's proactive work was done, or was caused to be done if not. In other words, they must know that they are looking at the case of "there was less work to be done."

Forecasting the year's variance

Variance management has two timeframes. First, what happened, why, and what are we going to do about it? Second, knowing what we know

now, what variance from the budget can we expect for the remaining and total year, and what are we going to do about it?

The variance report dealt with the first timeframe. Now we must deal with the second; remaining and total year. It is important to do so because the forecasts that are possible through the traditional variance report is misinformation in an uncertain world.

With the traditional-based forecasts, the firm will make decisions with misinformation that will likely be off target, thus, potentially damaging. At the least the firm will squander its energy solving the wrong problem. Alternately, taking no action for lack of good information is potentially damaging. The firm needs a way to break out of this predicament.

In a perfect world, the firm would rebudget each month as the year unfolds. The variance system serves this purpose by including the capability to forecast the remaining year based on what has happened to date and emerging indications of change in the business and resources environment. In other words, the system is built to forecast how the remaining year will vary from the budget. When the forecast is placed with the year-to-date outcomes, the firm will have a forecast of how the total year may vary from the budget and affect the firm's total returns. Most important, it is actionable information.

The difference between information and misinformation as a forecast of the year is clearly apparent in Figure 8-11. On the left side we see the cases that are the only means possible through the traditional budget and variance system.

One way (upper left) is to accept the budget for the remaining year as the forecast for the remaining year. It is added to year-to-date result. When subtracted from the budget, it is accepted as the forecasted variance for the year. The other way is to accept the budget as if it still correctly depicts the year's outcome. The year-to-date is subtracted from the budget and the result is accepted as the forecast for the remaining year.

These may partially reflect the real case. However, if applied overall, the actions the firm would take on the results or the inability to recognize the true necessity for action can be destructive to the year's returns.

The alternative is the right side of the figure. Year-to-date is, of course, now fact. What the remaining year will bring is not. If we were rebudgeting we would no doubt make some changes; which is what we do now. The resulting forecast for the remaining year is added to year-to-date result. The resulting information is a forecast of the year's variance. Better yet, the information is used to reach a better outcome for the remaining and total year.

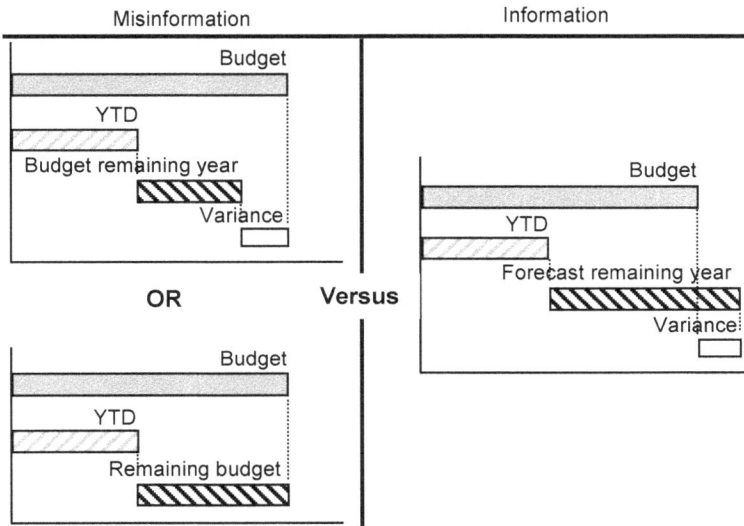

Figure 8-11: Forecasting the remaining and year's variance.

Therefore, it is important that the variance system makes it possible to conduct monthly budget-like decision cycles as the year unfolds. Because the budget and variance are built on a financial-statements-based business model, the capability to forecast the year's variance as actionable information can be built into the variance system.

The key is to identify the range of cases as uncertainties that would drive variance. This is determined when the budget and variance system is being designed. With that assessment we design views in the variance report that allow the user to set what-if-type expectations for the remaining year. The designed interactive views are included in a forecast section of the monthly variance report.

An effective method to automate the ability to forecast the remaining year is to form a set of realistic possibilities for each case that has been identified as an uncertainty. They are placed in the forecast section, each with an adjustable range of the possible outcomes. For each question the user makes selections based on their personal view of the case. Once the viewer makes selections, the remaining and year's variance is forecasted along with the details of the variance.

The forecast of variance should roll up to a returns model such as Figure 8-12. With it, the firm steps beyond forecasting purely changes for workload, resource and dollar variances. The firm must be able to measure the meaning of the forecasted variance to business returns.

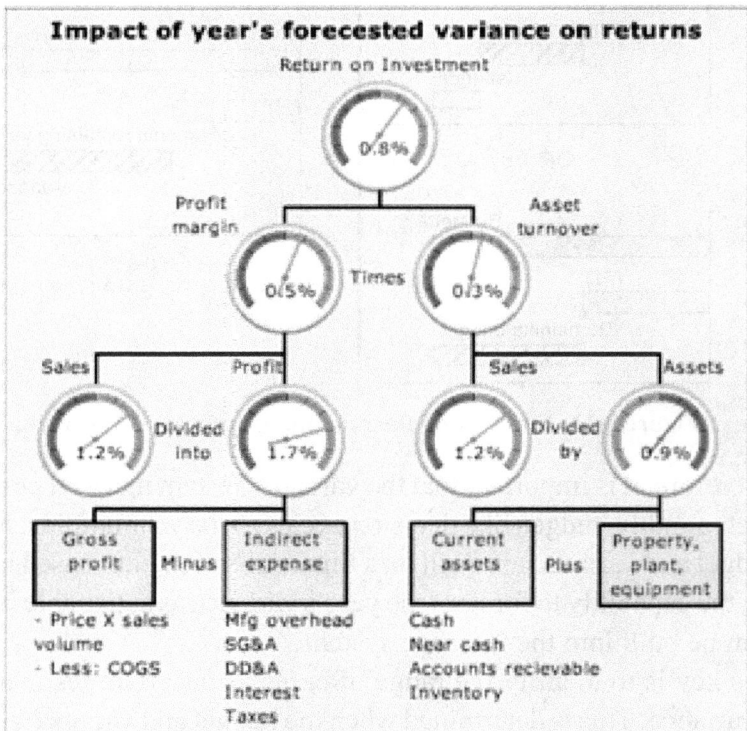

Impact of year's forecasted variance on returns

Return on Investment — 0.8%

Profit margin — 0.5% — Times — Asset turnover — 0.3%

Sales — 1.2% — Divided into — Profit — 1.7%

Sales — 1.2% — Divided by — Assets — 0.9%

Gross profit — Minus — Indirect expense

- Price X sales volume
- Less: COGS

Mfg overhead
SG&A
DD&A
Interest
Taxes

Current assets — Plus — Property, plant, equipment

Cash
Near cash
Accounts recievable
Inventory

Figure 8-12: Measuring the year's forecasted variance as returns.

The model of Figure 8-12 is important because variance as dollars do not just roll up to returns through a single path through the firm's financial statements. Variances will roll up to variously affect average sales price, sales volumes, cost of goods sold and other lines in the income statement. They can concurrently roll up through the balance sheet to affect the working capital, and property, plant and equipment accounts. Of course, these are the relationships upon which the budget and variance system was built on, down from the top. Now the same model allows the firm to view the full ramifications of the year's forecasted variance; back up to the top.

This is important because making decisions and taking action to change the year's outcome is like everything else in managing an enterprise. The firm must decide if the action is worthwhile as measured by its ramifications for returns. The returns model on top of the variance forecast gives the firm a means to quickly evaluate the relative importance of its concerns for the remaining year.

Sections and frontend to the variance

The variance report and forecast is an electronic-based document which can be produced as hardcopy. After time, its many sections will settle on purpose, scope and format. Change will be driven as the firm grows in its organizational ability to manage maintenance as part of the business.

The variance document will have sections that generally match the three circles of Figure 8-4. One section and its subsections will present management with variance matrixes matching the workload lines for direct work by trades. Sections for the workload of the outer two circles will also be provided. However, their variance formats will be much more basic. A feature most occurring in all three sections, especially direct work, will be the ability to drill down from variances and subvariances of individual workload lines to their root causes.

The section and subsections to forecast the remaining year and total year will span all three circles. What is included and how it is formatted will be unique to the firm. The content will allow for a great deal of interactive, what-if thinking.

The final section is the frontend section with potentially many subsections. Through them the user is able to view information in different formats or make "on-click" choices for drilldown, rollup or slice-dice.

These are the sections that give information its value because they allow us to put it to use.

As an old saying goes, "Thinking of the question is more difficult than answering it." Managers tax their brains to think of the question they should ask of the information in front of them. The frontend sections are designed to indicate what questions should be asked. The section will include dashboard-type subsections with such a purpose. They are necessary because the variance report's information is so vast it is akin to searching for 30 gold needles in 1,000 haystacks.

Figure 8-13 shows one such subsection formatted as a chart. With it, we can search through haystacks "by-click" from a menu of combinations. The result is the ability to drilldown, rollup and slice-dice. The user is looking for the "poke in the eye." When poked, the user will be able to drill down to what is behind it.

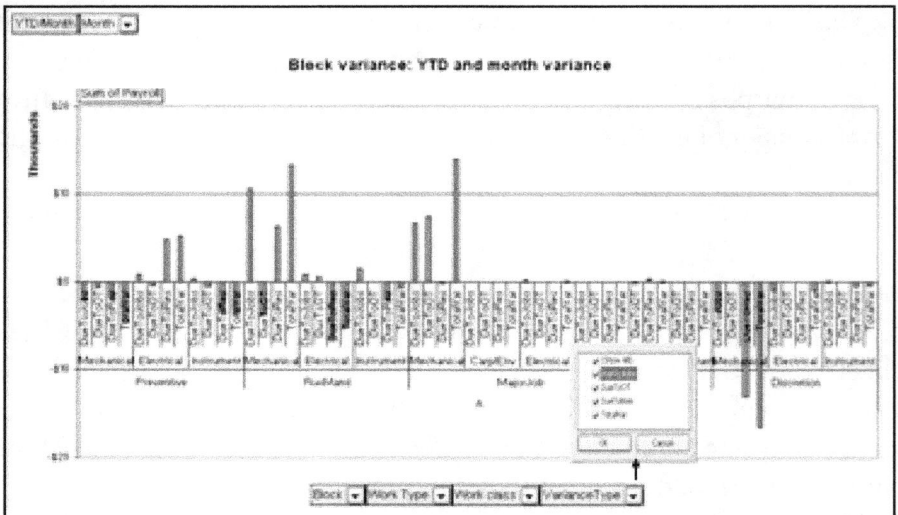

Figure 8-13: Dashboard to find questions to be asked.

An earlier section mentioned that the key is to look for important sub-variances below the individual workload lines of direct work. In this case the chart allows its users to do that; viewing subvariance as if a Rubik's Cube. The possible permutations of variance are production area, work-type, trade-type, period, and variance and subvariance. The chart may come with sibling charts to provide trend lines with the same menu of choices.

One likely section of the variance document will show variance on the original budget and variance that is outside the budget. If a subsection does not make the distinction, the view of variance is distorted.

An example is an unforeseeable, abnormal event in the plant, i.e., a local power failure results in substantial maintenance work to recover. The event is not included in the maintenance budget because it is not realistic for each business function to budget such contingencies. They are, instead, budgeted at the plant and corporate levels.

Another example is work that was budgeted for a turnaround. A decision later on in the process of planning or executing the turnaround may transfer some work to the backlog for running maintenance.

These cases are not true variances to the original budget. Making the distinction sustains and protects the integrity of the firm's running determination for whether it is succeeding at its business and resources strategies.

There are many possibilities and this book will not try to imagine them. When the budget and variance system is designed, the builder will poll across the firm to determine what they should be. This ensures that they will be molded to serve the needs of those who are touched by the system.

Timeliness of reports

The best, most perfect information has no value if the ship has already sailed. One thing is obvious from the explanation of the budget and variance report. The discussion of maintenance will be permanently changed. However, if the information that fuels the discussion is slow in arriving, there will be mostly discussion without much action and payoff.

The information contained in the variance report is powerful and immense. That does not translate to the need for skilled, substantial effort to generate the report each month. Modern-day ERP-type technology (see Chapter 10) allows variance report and forecast to be prepared with almost 100 percent automation. Furthermore, the report can be distributed with it sections automatically organized in different sequences and formats to match the varying interests of its recipients. Therefore, preparation and distribution as an obstacle to timeliness is virtually eliminated. Furthermore, a clerical position can easily take on the role of generating and distributing the report.

The limited value of the traditional variance report for managing maintenance is further reduced by the accounting closing process. It is not complete for many days, possibly several weeks, after the last day of the accounting period. When its information is finally available, the ship has already sailed.

This is not the case for the workload-based variance report and forecast. This is because it taps into some of the same data of the accounting system, but is not held back by its closing process. Furthermore, the data captured in the traditional accounting system is typically fully available within just several days after the end of the accounting period.

Consequently the time from the month's close to the time the workload-based variance information is in hand is only several days; at the most. Only several hours of that time is taken to generate and distribute the report. The remaining lag is largely associated with recording final data such as trade hours in the accounting system. However, the lag rarely causes the report to be stale. If it did, the report's builder would design a way around it.

Steps to build the workload-based budget and variance

Firms follow several well traveled paths to improve maintenance efficiency and equipment effectiveness. This book takes the game up to the next level as it describes the path to managing maintenance as part of the business rather than manage maintenance and equipment.

However, this chapter's description of budgeting and variance reporting and forecasting clearly exposes the deal-killer for any chosen program. It is hard to envision much working out without the body of business information provide by the described workload-based budgeting and variance reporting and forecasting system.

We have all observed or been engaged in maintenance programs. Imagine how they would have been different. Before kicking off, the budget analysis process the firm would have determined exactly how the its financial statements and returns would be different; and feasibly so. The budget would have been laid out upon what is required to realize the difference. Thence, routine variance reporting and forecasting would have ensured that what was feasibly expected would have been delivered, sustained and grown.

Therefore, the prerequisite accomplishment of any successful maintenance program is to build the firm's ability to conduct routine workload-based budgeting, and variance reporting and forecasting. The ability is the platform on which any program is evaluated, implemented and normalized. Furthermore, the ability will reduce substantially the magnitude and scope of all programs as they are focused, formed and tested upon what matters for business success.

This section will describe the steps to build the budget and variance system. The deliverable is a working budget, and variance report and forecast. However, in contrast to the overall book, it will describe the process as if we are building the firm's budget and variance system for the first time. However, it will also become apparent that the disciplines explained by the other chapters are is some form pulled into the process; because they matter.

Work steps

The work steps to design, build and implement the firm's budget and variance system and it processes are as follows (see Figure 8-14):

1. Conduct introductory sessions with stakeholders to explain how workload-based budgeting and variance reporting and forecasting work.
2. Survey and understand the firm as a competitive, operational and financial beast and its current and anticipated business cycles.
   a. Interview stakeholders across the firm.

b. Mine the firm's data to bring facts to the interviews and confirm the perceptions revealed by the interviews.

3. Establish the business and resources strategies the system will be designed to manage.

4. Blueprint the firm's budget and variance system and its processes.

   a. Survey the plant and firm-level IT systems to identify the system through which relevant data is captured, locate their databases and establish how its data tables can be made readily available to the budget and variance system.

   b. Establish the means by which the firm's budget and variance system will routinely reach into the firm's various databases for its needs.

   c. Identify and define changes to the firm's existing work processes for the purpose of eliminating important data weaknesses.

   d. Define the audit and control processes to ensure the continued integrity of the overall budget and variance system.

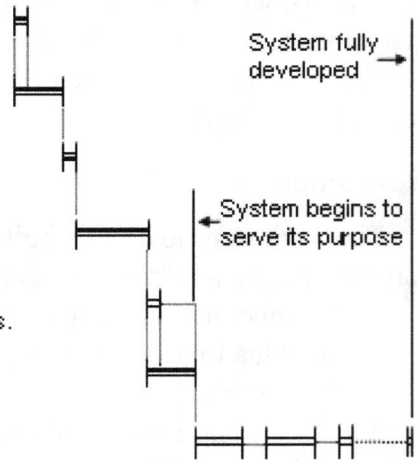

1. Conduct introductory sessions to explain workload-based budget and variancing.

2. Understand firm as competitive, operational and financial beast.

3. Establish business strategies the system will be designed to manage.

4. Blueprint the firm's budget and variance system and its processes.

5. Implement process changes, data cleansing and audits for data weaknesses.

6. Build, distribute and finalize the firm's initial maintenance budget.

7. Build and distribute the firm's initial four monthly variance reports and forecasts.

System fully developed

System begins to serve its purpose

Figure 8-14: Steps to build the budget and variance system.

e. Draft a blueprint of the complete budget and variance system and processes in accordance with the findings of the preceding tasks.

f. Finalize the blueprint with the firm's management team and other stakeholders.

5. Implement process changes, data cleansing and compliance audits to eliminate the data weaknesses identified by Step 1.e.

6. Build, distribute and finalize the firm's initial maintenance budget and its embedded business model.

   a. Build the interactive budget and its embedded business model as blueprinted.

   b. Distribute the budget to management for its initial budgeting cycle.

   c. Finalize the going-forward budget based on management's decisions.

7. Build and distribute the firm's initial four monthly variance reports and forecasts to management in accordance with the monthly cycle.

   a. Month one after budget: Build and deliver the first month's <u>single month</u> variance report and forecast.

   b. Month two after budget: Upgrade and deliver the monthly report to include its <u>year-to-date</u> and <u>trend-line</u> sections.

   c. Document the work steps a clerk will follow to generate and distribute the monthly report.

   d. Month three and four after budget: Train, hands-on, the clerk personnel who are assigned the task of generating the monthly report.

Deliverables

The deliverables of the steps are as follows:

1. Detailed blueprint of the budget and variance reporting and forecasting system and its annual and monthly processes; including its audit and control processes.

2. Preliminary and final maintenance budget and its business-model.
3. First through fourth months' variance report and forecast.
4. Documented steps to generate and distribute the annual budget and monthly variance report and forecast.
5. Personnel trained to generate and distribute the annual budget and monthly variance report and forecast.
6. All processes up and functioning for the routine budget, variance and audit cycles.

Chapter 9
Structuring Five Business Subsystems

Up to this point structuring the maintenance organization has been implicit. As the firm executes the returns of its core, synergistic business strategies for maintenance, it will put in place the organizational elements associated with realizing them.

Firms do a pretty good job of laying out their organizational structure. However, structures are typically designed without overt consideration for the potentially harmful, but important, dynamics of what this book will call the five business subsystems.

Rather than explain in depth the entire process of organization design, the book will focus on the five subsystems. This is because the firm must be able to consciously recognize the five subsystems and their dynamics as part of assuring that the firm will succeed at managing maintenance as part of its business.

The chapter will begin by summarizing the general process to design an organization's structure and point to the step in the design process where the analysis and design for the five subsystems should take place. The chapter will then introduce and explain each subsystem and how, through their respective dynamics, they work against each other: actually a good thing, but must be kept a fair fight. Finally, the chapter will draw conclusions which are generally the case for a maintenance function fully engaged in the firm's business success.

Generic steps to organization design

The approach to design an organization's structure is somewhat universal. The chapter will not describe it. Instead, this section will summarize the approach as a means to identify at what step the five subsystems are consciously designed into the structure.

The steps to design an organization structure for the maintenance function are as follows:

1. Establish the strategic direction for the maintenance function as part of the business.
2. Flowchart the maintenance function's cross-organizational processes.
3. Categorize the importance of maintenance function processes: critical, major and minor.
4. Determine the structuring rules for the roles and processes of the maintenance function per the five business subsystems.
5. Determine the structure of information and decision flow.
6. Layout the cross-organization structure for the maintenance function.
7. Evaluate the cost of the structure.

Step 1: Establish the strategic direction for the maintenance function as part of the business. The firm first sets direction for the maintenance function. It is the expression of what the maintenance function is to accomplish strategically for the firm as a competitive, operational and financial beast competing for returns above its industry's average. These details were developed by the steps and activities that were explained by the chapters leading up to this one.

Step 2: Flowchart the maintenance function's cross-organizational processes. A step in design is to flowchart the processes of the maintenance function. This will have been accomplished as the firm designed the processes associated with its core business strategies for maintenance and their substrategies.

Step 3: Categorize the importance of maintenance function processes: critical, major and minor. Based on the direction set by the first step, the firm will categorize the processes of the maintenance function according to their relative importance. Importance is categorized with respect to how quickly the firm's strategies would fail in their business purpose if a process failed to thrive.

A good method is to classify them as critical, major and minor. A process is critical if its failure would immediately result in lost business results. With major there would be an eventual loss and with minor there would not be a loss.

Step 4: Determine the structuring rules for the roles and processes of the maintenance function per five business subsystems. Organizations are a network of roles that can be recognized as falling within one of five business subsystems. Many of the roles necessarily and naturally conflict. In fact, it is important that they do. However, the trick is to structure them so that the conflict does not become destructive or fatal to the firm's ability to manage maintenance as part of the business. This step inspects very carefully the processes with respect to the five subsystems. The goal is to set rules or guidelines for how the roles of each subprocess both can and must not be structured.

Just as important, the investigation will reveal missing subsystems and roles. As this chapter unfolds; frequently observed such cases will become apparent. Another outcome will be that we understand the true purpose of different processes and roles to business success as we come to see them in a different light.

Step 5: Determine the structure for information and decision flow.[4] The flow of information and decision-making ties processes and roles together. The step determines the structure types on which information and decision-making are connected. The ultimate structure is a permutation of structure decisions: upward referral, self-containment, cross-organization relations, information systems and lowered performance.

Step 6: Layout the cross-organization structure for the maintenance function. With the findings of the previous steps the organization designer will make choices for a mixture of structure types and how processes and roles are attached to the structure.

---

[4] For an explanation of this step see page 257 of the book titled, *"Availability Engineering and Management for Manufacturing Plant Performance"* by Richard Lamb.

Step 7: Evaluate the cost of the structure. Structure has measurable cost. The more power, the greater the cost. The final step will evaluate the cost of the proposed structure and possibly be driven to explore alternatives to the initial design.

This is the generic process for organizational design. It is observed typically; except for the fourth step; five business subsystems. Consequently, the chapter is concerned with explaining the step that deals with them.

The concept of the five business subsystems

Explaining the principles and approach to analyze the firm's processes with respect to the five subsystems elicited the question, "What do people say when a process or role is weak or absent." The answer demonstrates the power of the method. It is more important what was not said, then what was said. This is because the absence of comment reveals why the firm's organizational result has not come to match its organizational intent.

This highlights the purpose of the step in organization design. We have already determined everything the maintenance function must become to be a player in the firm's overall competitive advantage. If important processes and roles have slipped under the radar or been structured inappropriately, subsystem analysis will reveal it.

Five business subsystems

As shown in Figure 9-1, the five inter-influential business subsystems[5] are as follows:

- **Production**: Concerned with what is produced by the firm or function. It is not to be confused with the firm's production operation.
- **Production-support**: Acquires resources for the production subsystem and wins support and acceptance for its work.

---

[5] Katz, Daniel and Kahn, Robert L. *The Social Psychology of Organizations*. 2nd edition. John Wiley & Sons. New York. 1978

- **Integrity**: Ties people into their roles and, thus, maintains the integrity of the processes of the maintenance function.
- **Adaptive**: Concerned with necessary change, whereas, the others are not.
- **Managerial**: Directs, integrates and adjudicates the other subsystems.

The principle

There are two principles that drive subsystems analysis. The first principle is that all of the five subsystems will exist in the firm that is normally successful. This applies to the firm as a whole and for each function. When some speak of "balance" this in a nutshell is what the five subsystems represent.

The second principle is that each subsystem is concerned with its own survival. This results in a characteristic dynamic through which each will seek to maximize itself in the organization. More important, the most fundamental action each subsystem takes to ensure its survival is to literally weaken or kill off other subsystems. As this happens a good ear will notice many things not said. It will also notices how what is said, is said.

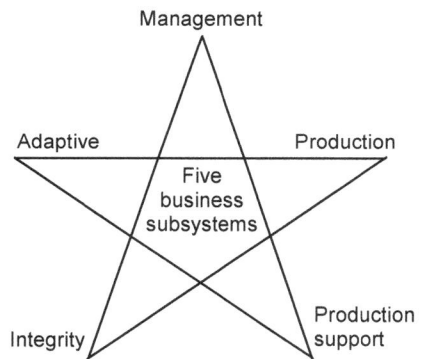

Figure 9-1: The five business subsystems of an effective organization.

As a method, the principle is simple. When we map the lead abilities to be put in place as part of each returns execution initiative (see Chapter 7), we will evaluate whether the five subsystems are alive and well. At the same time we will conduct our assessment with an eye and ear to whether or not the five subsystems exist in the larger organization, giving homes and protection to the subsystems of the subject incremental returns.

Overall, the firm's management must know that the conflict of the five subsystems is an ongoing part of doing the day's business. At the same time management must be ensured that the conflict is a fair fight. When we find frustration and failure in a firm, it is not uncommon to find that this is not the case and, accordingly, one or more of the subsystems has been weakened or eliminated by a dominant subsystem.

The system of the five business subsystems

This section will explain each of the five business subsystems, their dynamic and their typical roles. The five business subsystems are universal. However, from here forward the subject will be presented in the context of managing the maintenance function as part of the business.

Production subsystem

The production subsystem is concerned with the core "production" activity of the firm's overall maintenance function. However, we should never assume, there may be others. The subsystem is responsible for engaging the resources provided by the firm to execute the work selected to be done each day and do it right the first time.

Typically the activities to do this make up the central productive process of the maintenance function. The firm's overall goal is that the work done is aligned to the firm's business strategies for maintenance.

However, defining or viewing the firm's overall maintenance function as the maintenance productive process is harmful to the firm's success as a business. It is also a typical mistake. The result is that the maintenance function may come to operate as if the execution of maintenance work is the only thing that matters; reducing the purpose of all other processes to serving the execution of work as the production subsystem wishes it to be done.

The dynamic of the production subsystem is to maximize the proficiency of its work in terms of the accomplishment of each maintenance task. Accordingly, it will drive toward developing standard skills and methods and assuring that what work engages them is held constant in its nature.

There is a trap here. The drive to proficiency does not mean that the production subsystem will strive to gain the highest level of potential performance and expertise. To understand how to maximize proficiency we only need to remember the Ford Model T: one model, one color.

Consequently, programs to improve the overall maintenance work management process, aligned to business success, can easily become arrested in their development. This is because striving to maximize proficiency is made more challenging when work must deal with a range of outcomes beyond "one model and one color." Staff and trades driven by proficiency can easily become negative in their attitude toward higher-level performance.

This suggests the possible damage of defining the maintenance function by its production subsystem. When this is the case the subsystem will have an open path to dominating and crushing other important contrary dynamics across the maintenance function. In other words, it will diminish and destroy other roles that make it more difficult to maximize the subsystem's quest for proficiency.

The primary activities or subprocesses of the subsystem will be the assignment of work, trades doing assigned work, and the supervision and tracking of work. The primary judgment will be whether the day's or week's assigned workload is executed and done well.

It is also important to confirm what the subsystem defines as "executed." The production subsystem may not include all stages of a job in its self-defined measure of proficiency. An example is to put a repaired asset back in services but leaving the remaining stages of the job undone; catch as catch can.

The dynamic of the production subsystem will be opposed to the dynamics of the integrity, adaptive and management subsystems. The integrity subsystem will be contrary to proficiency in the context of disallowing loose measures and standards. For example, the integrity subsystem will resist the execution of work with excessive trades and the under- and miss-utilization of trades. Another example is to block gratuitous rush work. The integrity subsystem is also contrary to the production subsystem because it will push and enforce processes that sustain the overall maintenance function's ability to deliver on its business strategies.

The adaptive subsystem will be contrary to the dynamic of the production subsystem because it may cause work decisions to be made with changing criteria as the firm's business strategies change. It may also shift the makeup of work over time. At the same time, adaptiveness applied at the job level will push the subsystem to do the same job in multiple ways, driven by business thinking, rather than one size fits all on which proficiency is most easily sustained. At a higher level the adaptive subsystem will change the work mix and rules for recognizing, approving and acting on work.

The management subsystem is contrary to the dynamic of the production subsystem for a simple reason. If it is effective, it will ensure the survival of conflicting dynamics across the maintenance function; including the integrity and adaptive subsystems. As a point of reference, if the management subsystem has been eliminated by being pulled into the production subsystem, ruling against the integrity and adaptive subsystems will be the normal case until they eventually have little affect on the overall maintenance function. At that point the maintenance function is the production subsystem.

Production-support subsystem

The production-support subsystem acquires resources for the production subsystem and wins acceptance of its work. Thus, its actions as processes are direct extensions of the production subsystem. This is the case as they determine and acquire resources to do work and gain acceptance for the finished, or unfinished, work. In the last case, its dynamic is to convince the remaining plant that "what it got was what it wanted."

It is noteworthy that the subsystem is not a force for change. This is because its fundamental dynamic is to sustain field maintenance processes as they are, rather than what they could or should be. In other words, its dynamic is to allow the production subsystem to conduct its processes with maximum proficiency unfettered by other business issues.

The functions associated with the subsystem include those for identifying and gathering all resources for short- and longer-term requirements. In this capacity, the dynamic of the production-support subsystem is to pressure for excess resources and resist dynamics that attempt to optimize the resources on hand with a sharper balance between workload and actual need. Consequently, the goal of its dynamic is to prevent the production subsystem from being encumbered by the need to be more sophisticated in its practices to determine and acquire resource needs.

The importance of the production-support subsystem to the production subsystem's output makes its value highly tangible and visible; unlike the remaining three subsystems. Therefore, the two subsystems are a big threat to managing maintenance as part of the business. Their direct and tangible nature allows them to easily dominate conflicting roles in other subsystems.

The result is that it is common to find failing or poorly performing organizations whose core production activities are the epitome of excellence. The dynamic for proficiency has come to dominate the conflict. For example, in such a firm the maintenance function will focus on the work accepted to be executed on each day. It will seek to have available excess resources, thus, assuring performance without requiring sophisticated management practices to execute it.

An example of defining functions per the name of the department is maintenance parts and materials. The process is doomed if it is interpreted as production-support rather than recognized as part of the integrity subsystem. That is because, if it where a production-support-type subsystem, its thrust would be to supply the production subsystem's processes. It would be not be concerned with, and even averse, to doing that optimally with respect to the firm's income statement and balance sheet.

The primary activities or processes of the production-support subsystem recognize, classify and approve work for execution, and evaluate and pronounce work as complete. These processes are integral to establishing resources to be engaged by the production subsystem and when they must be available.

The processes of the subsystem also include job planning, but in a limited sense. It is to determine the list of resources, although issues of what is business-optimal reside within the domain of the integrity and adaptive subsystems. This is why it is common to find job planners tied up supporting jobs rather than planning the "next" job. It is akin to boxing; lots of shots to the body, don't let him breath.

Scheduling process will also be a part of the production-support sub-system, however, to a limited extent. It will be concerned with when work will be done so that resources will be available. The concern for the availability of resources does include the concern for what are business-optimal resources to be made available. Instead, processes for the integrity and adaptive subsystems will be concerned with determining and operating at optimal.

The mention of job planning and scheduling demonstrates a point for the five subsystems. A single person or position can have roles within a process that stand in conflicting subsystems. The issue for organizational design is to break up the roles or place them within the structure in a way that that they cannot be easily undermined in their business purpose. For example, the roles of the job planner are potentially most significant to the firm's returns with respect to the integrity and adaptive subsystems. Thus, structure them as part of one of the two rather than the production-support subsystem.

We have all seen firms that charted their maintenance work management process from end to end; but still could not seem to get it to work. In some cases, the CEO makes appearances to mandate the process; but it still did not get up and run. The dominance of the production and production-support subsystems is most often the reason. The process is world-class on paper but the wolf is ultimately still in charge of the sheep farm. Wolfs have not only eaten the integrity and adaptive subsystem, but also the management subsystem.

Integrity subsystem

The roles of the subsystem are directed at the organizational "equipment" for getting the firm's work done. Across the maintenance function, work is the collective actions of humans with respect to established processes and roles. The "equipment" which must be "maintained" is people.

There is no guarantee that people will accept, perform and remain in their roles and comply with processes. In that context the integrity subsystem's role is to recruit, incorporate, motivate, develop, reward and monitor. The result is to tie people into the overall naturally conflicting requirements of the maintenance function as part of the business.

An example tells the story. The production-support subsystem deals with the provision of inputs to the production subsystem. By comparison the integrity subsystem is concerned with whether the inputs are appropriate.

Accordingly, the functions and elements of the subsystem include human resources management, procedures, training programs and internal audit and control processes. In fact, the details of audit and control suggest that the core process of maintenance as part of business success is not production and production-support; it is audit and control. Interestingly, little of it can be found in most maintenance functions.

The fundamental purpose of the subsystem is to sustain integrity through the stability and predictability of roles and, thus, processes throughout the maintenance function; where ever its parts are located. Therefore, its dynamic is to preserve a state of equilibrium.

Its dynamic is to attempt to formalize all behaviors. Thus, its organizational survival is insured as all things are held as they are and restricting change.

It is important to recognize that the subsystem will strongly resist change for the simple reason is that its survival is threatened by change. With change, some part of its activities may cease to be relevant. Alternately, demands may be made for activities for which it is not currently equipped to handle.

These threats are significant to the integrity subsystem because some of its parts will be killed off or disrespected. Just as survival is a driving dynamic of all subsystems, the integrity subsystem can also easily become absorbed in its survival. To do that it will use its stature to keep current organizational elements in place; even as their relevance to the business purpose of the maintenance function diminishes and becomes an obstacle.

This suggests the nature of dysfunction if the integrity subsystem were allowed to dominate. The maintenance function's processes will become increasingly rigid. The maintenance function will lose its ability to respond to changing business and operating conditions, initiatives to improve plant production and maintenance, etc.

Typical roles and processes of the integrity function are to evaluate and conduct job plan requirements, close completed work, variance reporting and control, integrated schedule and productivity analysis, and process audit and control.

The process to evaluate and conduct job plan requirements is the act of determining the proper resources in terms of quality, quantity and timeline. It will also seek to ensure that all elements are defined such that they can be ensured of being part of the job's final execution and data that is spun off by the plan and its execution.

The closing process is an extension of this thrust. It ensures that all details on which integrity will be sustained are captured. It also is an opportunity to confirm that procedures, with important ramifications, have been followed.

Variance reporting and control is also a process of the integrity subsystem. Through it, the integrity subsystem will confirm that resources involved by work match the firm's resources strategies rather than dance to the tune of the proficiency dynamic of the production subsystem.

Whereas, variance reporting and control is an example of confirming integrity at monthly intervals, integrated schedule and resource productivity evaluation is a shorter-term view. Through it, the integrity subsystem confirms some of the same issues. It will discover whether apparent success is actual success. In other words, it will counter the dynamic of the production-support subsystem to convince the firm that it got what it needed; when in fact it did not.

The integrity subsystem will also be home to the processes to audit and control compliance with processes across the maintenance function. This is important because they have been designed to collectively make and manage the maintenance function in the firm's business success. This includes the integrity of the variance reporting and schedule evaluation processes.

As mentioned earlier, the subprocesses of the integrity subsystem are contrary to the combined dynamic of the production and production-support subsystems. Their ultimate placement in the organization will decide whether or not the integrity of the overall maintenance processes will be sustained or undermined. It is very common to discover that the subsystem is weak or largely absent. Maintenance experts are frequently mystified why valuable improvements once in place and fully functional are later found to be in disrepair or have actually returned to zero; this is why.

Adaptive subsystem

The adaptive subsystem and, thus, its dynamic are concerned with spotting the need for change when it is necessary. The others are not concerned with the need to spot and respond to necessary change. They are concerned with functioning and practices as they are. Consequently, a subsystem must be allowed to exist in the overall maintenance function that seeks and identifies change in the firm's business and maintenance environment.

The subsystem must see both the short- and longer-term big picture and vision; including the firm's financial situation. Consequently, many of its processes are actually the responsibility of maintenance top management. However, the processes require specialists to conduct them on management's behalf. This is the case for strategic planning for maintenance as part of the firm's business success, financial-statements-based analysis and workload-based budgeting.

At another level, the adaptive subsystem has an equivalent role one job at a time. As a subrole in job planning, the adaptive subsystem is visible whenever the planner develops strategies for a job or group of jobs because the one-fits-all case is not the best option. The process to close work orders also has an adaptive element as it is intended to cause the firm to learn from its experiences.

These are reasons that job planning must be kept separate from work execution and may be somewhat threatened by the integrity subsystem. The production subsystem can regard them as a threat to established proficiency. The integrity subsystem can regard them as a threat of revealing the need to change what is being complied with.

At the middle range, the adaptive subsystem is concerned with the firm's maintenance workload linked to business strategy for maintenance and the year's business plan. At this level, the adaptive subsystem will also determine resource strategies with which the workload will be delivered. This is why the budgeting process is part of the adaptive subsystem.

Another role of the adaptive subsystem is the care, feeding and utilization of tools and systems to mine data and conduct decision analysis. In other words, it is the guardian and steward of the tools of change. These tools cause the adaptive subsystem to be regarded by the others as a threat. It is no surprise that in a world of maintenance dominated by the production subsystem, these tools rarely exist, nor the expertise in building and using them. The information from what tools are seen can be found is mostly nonthreatening to the status quo.

The integrity and adaptive subsystems expand the basic organization. This is because they add specialized activities that must exist to develop, reach and sustain the maintenance function as it is engaged as part of the business rather than relegated to merely managing a necessary evil. Consequently, both subsystems are vulnerable. Their contribution to organizational result is short- and long-term, tangible and intangible. Their contribution is not easily measurable by simple cost-benefit calculations. We have all seen the evidence of the threat to their continued survival. When there is cost-cutting and down-sizing the players and roles of the subsystems are often the first to be cut; that is if they were ever allowed to come into existence.

The consequences of succumbing to this vulnerability can have a permanent effect unless it is recognized and reversed. Other subsystems will become dominant as their dynamic prevents or destroys both subsystems.

Once lost, the established dominance will easily be able to prevent or make very difficult their resurgence.

Management subsystem

The management subsystem stands over the other four subsystems. Its dynamic is to integrate them. Accordingly, its actions affect the overall maintenance function, establish rather than implement rules, and formulate rather than implement strategies and results.

The management subsystem will strive to optimize the entire system by suboptimizing and constraining the dynamics of the other subsystems. However, the subsystem also depends upon natural conflict between their dynamics to sustain the optimization. Consequently, a central role for the subsystem is to develop the organizational structure that enables a fair fight.

This highlights the reason to understand organizational dynamics. If the conflict has resulted in an overly dominant subsystem, the dominance is a symptom pointing to a weak or nonexistent management subsystem.

The management subsystem will include three basic roles: legislative to make "laws," executive to over see the execution of the laws, and judicial to adjudicate when the natural conflict between dynamics cannot by settled by its participants.

To fulfill its role, the subsystem will set and confirm the execution of policy and business strategy for maintenance. The requirements will be conducted on fact-based findings developed through the adaptive and integrity subsystems; if the management subsystem has successfully enabled them to exist in good form. That is a reason why the adaptive and integrity subsystems are implemented through the management subsystem. The decision to adopt their findings is the role of the management system.

Where the activities of the managerial subsystem are located will reflect the firm's overall organization design. However, regardless of location one criterion applies. Positions that are responsible for the production and production-support subsystems should not also do double duty as the management subsystem. The risk of organizational dysfunction is too great.

The criterion is not the case for the adaptive and integrity subsystems since many of their roles are actually specialized extensions of the managerial subsystem. If the two subsystems are marginal, so too will be the management subsystem. Therefore, structuring the management subsystem to also be responsible for the adaptive and integrity subsystems will not undermine them. This is because the structuring actually allows the management subsystem to protect the processes that are crucial to its own dynamic; integration and optimization.

The adaptive subsystem will conduct the analysis required to formulate business strategies for maintenance. In turn, the management subsystem ultimately makes the keep-or-kill decisions. In this role, the management subsystem and adaptive subsystem are actually a single subsystem; one conducting decision-analysis, the other conducting decision-making.

Closely following strategy is to set the maintenance budget. Strategy decides the workload lines of the budget. Resource strategies are relatively independent of the workload-based lines of the budget. Therefore, following analysis by the adaptive subsystem, the management subsystem will make the final decision for resource strategies and the adaptive subsystem will build them into the budget.

The management subsystem will also have the role of causing action on variance reports and forecasts. They may reveal needed decisions that are only the management subsystem's prerogative because they affect the entire maintenance function as part of the firm's business success. As the firm reviews variance information, through the integrity and adaptive subsystems, the ramifications and necessity of action are evaluated for decision-making.

The management subsystem is also responsible for setting and enforcing rules and process for the maintenance function. The integrity subsystem will operate the audit and control system that seeks out noncompliance. Therefore, like the adaptive subsystem, the integrity subsystem is also an extension of the management subsystem. Accordingly, the management subsystem will make decision and act on the findings made possible through the processes and information systems of the integrity subsystem.

The description of the four other subsystems shows that they are essentially contrary forces for business success. The firm depends heavily on an ongoing conflict between them to be successful as a business. Because of the huge value of the conflict, it is the management subsystem's role to monitor and manage the conflict. In the role, the subsystem watches for impasse and unfair advantage and steps in to adjudicate when this is the case.

Findings from subsystem analysis of maintenance

The implications of the five business subsystems are fatal for the function if ignored. The most noteworthy observation is that firms have always structured their maintenance function to manage maintenance work rather than be a full player in the firm's business success. This is a problem because firms have typically expected the returns that can only come from managing maintenance as part of the business.

The subsystems analysis of this chapter is not intended to give us a set of hard and fast rules for structuring a maintenance function. However, we can establish some general rules while recognizing organizational roles that are mandatory to managing maintenance as part of the business. Another view is that we will see why maintenance functions never seem to get beyond managing a necessary evil; better yet, we will tear down the wall holding them back.

This section will diagnose what a business-driven maintenance function's structure and roles must be; conceptually. The diagnosis will begin with the combined production and production-support subsystems. It will then look outward to the surrounding three subsystems. The diagnosis will move on to define the counterbalancing subsystems to the combined production and production-support subsystems: the adaptive and integrity subsystems. Finally, it will draw general conclusions for structuring overall.

Chapter 9

Production and production-support subsystem

The core production, in most cases, of the maintenance function is the field work to sustain the performance and condition of production equipment and facilities. Most firms can safely combine most if not all of the roles of the production and production-support subsystems. As a unified subsystem, the firm must expect that is will focus on the proficient execution of work. This is because it is their combined natural dynamic for growing and surviving as subsystems.

The elements of the unified subsystem are charted in Figure 9-2. At the top of the combined subsystems will be management roles that are concerned with executing the firm's maintenance work. Higher management in the maintenance function will hold the manager accountable for delivering the firm's maintenance workload within the boundaries set through the other three subsystems. Of course, the managers of maintenance work generally embrace such boundaries because they are part of putting points on the board. Furthermore, they were engaged in negotiating them.

The combined production and production-support subsystems will entail four groups of processes and roles. First is work generation. Second is planning, organizing and controlling the work approved for execution through to completion and closure details. Third is to execute the administrative, logistic and active tasks of conducting the work. Fourth is the management of personnel engaged directly and indirectly in the work.

The work generation group will classify work, set its priority and approve it. The combined production and production-support subsystems will attempt to maximally enforce its dynamic for maximum proficiency at this stage by its choices and decisions. However, at this stage the firm at times needs there to also be decisions for accepting and prioritizing work based on business ramifications. Consequently, as Figure 9-2 shows there is a line of influence from the "strategic decisions" step back to the adaptive subsystem. An example and common conflict managed along the dotted line is when some roles wish to delay work, whereas, others do not. This conflict is resolved with the aid of decision-support tools; most home-based in the adaptive subsystem.

```
Maintenance work management
 ├─ Trades administration ─ ─ ─ ─ ─ ─ ─ ─ ─ ─ ─ ─  Dotted line to:
 │                                                 Integrity and adaptive subsystems
 ├─ Work           ┬─ Identification.
 │  generation     ├─ Strategic decisions. ─ ─ ─ ─ Dotted line to:
 │                 │                                Adaptive subsystem
 │                 ├─ Classify, approve.
 │                 └─ Prioritize.
 ├─ Plan, organize ┬─ Job plan.  ─ ─ ─ ─ ─ ─ ─ ─   Dotted line to:
 │  and control    │                               Integrity and adaptive subsystems
 │                 ├─ Pick and schedule.
 │                 ├─ Gather resource.
 │                 └─ Monitor, direct execution.
 └─ Work           ┬─ Administrative.
    execution      ├─ Logistic.
                   └─ Active.
```

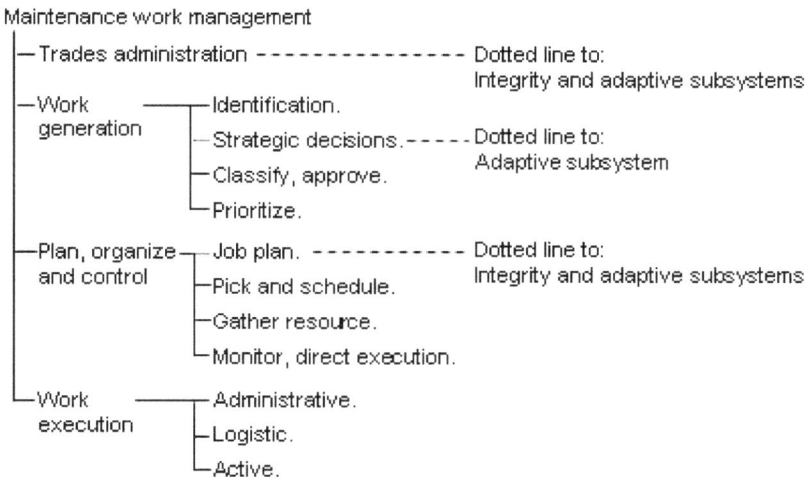

Figure 9-2: Combined production and production-support subsystems for the maintenance function.

The second group of roles and processes of the combined production and production-support subsystems is to plan, organize and control work as it is taken from backlog. These are roles that gather resources made available by other roles, place jobs on the short-term schedule or pick work real-time from a list, and supervise work as the trades execute its administrative, logistic and active steps.

Job planning is also shown in the group. However, subsystem diagnosis would guide us to recognize that an important purpose of job plans is to prevent unfettered proficiency. This is because job plans define and quantify productivity for each job; making proficiency a more challenging achievement.

Job planning will also be contrary to unfettered proficiency when it looks beyond a "one-suits-all" plan to one that recognizes business issues that must influence the subject plan. Consequently, the job planning process is integral to work management, but is actually a window into the combined adaptive-integrity subsystem.

The third group of processes and roles is to execute work. This is the producing core of the overall maintenance function.

Finally, there will be roles within the combined subsystem for personnel management. However, they will be constrained by two other subsystems. Through the adaptive subsystem, the maintenance function will set resource strategies and targets that determine the productivity of trade resources.

Meanwhile, and important to the function's ability to set strategy, the integrity subsystem will confirm, through its audit and control processes, that trades are not being under- and miss-utilized. Meanwhile, and not shown in the figure, the firm's human resources function is another part of the integrity subsystem for trade resources. In this case we see an example of a part of the integrity subsystem residing outside the maintenance function.

Subsystems surrounding production and production-support

The recognition that there are five business subsystems and that the production and production-support subsystems can be safely structured together reveals a basic truth. There is much more that must happen across the maintenance function if it is going to be able to take a role beyond being merely managing a necessary evil. Figure 9-3 shows the surrounding structure.

Essentially, maintenance as a business function must be structured to be one of the firm's primary functions. As such it will be a peer function to marketing and sales, production and logistics. There is no one structure solution to meet this requirement

In some firms the functions may be structured within supply chain management. In others, several along with the maintenance function may be classified as manufacturing (i.e., Figure 9-3). The big point is that the maintenance function should not continue to be mistaken for maintenance work management.

At the top of the maintenance function is the management subsystem. Underneath the subsystem there are two branches of subsystems. One is universal in industry the other, manage business success, is not. When it is not recognized, the management subsystem is absorbed by the branch for the management of the work. It becomes part of the production and production-support subsystem reducing the firm to managing a necessary evil.

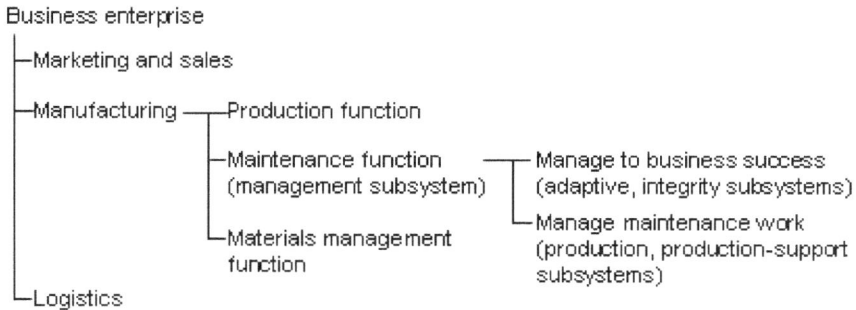

Figure 9-3: Subsystem super structure for the maintenance function.

The branch to manage business success, which is largely unrecognized in industry, institutionalizes the adaptive and integrity subsystems. They are essential to allowing function management, as the management subsystem, to manage maintenance as part of the business. It is simple math. If one or more of the management, adaptive and integrity subsystems is somehow undermined, then all the firm will have is maintenance work management; albeit maximally proficient.

Adaptive and integrity subsystems

Figure 9-4 shows the generic multi-subsystem structure of processes and roles for the adaptive and integrity subsystems. Just as it is safe to group the production and production-support subsystems in the maintenance function's structure, it is safe to group the adaptive and integrity subsystems.

However, there is a conflict between their respective dynamics that must be recognized and monitored if this is to be the case. One subsystem is about change, the other about constancy. However, it is normally easy to manage the conflict through the management subsystem. This is so because both actually do specialized work that is an extension of the dynamic of the management subsystem for its survival and success.

As we inspect the figure, it is apparent why maintenance has a history of being regarded as only a necessary evil. The processes or roles shown in Figure 9-4 have been mostly disenfranchised if not missing in action. This has relegated maintenance to managing a necessary evil rather than being a boardroom matter of interest; as it should be. Dealing with equipment maintenance as a headwind to operations is "table stakes" to business operations, but it is still a far cry from managing maintenance as a part of the business.

Departments for maintenance and reliability expertise and practices have a history of struggling to establish their value in the minds of firm senior management through the value of what they advocate. This is made doubly difficult as the production and production-support subsystems pressure to undermine the survival of these departments for reasons explained earlier in this chapter. Why this is the case is visible in Figure 9-4.

The processes and roles of the figure belong to these departments. However, few of them have been recognized as a "must-be." Instead, these departments have limited themselves to general internal consulting and implementing best practices for job planning and scheduling, forming equipment reliability and maintenance strategy, work management process, and EAM/CMMS.

There are five groups of processes and roles within the combined adaptive and integrity subsystems. They are strategy and change, audit and control, implementation, information systems, and parts, materials and services.

The strategy and change group is concerned with the long to short-horizon, and wide to narrow-view. At the longest and widest is business strategy for maintenance as part of the business, workload tied to the strategy and the year's business plan, and the associated resource strategies with which they will be accomplished through the workload.

At the short-horizon, narrow-view is planning jobs with respect to business implications. Planning also sets the details of productivity for individual or groups of equivalent jobs. Without this placement, job planning will be reduced to supporting the Model-T Ford strategy for ensured proficiency: one model, one color, and be reduced to supporting the actual execution of work.

Maintenance adaptive-integrity subsystems

```
— Strategy, change —— Business strategy.
                    — Workload per strategy
                    — Resource strategy.
                    — Budget and variance forecasting.
                    — Job plan as business.

— Audit, control —— Variance reporting and analysis.
                    — Integrated schedule and productivity
                       reporting and analysis
                    — Process and rules compliance audit.

— Implementation —— Business, resource strategies.
                    — Practices, skills.
                    — Process and systems

— Information ——— Budget and variance (workload-based).
   systems         — Auto audit.
                   — Reliability engineering.
                   — Process frontends.
                   — Databases.
                   — EAM/CMMS.

-- Parts, materials, ◄— From materials and services
   services              management function.
```

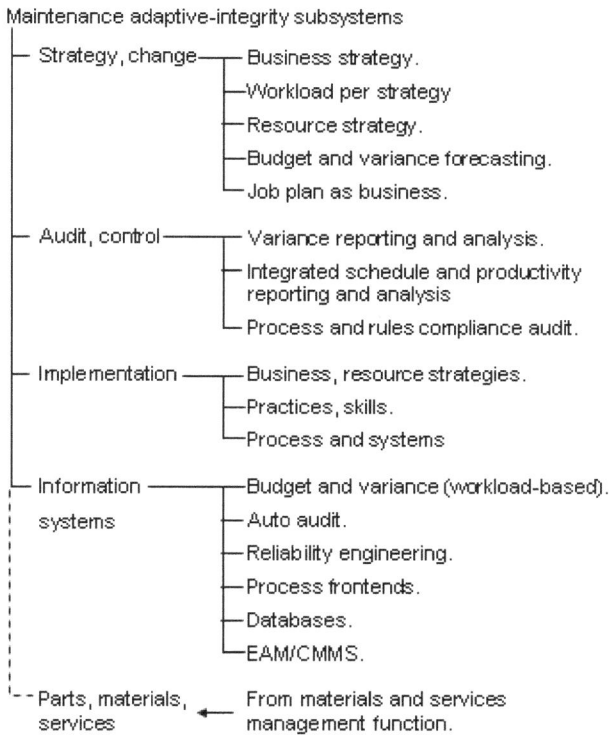

Figure 9-4: The structure of the adaptive and integrity subsystems.

In the middle-horizon and middle-view is designing the maintenance strategies for groups and individual equipment. This may be driven by both the short and long-horizon and have wide to narrow view. The maintenance workload changes as a result.

Workload-based budgeting resides in the strategy and change group. It provides the body of information with which the firm will manage its strategy and year's business plan. As an extension to budgeting, it includes variance forecasting which is also an extension of the monthly variance report.

The second group is internal audit and control. Its processes and roles assess, design and operate the audit and control systems. Without them, the firm has a plan, but not the assurance that they are actually working the plan; or that the plan is a good one or still relevant. The group includes variance reporting, audit and control, and integrated productivity and compliance analysis of the weekly schedule.

In Figure 9-4, the strategy and change and audit and control groups are distinctive. However, their activities and processes will often appear as singular to the casual glance. For example, budgeting, and variance reporting and forecasting look to be one process. As the structure of the maintenance function is defined it is important to make these distinctions. If we do not, we may overlook something subtle and simple for success.

The third group is the development and management of the ERP-type and other computer-based information systems needed to allow the overall maintenance function to fulfill its business purpose. The systems include workload-based budget and variance, auto-audit, asset reliability and maintenance strategy management, specialized process not supported by EAM/CMMS and current tables in the firm's databases. This group highlights the importance of engaging ERP-type technology to manage maintenance as part of the business rather than only managing a necessary evil; something not possible with only EAM/CMMS.

The fourth group in the combined adaptive and integrity subsystems of the maintenance function's structure is the implementation of the processes, methods, tools and systems of the subsystems across the function. This is typically the greatest historically observed role of corporate reliability and maintenance departments. However, as mentioned before, implementation is largely limited to maintenance and reliability best practices and the EAM/CMMS.

The final group includes the provision of maintenance parts, materials and services. These processes and roles should not be confused with the production-support subsystem which is part of the core productive process of maintenance. Instead, as part of the integrity subsystem, they ensure that resources gathered to conduct work follow procedures needed to control assets and the expense of acquiring and holding them. Notice in the figure the broken line to the group. This identifies the processes and roles as an important part of the maintenance function; however, its integrity is often ensured when firms structure their specialized management elsewhere in the firm and outside the maintenance function's structure.

General structural conclusion

There are no hard and fast rules for structuring the maintenance function with regard to the five business subsystems. The Figures 9-3 and 9-4 suggest some principles. However, the firm's overall structural case will decide exactly what the maintenance function's structure will look like.

For example, a firm may have structured its manufacturing function as two dimensions. One will be the actual operations; the other will be concerned with the excellence of operations. In fact and interestingly, this represents managements' gut-level sense of the conflicting dynamics of the universal five subsystems. Accordingly, the five subsystems for the maintenance function may reside separately located along both dimensions. When this is the case, the firm will somewhere structure the management subsystem such that will its cause the firm to manage maintenance as part of the firm's business success.

This section has carefully avoided defining what must be done. At the same time, it has pointed to what should not be done. The five business subsystems were shown as interrelated in Figure 9-1. They can now be transformed to a basic pattern for the subsystems with respect to a successful maintenance function. Figure 9-5 shows the outcome.

The management subsystem will somehow rest at the top of the overall structure; regardless of the structural location of its roles. The remaining four subsystems will fall along two branches.

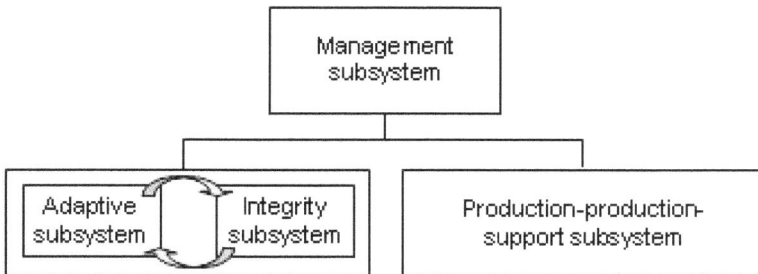

Figure 9-5: Generic structural conclusion for the maintenance function.

On the first branch, the dynamics of the production and production-support subsystems do not fatally conflict. Both advocate for the dynamic of the production subsystem which is to be maximally proficient in the execution of maintenance work, unfettered by other boundaries and constraints; including productivity.

This drives us to recognize the second branch. Its structured processes and roles will be the boundaries and constraints to the proficiency dynamic such that the firm can aspire for its maintenance function to be "good business." Consequently, the adaptive and integrity subsystems reside on the second branch. Their conflicting dynamic is manageable; making it possible to place them on the same dimension.

Putting the five subsystems to work

The previous sections introduced a concept that looms big in winning the bet for whether or not a maintenance function will succeed in managing itself as part of the business rather than continue to be relegated to managing what is regarded as a necessary evil. The next question is how do we put it to work?

Let's tackle the point with a particular concept; as our children say, "Pretend that..." In this case, pretend that the firm is transitioning from one that only manages maintenance as a necessary evil to one that manages maintenance as part of its business success.

There will be two stages. First is to transform the firm's structure for the maintenance function as it is now to one that with its subsystem dynamics aligned to be successful in the new vision for maintenance as a competitive advantage.

The second assumes that the realignment is made and the firm is in progress of executing returns. Consequently, one or more return execution initiatives (REI) is underway as explained in Chapter 7. Accordingly, structuring would be part of an REI as required to begin to generate the returns of the execution initiative.

The steps are as follows:
1. Layout the subsystems-based structure of processes and roles for the maintenance function in the overall firm.

2. Map the firm's existing maintenance processes and roles upon the subsystem structure.
3. Map the abilities of the subject return execution initiative upon the subsystems-based structure; noting what is not represented.
4. Act as necessary to effectively generate the organizational of outcome of the subsystems-based structure.

Step 1: Layout the subsystems-based structure of processes and roles for the maintenance function in the overall firm. The firm is beginning with a maintenance function structured without regard for the five business subsystems. Therefore, the step will mold the structural elements and concepts shown in Figures 9-2 through 9-5 to match the firm's overall structural case. The deliverable will be a skeletal perspective that will be settled with the firm's senior management.

Step 2: Map the firm's existing processes and roles upon the subsystem structure; noting what is not represented. Once the subsystems-based structure is settled with senior management the next step is to map, according to the principles of subsystems, the processes and roles of the maintenance function as they currently exists. One outcome is that missing roles will become apparent.

Step 3: Map the abilities of the subject return execution initiative upon the subsystems-based structure. Chapter 7 explained the approach to incrementally execute the returns of the firm's strategies for maintenance rather than implement the strategies. The process was to map the abilities that must be put in place to roll up collectively to generate the targeted incremental returns.

The purpose of this step is to map the abilities onto the subsystems-based structure established by the first step. This is an important step to generating the returns. It is possible to design well the lead abilities to returns, but cause them to fail to fulfill their business purpose because they have not been structured to be successful.

Step 4: Act as necessary to effectively generate the organizational of outcome of the subsystems-based structure. Restructuring does not always result in new organization charts and calling in office movers. In some cases, it may be to merely do something different with one's days, starting tomorrow. Accordingly, the final step is to act as necessary to fulfill the subsystem-based structure of processes and roles for the maintenance function.

Chapter 10
Audit and Control for Business Returns

To this point the book has introduced and explained all that is developed for the maintenance function to be managed as part of the business. However, there is an additional requirement and the subject of this chapter.

No matter how good an operational solution, it must be kept in good working shape to deliver its intended results. If the roles along the processes of the solution are not "firing" as they should, the maintenance function will evolve back to merely managing a necessary evil, rather than remain a boardroom topic.

The chapter is about developing the system of audits and controls for the processes across the maintenance function. More specifically it is about holding people in their roles. This is essential to success because any process is a sequence of human micro-roles. The previous chapter explained that holding people in their roles is the purpose of an enterprise's integrity subsystem.

To meet this requirement, it is necessary to design and manage two processes in addition to those already designed to manage the maintenance function. First is the process of audit and control directed at the maintenance function's processes. Second is the process to audit the audit and control system itself.

The chapter will explain audit and control in the context of describing the stages the firm must pass through to first design and then operate the two processes. When in place and operational they will protect the firm's ability to generate the returns it has come to know are possible through its maintenance function.

Chapter 10

The capacity to audit and control the maintenance function, and build the ability to do so, has been hugely advanced and made easy by information technology. This aspect of audit and control will be spoken to in this chapter with respect to what is made possible through ERP-type (enterprise resource planning) information technology. However, the subject of ERP will be more deeply explained in the next chapter.

Four stages of audit and control

There are four stages to initially design, implement and manage the audit and control system. Subsequent, scheduled and planned audits of the system will periodically drive the firm back through them to confirm that the system has sustained its integrity and is effective, as well.

A firm's control environment may change as there is competitive, operational and financial change for the firm. When this happens, the system of audit and controls will be updated as needed to continue to protect the firm's returns.

For the maintenance function, the overarching purpose of the system and, therefore, its stages remains constant. It is to ensure that the returns made possible through the maintenance function will be realized. It is also to ensure that the returns realized are actually the result of what was to expected to generate them; not just the result of "sloppy pool."

The four stages and their design issues are as follows:

1. **Assess business risk:** Where would discrepancies in the processes, conduct and outcome of lead abilities present a significant, pervasive risk to the returns the firm has executed?

2. **Define audit points:** What does the firm need to know to periodically and continuously ensure that the discrepancies are not occurring?

3. **Design system of controls:** What controls must the firm put in place to fulfill the firm's needs at each audit point?

4. **Manage integrity of audits and controls:** How will the firm manage and ensure the continuing integrity of its ability to audit and control maintenance as part of the business

The first three of the four stages layout and make operational the audit and control system. The fourth stage will push the firm to revisit the first three as it periodically audits them. It also audits itself as accountable for managing the overall audit and control system and its continued integrity.

Let's make note of a reality before leaping into explaining each stage of audit and control. Modern-day information technology makes it possible to automate much of the audits and controls needed to manage maintenance as part of the business. In some cases, the engagement of people (roles people must be held to) is virtually eliminated by the automation that technology makes possible. Furthermore, because of technology, audit and control is not limited to what has become standard functionality for state-of-the-art EAM/CMMS.

As the chapter unfolds, read it with the confidence that what is a great amount of process activity is a minor amount of human activity. The next chapter will describe the ERP-type technology that makes this the case; just as it does for everything else presented by the book.

Stage 1: Assess business risk

Developing the audit and control system begins with a question. Where would discrepancies in the processes, conduct and outcome of lead abilities present a significant, pervasive risk to returns? Stated otherwise, we are concerned with the risk of failing to receive the quantified returns which the firm has determined are possible through maintenance and has built its ability to reach and sustain.

There is a second related risk to be managed. It is the risk that the returns that are being generated are not being driven by what the firm thinks is driving them. This introduces a third risk. It is that there are additional returns to be had, but the firm is not aware of them and, therefore, not able to generate them at will. We could say this is the risk of failing to find all opportunities to prosper.

Accordingly, the purpose of risk assessment is to locate across the maintenance function's processes where there are chinks in the armor that may allow what is a risk for returns to become a reality for returns. To do this, the business risk assessment stage of audit and control traces back from returns to the flowcharted roles along the processes of lead abilities that drive them.

Risk assessment begins by defining the risk to be guarded against. The previous three questions of risk is an example of such a statement. However, the statement will vary from firm to firm and be more specific with respect the firm as a competitive, operational and financial being.

Recall that included in the statement of design issues for business risk assessment is the term "significant." Consequently, we trace back from returns through to roles along the processes of lead abilities. As we do we are in search of where would discrepancies prevent the change that has been determined is possible for the firm's financial statements.

The search for the defined risk begins with the financial statements. A financial-statements-based model is used for risk assessment. This is the same model that was built by upstream work described by previous chapters for the purpose of bringing the maintenance function to be part of business success. It is now put to work to assess business risk.

The first question to be answered for "significance" is which line items and accounts of the firm's financial statements are the firm's returns most sensitive to. The second question to be answered is which of these line items and accounts are most sensitive to the firm's business strategies for maintenance. The third question is if the sensitivity is immediate, eventual or minimal to discrepancies in the conduct of the strategies.

It is now necessary to locate precisely the firm's significant risks and determine if they are pervasive. The sources reside in the lead abilities to the returns. To find them, we use the interface map which was developed upstream except that we will now use it to develop the audit and control system. The map rests between the financial statements and the lead-abilities map.

The interface measures maps begin where the line items and accounts of the financial statements end. From the line items and accounts of the financial statements, we trace along the forking trails of the interface measures map. The trailhead through the lead abilities map begins at the end of each trail through the interface measures map. We continue to trace along branching trails through to the lead-most or trails-end abilities of the map. The sources of risk to returns reside in the processes of these lead abilities.

Chapter 9 explained that the integrity subsystem owns the audit and control system. Its job, assisted by the management subsystem, is to protect it and ensure that it is not undermined by other business subsystems. Its survival, in good form, is important because the overarching purpose of the integrity subsystem is to hold people in their roles.

This is a critically important purpose because every "box" in the flow-charted process of each lead-ability to returns is a human role, unless automated. A human role can be as small as the "click" of a button making something happen.

Therefore, the business risk assessment will inspect each ability's flowcharted process as chains of micro-roles. The inspection will seek cases where discrepancies in the conduct of a role would travel upward to returns through the lead-abilities and interface-measures maps and the line items and accounts of the financial statements.

At each human role, the risk assessment will determine if the affect on returns will be significant. At the same time the assessment will ask another key design question. Is there a pervasive chance the discrepancy will occur? If the determination is affirmative, along with significance, the risk assessment has located a risk that must be contained by audit and control. The audit and control system will be designed to control or block the discrepancy or minimize the consequences.

This description will no doubt conjure up pictures in the readers' minds of hundreds of controls to be managed. This sound like a deal-killer; but wait! As mentioned before, ERP-type technologies are a large part of an audit and control system. This is because most of the controls can be automated: reducing the human workload to almost a nonevent. This is such an important point that the chapter will repeat it throughout.

Stage 2: Define audit points

The risks to returns that are both significant and pervasive are now on the table in the light of the day. We must now ask ourselves the next question. What do we need to know to be ensured that discrepancies are not occurring? In other words, what does the maintenance function and the larger firm need to know to be ensured that the returns that are possible and reported will be what they should be.

This is information allowing the firm to know that what must be done; is done. If done, the firm needs to know that it is done correctly with respect to guidelines. The firm also needs to know it was done in the correct or intended time frame.

The purpose of this stage is to define what exactly must be audited and controlled with respect to the identified significant and pervasive risks. In other words what must the firm know to be ensured that its lead abilities, as sequences of human roles are taking place as they should; putting points on the scoreboard of returns?

This is a good point to introduce a tool for building the audit and control system. It is the table of audits and controls shown in Figure 10-1. A table is built for each lead ability that has been found by the business risk assessment to be a source of risk to the firm's returns. The first column lists the "boxes" of the flowcharted process. The second is a short description of each flowcharted box. The firm already has the details on which to build the two columns. They have been prepared by upstream activities to detail business strategies for maintenance.

Process task	Task description	Found risk	Discrepancy to avoid	Information need to spot discrepancy	Cont
	tion spot ancy	Control	Means of control	Information plan	Confirmation of control integrity

Figure 10-1: Table of audits and controls.

The remaining columns capture the results of each stage to develop and manage the audit and control system. Accordingly, the next column will record the results of the risk assessment. The record will also note if the risk is significant and pervasive. If not, it should be noted that it is not, and why.

The next column, associated with the stage to define audit points, will describe the nature of the discrepancy. Examples are to bypass the step, override the logic at branches, make incorrect entries, fail to be timely, etc. Notice that each is a case of "human activity" on which the firm's fortune is resting

The next column records what the firm would need to know to avoid or diminish the occurrence of each discrepancy. The answer falls into two groups. First is what do we need to know will never be the case. In these instances, the firm knows its controls will block the occurrence of the subject discrepancy. Second is what do we need to know when a discrepancy is the case.

Modern ERP-type software makes it possible for a large number of discrepancies to be included in the first group. In these cases, an information system's front-end view, program and back-end tables are configured to disallow discrepancies along the process of a subject lead ability. For example, a person engaged in a process cannot move to a next step before doing what is required in the current step. Another example is to disallow data entries that are clearly inconsistent with data to be captured at the steps along an ability's process.

In such cases, that these types of controls are in place is all the firm needs to know. When the audit and control system is periodically audited, the purpose will be to confirm that collusion has not overridden a specific control; something that is also electronically easy to confirm.

The second group requires that we must view and possibly evaluate information to know what must be known. At one extreme we must review reports: in fixed and interactive formats. The budget, and variance report and forecast are examples.

At the other extreme of information is exceptions reporting. This is the case of information that must only be absorbed when a discrepancy is actually the case. No news is good news. Exception-type information appears to inform players across the maintenance function and possibly the firm that a discrepancy has recently happened or is now happening.

The exceptions-type group of information is also a large part of all that is needed to deal with discrepancies. Once again, modern ERP-type technology makes them possible and powerful. Just as important, the capacity to automate also reduces the human energy to produce them to almost a nonevent.

Stage 3: Design the system of controls

The third stage translates the upstream stages to a designed and working system of controls and distributed information. The design details of this stage are added to the audit and control system table of Figure 10-1.

Each control and its distributed information are very specific. The stage will also lay out the overall process that unifies and manages the controls and their information. The stage ends with installing and making operational the system of controls and information, and the unified administrative process.

Control types

There are three types of controls. In the general order that they are developed as follows:

- Feedforward.
- Concurrent.
- Feedback.

Feedforward controls. Feedforward control sounds exotic, possibly like rocket science. This is especially so to the ear of production process control engineers. In their world, feedforward control is a vision to be able to adjust the process in anticipation of the consequences of what is happening in real time.

However, feedforward in the context of audit and control is simply a control designed in anticipation of discrepancies with the intent to prevent them, thus, blocking or diminishing risks to returns. In other words, the audit and control design stages have found a likelihood or potential for people to digress from a process or standard.

An example of feedforward control is a process flowcharted to help personnel stay on track as they conduct their roles. Another is controls that require an entry before the human is allowed by the system to go to the next step (micro-role) in a process.

Feedforward controls have evolved to be a substantial possibility for control systems. Modern ERP-type technologies are easily configured to guide people through processes and control what is allowed. Accordingly, controls are configured in the technologies to block or prevent the anticipated discrepancies. As they are, human energy to conduct a feedforward control is reduced to virtually zero.

Concurrent controls. Concurrent or real-time controls monitor activities (micro-roles) in the present to prevent them from digressing too far from the standard set for them.

When there are discrepancies, this type of control will depend heavily upon exceptions-type reports and notifications to be transmitted to preestablished players across the firm. Some players will be accountable for taking action to remedy off-standard activities and prevent it from happening twice in a row. Others will be people who want to be aware of discrepancies because of their stake in the returns that are threatened by them.

Who receives exception reports and notifications is determined in the design of concurrent controls. The details will be recipient-specific with respect to channel, content, format and interactivity. Once again, ERP-type technology makes great things possible while minimizing close to zero the human energy to do so.

Feedback controls. The third type of control is feedback to provide information on completed activity. This type of control allows the firm to change its results by learning of and from what has happened. Furthermore, they allow the firm to control its destiny; repositioning how it will tackle its remaining year and longer-term future as the year unfolds. Learning and positioning through feedback controls allow the firm to reach and remain at the pinnacle of its possible returns.

This type of control tells the firm if it is succeeding, and why and why not. This highlights an importance of the feedforward and concurrent controls to business returns. They eliminate the noise that would render feedback less meaningful or make it outright misinformation.

An example of the role feedforward control is the work types on which the workload-based line items of the budget and variance system is built. As the firm reviews and acts on variance, it needs to know that new work types have not been slipped into the system; distorting the firm's view of its reality as they pass under the radar. An example of the role for concurrent control is to prevent data from being entered off-standard and distorting the firm's feedback information.

In other words, the feedforward and concurrent controls, as upstream to feedback controls, give the firm confidence that information which is feedback on success means what it means. This is important because it is a difference that gives the firm the option to manage maintenance as part of its business.

Design controls and their umbrella process

The stage will extend the table of Figure 10-1 with the details of the controls for each audit case. The previous stage determined what the firm needs to know, as an audit, to ensure that its processes are functioning without pervasive, significant discrepancies. This stage will identify case-specific controls with respect to type of control, human and technological means, generated information, if any, and reporting scheme.

The reporting scheme will detail the "who, when, what, format and how" of the generated information. "When" includes whether information is to be available by event, schedule or on-demand.

To this point the system of audits and controls has been detailed. The focus has been individual audits and controls. The next step is to flowchart the roles and responsibilities to the conduct the audits and controls as an overarching system.

All maintenance professionals are familiar with the process charted to manage maintenance work. Similarly, the audit and control system designer will map out the umbrella process for the entire collection of audits and controls. The result is to tie them together as a system of activity.

As returns are executed, these controls will be put in place as part of lead abilities. However, before then the processes across the maintenance function that were charted with respect to each business strategy are subjected to a final exercise. It is to review each flowcharted process to determine it needs to be modified to reflect the audits and controls before it can be considered complete.

Implementing the system of audits and controls

The stage is completed when the audits and controls are in place and their information is being generated in the context of a unified, umbrella audit and control process. However, the installation of audits, controls and process will be staged.

Chapter 7 described the approach to execute returns rather than business strategies: if we want results we should execute results. This chapter spoke to audit and control with respect to the processes of human roles for individual business strategies. Consequently, audits and controls will be designed initially as part of the detail of each strategy. Over them will be designed an umbrella process.

However, the audits and controls will largely be installed and made functional in the context of individual returns execution initiatives (REI). Accordingly, they are implemented directly linked to the returns they were designed to protect and ensure. As REIs are constructed, the overall umbrella system will absorb each new set of returns-specific audits and controls; causing a buildup in the system and its process to serve them.

Stage 4: Manage the integrity of audits and controls

Who is taking care when the care taker is taking care? The final stage is to deal with this question.

The audit and control system is function and process just as are the processes it audits and controls. If the audit and control system begins to experience its own discrepancies, so will discrepancies begin to appear across the processes it was intended to protect.

The fourth stage to develop the system adds two columns to the audits and controls table. For each line of the table, we must now ask ourselves how we would know if the audit and control system is working. The final column will define the means by which the firm will be able to answer the question.

An example is a control that tests for untimely action in a process and generates an exceptions report when it is past due. The audit of the control may be a push-button or automated query of associated data tables to identify such discrepancies for the purpose of confirming that the audit and control process responded as designed.

Another example is classifications such as work type. The control can be to configure all systems across the maintenance function to accept only a preestablished set of titles. All others would push back and disallow the person engaged with the system to move to the next step until an appropriate title has been selected.

The audit plan for the control may be a data query to reveal any appearing work types outside of the set that was established since the time of the last audit. If a new title is revealed, the audit process will confirm that it was changed in accordance with procedure.

At this point in the four stages, the audit and control table is complete. The next requirement is to chart the overall plan to audit the audit and control system. The audit plan will bring together the details of the final two columns of the table: how to know the control is working and the process to make the determination. The audit plan will bring them together as a plan that specifies details such as interval, involvement and how the result will be presented to senior management.

Planning an audit begins by evaluating the firm's environment for internal controls because the assessment influences the audit plan. The first concern is the general or atmospheric influences in the control environment. Issues include ethical values, commitment to competence, participation of firm leadership and audit entities, management philosophy and operating style, assignment of authority and responsibility, and human resource policies and practices. The evaluation will identify cases and change in the environment and cause the audit plan to reflect how they have reduce or strengthen protection against discrepancies.

The second concern for audit planning is the maintenance function's organizational structure. What is the function's structure and how is it structured within the firm's overall structure?

The evaluation of the structure is based on the principle of the five business subsystems (Chapter 9); have the dynamics of the respective subsystems been configured such that some are a threat to others. In turn, given the audit and control system, the planned audit will evaluate whether the structural case has placed any controls at the risk of being diminished or eliminated.

The final area of concern is the actual controls, their associated procedures and the system of procedures that manage and operate them overall as a system. The audit plan will define the procedures to be taken to confirm their continued integrity.

The final audit plan must be sensitive to the human effort required to periodically conduct it. Consequently, it will make maximum use of information systems technology. Just as audits and controls can be automated, so can the audit of controls be highly automated.

Table of audits and controls

All through this chapter, a table has been spoken of as a tool to collect the details for the system of audits and controls as they are formed and managed. Initially, its details will define the system of audits and controls to be installed. Subsequently, for cycles to audit the system, it will be the baseline against which audits will be planned and, thence, be updated by these audits.

We will now gather the columns for view in a single place. A table is formed for each process across the maintenance function. The columns of the table and their audit and control issues are summarized as follows:

Column	Audit and control issue
1. Process task	Name of the task as shown in the flowchart of the subject process.
2. Task description	Short description of the task.

3. Revealed risk   Task is found to be a pervasive, significant risk. The negative case is also recorded.

4. Discrepancy to avoid   Nature of the discrepancy to be avoided.

5. Required information   Information needed to avoid or diminish the occurrence of the found discrepancy.

6. Control   What the control will do, i.e., block an occurrence or report an exception

7. Means of control   How the control will be accomplished; including the use of ERP-type technologies and others.

8. Information plan   How the discrepancy will be communicated, if applicable: who, what, when and how.

9. Confirmation of control integrity   How the control will be confirmed and reported as working effectively.

At this point in the book, the entire system of "what must happen" has been introduced and explained both in principle and how to bring it about. This began with how to determine what the maintenance function must accomplish and measure the business value of accomplishing it. It then moved on to executing returns and building the budget and variance system that quantifies what is success based on workload and allows the firm to determine and confirm that it is succeeding. This chapter has explained what and how audits and controls must be built to ensure that the well conceived means to make maintenance a part of business success will itself continue to be successful.

The next chapter will deal with the final topic for making maintenance a part of the firm's business success: ERP-type technology. It is an important extension of the discussion of this chapter, as it is for all others, because information technology makes strong audit and control possible.

Chapter 11
ERP Technology for Business Process

Peter Drucker, the father of management consulting, often said that there is nothing new under the sun in the principles and practices of business management. This is probably true. The disciplines that this book presents are surely not new. Accounting is several hundred years old. The ROI model explained in Chapter 5 was created at DuPont at the turn of the 1900s and first adopted as a standard practice by General Motors in 1917. The curriculum of modern business schools is largely the principles of the past renamed to sound fresh.

What is new is that computer technology has made it possible to do what we have known we needed to do for at least a hundred years. Until this became the case, much of what we had long known to do required far too much human energy and too much data to be doable.

At the mention of technology we think of computerized maintenance management systems, handheld devices and a few others. However, this is a very limited perspective of the universe. In fact, the content of this book evolved from a point in time in 2004 when the author was introduced to database management technology and continued on to understand the component technologies that make up the modern enterprise resources planning (ERP) system. Accordingly, the knowledge of managing maintenance grew from building a budget and variance system to dealing with the full set of management disciplines upon which maintenance is managed as business.

This chapter is not intended to be an in-depth text on information technology. Instead, it will present the basics a maintenance professional must have an awareness of to be relevant to the firm's business success. With it, the professionals will be able to speak to what must happen and how to make it happen as they lead their firm to managing maintenance as business.

The chapter will begin by explaining the concept of ERP and what a system looks like with respect to its component parts. It will then explain the concepts and tools that allow the firm to create and capture data, and convert it to information.

The EAM/CMMS is only designed to support a basic process and, thus, cannot support the full set of processes that must exist before maintenance can be managed as part of a business. Accordingly, the chapter will explain how the ERP-type components are utilized to make the processes possible.

Concept of enterprise resource planning technology

ERP is the acronym for enterprise resource planning. The overarching purpose of ERP is to integrate all activities of the business functions across the firm. Each function draws upon a range of applications that are relevant to its particular operation. Examples are product planning, parts purchasing, inventory control, product distribution, order tracking, finance, accounting and human resources. The application or system that we maintenance and reliability professionals are highly familiar with is of course the EAM/CMMS.

The activities of functions are integrated through data generated by one function, and used and updated by another. As the individual applications use common data they "talk" to each other. As they talk through data, the activities of divergent business processes are integrated.

The "EAM" (enterprise asset management) acronym that is replacing the acronym CMMS reflects that the latest generation of CMMS is consistent with the overall concept of ERP. As one of the organizational functions, its data flows into the firm's larger cross-functional database. An example of functional integration is that the maintenance management process and parts inventory management process are integrated because they draw, update and add to the data of the other. Another example is the EAM/CMMS and payroll systems.

An ERP system is essentially comprised of two systems. One is the specialized software of the firm's business functions, i.e., the EAM/CMMS. These are often called an application.

The other system is the database management system; also an application. This can be a little confusing to us "normal" people. We are all accustomed to thinking of both together as a single software arriving as a CD in a box. However, the desire for organization-wide integration requires that the capture and management of data be a specialized system or application in its own right.

We can further expand our perspective of an application. An application is actually two subapplications that appear as one to the user. One is the guts that electronically do the functional and database processes. The other is the front-end or window into each application. Through it, people interact with individual applications and data systems across the overall ERP system.

As will be seen in the last section of the chapter, this is a necessary distinction. This is because business strategy for maintenance requires the firm to step outside the standard applications; including the EAM/CMMS. When it does, what is needed is easily built with the components of ERP technology; including frontend-type applications.

If an application has a frontend, what is a backend? It is its database. We actually have the choice of working through the frontend or backend of an application. In the latter case, we are reaching directly into the database tables in which the data generated by the firm's functional applications is captured and managed. However, almost all of us typically touch data through a frontend action to the application.

However, if we wanted to, we could do the same thing at the backend as we do at the frontend. This is an important distinction. When the firm needs to build a specialized business process for managing maintenance as part of the business, "reaching" into the backend makes doing so relative easy.

Figure 11-1 is a simple view of an ERP system. The system resides upon the network. The network will likely include both an intranet and internet connected together largely indistinguishable to the user.

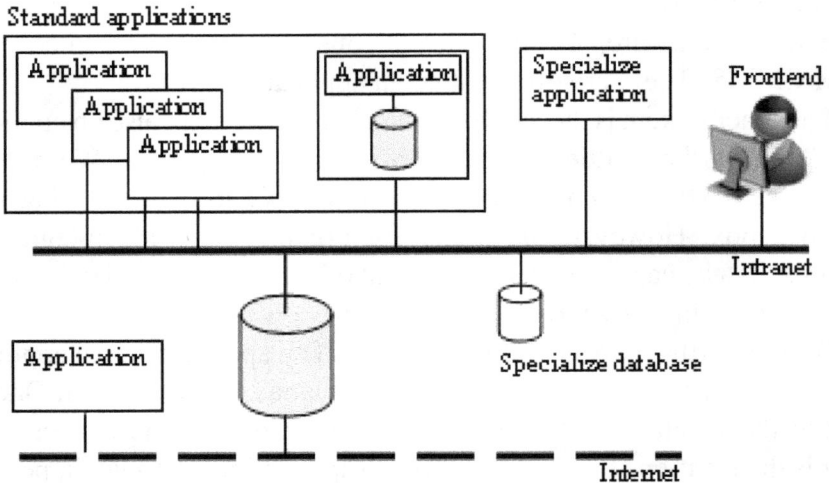

Figure 11-1: View of an ERP system.

Some systems may be located outside the firm on the internet. In fact, the application component of the modern-day EAM/CMMS is located on the internet. This allows it to be maintained and administered at a central location by its creator. Meanwhile, the database may reside inside the firm as part of the database system located on the intranet.

This trend for EAM/CMMS makes the idea of customizing a system to do more than what it has functionality been designed to do is largely unfeasible. Consequently, the point of this chapter is that the components of an ERP system allow the firm to put specialized business processes in place stand-alone from the standard systems; but still integrated through data. In other words, modern ERP-type technology allows the firm to step beyond merely managing maintenance as a necessary evil.

Functional and database applications, installed on servers, are located on the internal and external networks. The EAM/CMMS is one of the applications. Through the frontend or backend of the systems, users can reach into them from their workstations or other locations.

The data that is gathered into the application at an application's frontend and the data generated in the use of the application are sent to the database which is actually a set of tables. Some applications, such as an EAM/CMMS, have thousands of tables.

The figure shows several variations on the construction of function-based applications on the network. The "big dogs" will be strictly the working guts taking input through an associated frontend application and pulling and sending data to its appropriate tables in the database.

Another variation retains its data within the application. Some scheduling software does this. As a training text described one, "A brain on top of a database." However, through the tools of an ERP system, it easy to reach into the application-resident tables and join its data with data in the database management application.

A third variation is supplemental or home-grown applications. In these cases a mainline application does not have the functionality the firm needs to manage maintenance as part of the business. Accordingly, we build a special purpose application to serve the needs of a specialized business process.

The different components of ERP-type technology are utilized to create the specialized application. Examples are frontend or form technologies, database query tools, programmed micros and computational applications. The budget and variance application is an example.

These are not customizations of the firm's mainstream applications. It is using the power of the ERP-type technologies to achieve a purpose. In the grand scheme of the overall system they are relative minor even though they loom large for firm's ability to move its returns through its ability to manage maintenance as part of the business.

This is a simple working view of an ERP system. The remaining chapter will explain the concepts behind the components. The explanation will be for the purpose of giving the professional a basic understanding of how the third or home-grown type of application is built once a business process has been defined which it is to support.

From data to information

Given our history, many of us tend to think of data as magical; something we request from IT and wait a long time to receive. We often speak of measures, but silently doubt they can be actually achieved. In turn, our expectation of measures is KPIs because a EAM/CMMS gives them to us.

This has held back our field in the past even though data has become an easy deal. Consequently, listen to the day-to-day discussion of maintenance and one thing will become disturbingly apparent. There are many statements and long discussions that are not actually based on solid fact.

This section will get us over that condition by explaining data. Where does it comes from, where does it go and how do we get to it? Microsoft Access provides a training file we will use to demonstrate the answers to the questions. Although not an example of a manufacturing enterprise, the principles are still directly relevant to managing the maintenance function as part of the firm.

Databases and tables

A database contains tables. Each application in the ERP system has either its own set of tables or tables it shares with other applications. There are thousands tables associated with an EAM/CMMS. This is also the case for the firm's other mainline applications. The database is huge because the tables of each of the firm's ERP-based applications reside within it.

Tables can be seen in Figure 11-2. The demonstration firm has eight tables. Their titles show that they are tables related to applications for customers, suppliers, products, orders and human resources.

If we were mining data to form facts about maintenance performance, financial line items and accounts, etc., we would literally surf the tables until we find what we need to meet our needs. Fortunately, the application and its manuals usually provide us with clues for where to look among the tables. In the case of at least one EAM/CMMS, if we right click a box it tells us the field and table names.

Picture a home project. We often walk the aisles of the hardware store developing a solution as we do. In essence, this is what the tables are; aisles in the "data store." Our project is to solve a management issue.

There are two views of a table as shown in Figure 11-3. Let's look at the table view in the back part of the figure. A row is a record. A column is a field. A person's full contact information is an example of a record. A person's last name is a field in the record.

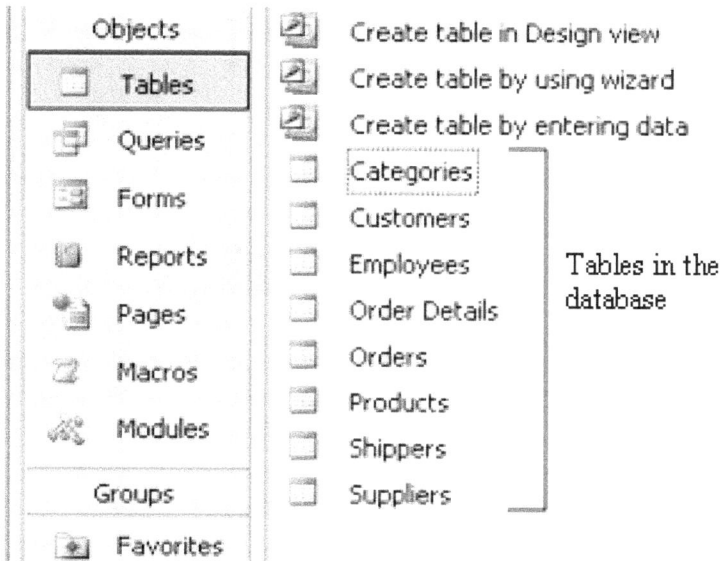

Figure 11-2: Data tables in a firm's database

Each time we make an entry as a user sitting at the frontend of an application, a field in a table will receive the entry. If it is a first-time event, a new row will be created. Thence, whenever an entry is made it will at the least update existing data in a table's field. Alternately, it may create a new row. Actually, our entries do both. They update a record in some tables and create new records in others.

The second perspective of a table is in the front part of Figure 11-3. It defines all fields (columns) of the table and their format. This is an important characteristic because it is what gives applications the ability to "talk to each other."

The formats of matching fields in different tables must match. If we are bringing two tables together from different databases, it may be necessary to revise a field's format in one of the tables. When this is the case, it would be done using the functionality of the database management system which is shown in the front-most view of Figure 11-3. If we are regularly bringing tables together for some purpose, we can automate the steps we would do manually to make the conversion.

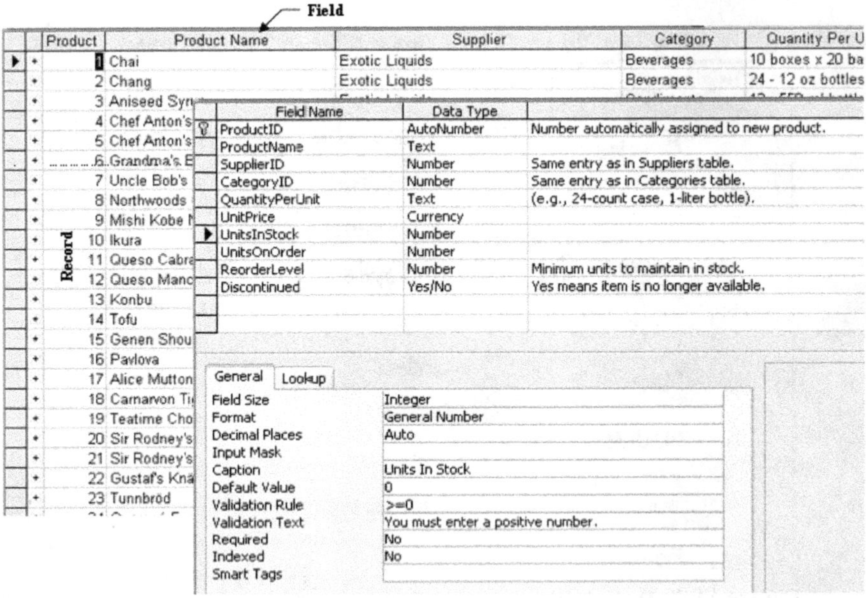

Figure 11-3: Table and field design of a data table.

In a database is captured all of an application's data elements as tables. The individual tables are setup based on the principles of relational databases. What this means is that rather than a database of individual tables or all data in one huge table, an application's database is a system of tables. As a system they have common fields between one or more tables, formatted to match each other. This is shown by Figure 11-4.

Each box on the figure is a table associated with one or more applications in a small ERP system. The lines between tables are called "joins." As an example, when entries are made in the application to a supplier's contact name the field will be updated. If a new supplier is entered into the system a row will open as the details of the supplier are completed. As the details of the supplier's products are entered in the application and flow to another table, the SupplierID field will link them. Each of the supplier's products would be a row in the products table.

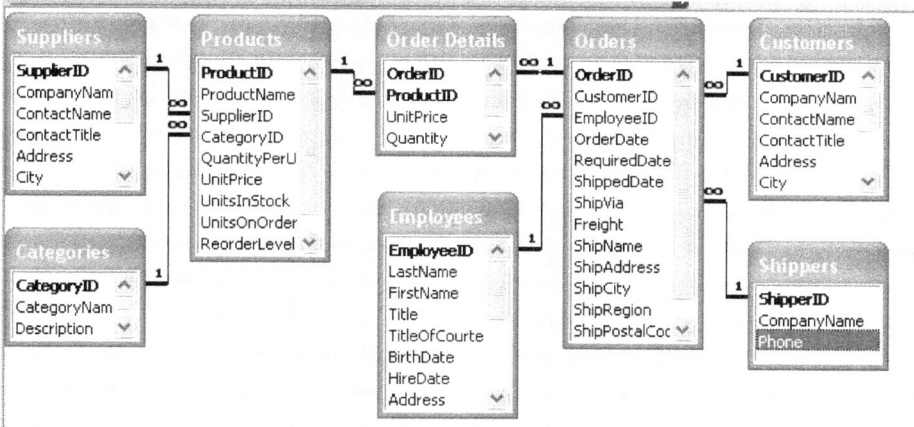

Figure 11-4: Interrelationship between tables.

Getting data from tables

So we have data, huge amounts of data. The previous explanation has shown us something very important: we can actually see data. Furthermore, the data is interrelated; giving us almost anything we could want from it. Therefore, the next stage is how do we get the data; actually touch what we can see?

It is noteworthy that the tables serve the needs of the applications that put them there. They were not set up with a concern for the records and fields specifically of interest to us. The difference is that we may want well less than 0.0001 percent of the data, even though what we want may engage hundreds of thousands of pieces of data.

Furthermore, it is out of the question to expect that we can cut and paste tables into a spreadsheet then sort, relate and format their data to serve our purpose. This is doubly out of the question because if we cannot get our data by click, our data needs are usually prohibitive.

This brings to the forefront the next element of ERP-type technology; data query. Queries are the means to reach into the database tables and pull the data into a single table. Figure 11-5 shows a built query. At the click of button; it will run and produce a table.

Here is what is happening. The upper section shows the tables that have been selected to be pulled into the query because they have fields of interest to the user. The lower section shows the fields that have been literally pulled into the actual query. Notice that the field and table are identified by the upper two rows. In a few strokes we have set up to sift from the many fields the data we need. We could also insert a column that calculates a result based on one or more of the fields (columns).

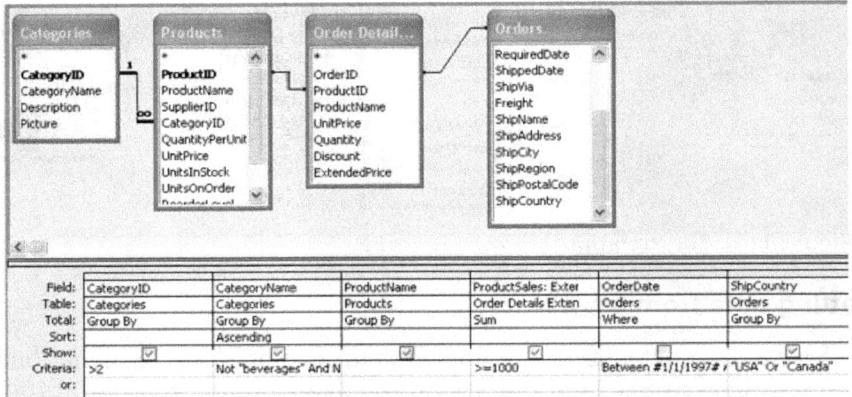

Figure 11-5: Query to pull up data fields from four tables.

Along the criteria row the designer has established which records with respect to each field are of interest. The criteria in each column works with all others to place the limits on the data. Any record that does not meet all five criteria will not be pulled from the database tables.

When the query is run a new hybrid table will be generated from the tables in the database. In this case the table is shown in Figure 11-6.

What can be seen in the figure is a table that has 29 rows (records) for 5 fields. If the four tables were joined and run without designating fields and criteria, the result would be many thousands of pieces of data as a result of dozen of fields and hundreds of rows; all of this from a very small set of tables.

The result is that, with a query, we have supplied ourselves with the table we need for our specific purpose. As a point of reference, when we are sitting at the frontend of an application our actions trigger preestablished queries whose resulting data table fills the boxes of the window we are interacting with. When the user moves on, the application will throw the table away to be regenerated with fresh data upon the next occasion.

Category ID	Category Name	Product Name	Product Sales	Ship Country
4	Dairy Products	Camembert Pierrot	$3,961.00	Canada
4	Dairy Products	Camembert Pierrot	$2,380.00	USA
4	Dairy Products	Flotemysost	$2,563.87	USA
4	Dairy Products	Gorgonzola Telino	$1,233.75	USA
4	Dairy Products	Gudbrandsdalsost	$1,494.00	USA
4	Dairy Products	Mozzarella di Giovanni	$1,218.00	Canada
4	Dairy Products	Queso Manchego La Pastora	$3,800.00	USA
4	Dairy Products	Raclette Courdavault	$2,065.80	Canada
4	Dairy Products	Raclette Courdavault	$4,922.50	USA
5	Grains/Cereals	Gnocchi di nonna Alice	$2,926.00	Canada
5	Grains/Cereals	Gnocchi di nonna Alice	$7,740.60	USA
5	Grains/Cereals	Gustaf's Knäckebröd	$1,008.00	USA
5	Grains/Cereals	Wimmers gute Semmelknödel	$2,726.50	USA
6	Meat/Poultry	Alice Mutton	$1,170.00	Canada
6	Meat/Poultry	Alice Mutton	$6,124.95	USA
6	Meat/Poultry	Perth Pasties	$4,997.60	USA
6	Meat/Poultry	Thüringer Rostbratwurst	$7,218.78	USA
6	Meat/Poultry	Tourtière	$1,092.75	USA
7	Produce	Manjimup Dried Apples	$1,908.00	USA

Figure 11-6: Table produced by the query of selected tables.

This is a good place to make a point. An application, such as an EAM/CMMS, its own queries. However to manage maintenance as part of the business, the firm will need its own. They will be formed as part of business processes and their home-grown applications that are built outside the standard applications of the ERP system. They will usually still reside within the ERP system.

Getting to the tables

We have seen where data resides and how to form tables with the data for our own purposes. A next question is how do we get to the data so we can build and run queries? The answer is easily.

Of course, the first requirement is to get clearance from the IT administrator to enter the database for tables. Many people in a firm already have such a clearance for the systems they work with. An example many of us are familiar with is that we receive a password to enter the EAM/CMMS which is actually a frontend to its database.

There are two choices for getting data tables: link and import. Figure 11-7 shows the case of how this is done in Microsoft's database management application; Access. The choices and how we navigate to them are shown are shown in the figure.

Once we select Import or Link Tables, we will navigate to the database file of interest. When the database is selected, we will be presented with a list of its tables from which we will select the tables of interest to us. If our choice was Link Tables, upon selection a link to the table is entered in the list of tables: note the arrow icon next to the table titled MAXIMO_WOSTATUS. If we had imported the table, it would be copied to reside in our database management application just as are the other tables in the Figure 11-7.

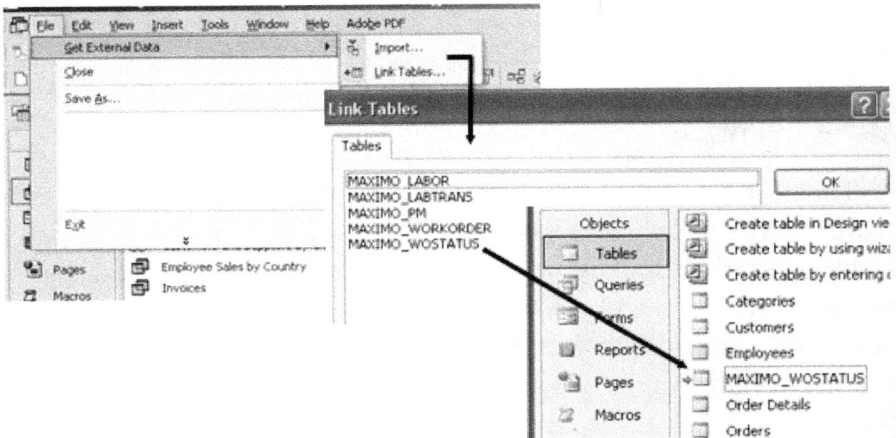

Figure 11-7: Gaining access to database tables.

How the tables are accessed to build or run a query will be different according to our choices. In the linked case, whenever a designed query to use the data is run, Access will navigate to the table and link up, run the query and then disconnect. By comparison, the import case actually pulls a copy of the table onto the users' database management application. Queries will continue to use the table's data until it is updated by a new import action.

Each case has its disadvantages and virtues. Importing means the data becomes old; possibly in minutes. However, when working with data to build a query this works well as it makes it possible to work the problem until solved, unencumbered by network issues. Alternately, linkage results in the latest data each time data is queried. If we needed a permanent picture of data at a point in time, we would also import rather than link.

Converting data to information

With data in a table, we still do not have the information we need to conduct analyses or a business process. It is Halloween: trick or treat. We are treated because we have the data we need. We are tricked because we still do not have any information.

The next question is how the tables we create with a query or raw tables are converted to information. The answer is different ways through the functionality of different available applications. Let's begin with the most direct which is to pull the data into a formatted report. Figure 11-8 shows the method.

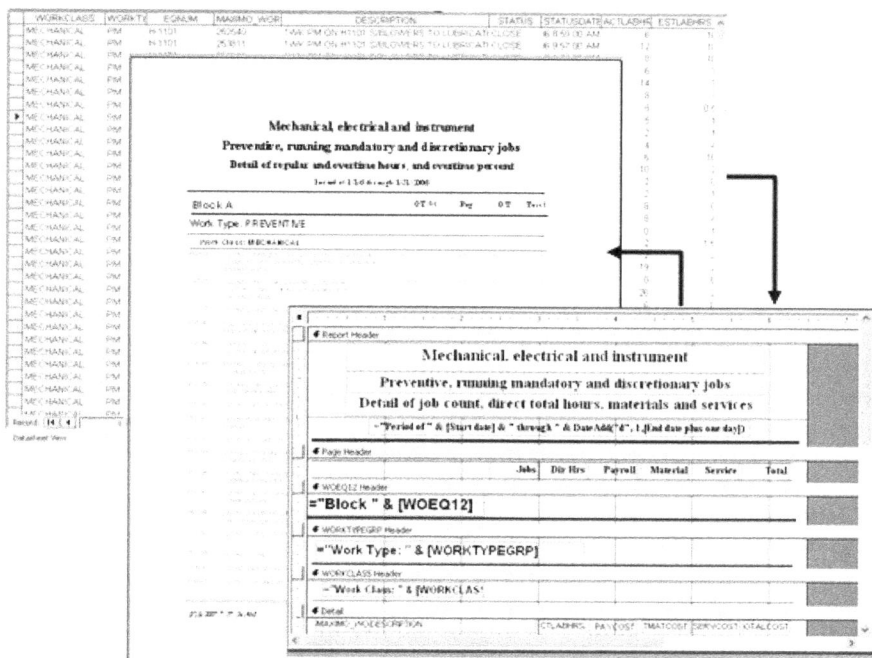

Figure 11-8: from data to information via report.

Within a database management application or other application types, such as Crystal Reports, the most basic method is to build a report. In the figure, the front part shows the design view of a report application.

The designer first identifies the query or database table from which the report will take its data fields. The developer places the fields on the report in accordance to what the report is formatted to present as information. The report is also built to present information in hierarchical groupings. An example is department, work type and trade type.

Upon run, the report reaches into the database or query-created table, shown at the back part of the figure, and pulls and places the data in the report. The result is the middle view of Figure 11-8. The report can now be had upon click. The shown report will be generated with the latest data if the query is connected by link to the database rather than connected to an imported file.

Report applications are available from many sources. A database management application may have its own. The figure is such a case. There are also specialized offering such a Crystal Reports which has become part of the SAP offering. The most advanced of the software gives its users a great deal of rollup, drilldown and slice-dice capability. They may also include query capability to reach into database tables so that we do not have to go through a database management application to build a report.

However, even the best of report technology has limitations. They are designed to group information in hierarchies. However, they cannot deal with complex reporting formats such as those of the workload-based maintenance budget and variance application. Another example is financial-statements-based models.

In the complex cases, we build queries to bring data into an application that will subject it to a system of algorithms. Rather than deliver a report, the home-built application will convert the data to the complex formats that make it information.

The budget and variance views shown in Chapter 8 are based on a spreadsheet application. Across its worksheets is a system of algorithms converting the queried data to a sophisticated, interactive electronic-based document.

There is a range interactive applications for transforming data to information without adjusting the design or rerunning the report. One that is most known is pivot-type reporting in spreadsheet applications that allow interactive choices as a user views tables and charts. The best of the query and report applications also include this type of functionality.

Pivot views of tables and charts provide an interactive means to re-view a great deal of information. The drop-down buttons at various locations on the table or chart provide the user with a menu of choices. This allows reporting such that variations in hard-formatted reports are not necessary. Instead, as shown in Figure 11-9, the viewer can rollup, drill-down, slice-dice and add-remove information as is relevant to them. Pivot-type information can be presented stand-alone or built into other home-grown application such as a workload-based maintenance budget and variance application.

Menus for rollup, drilldown, slice-dice

Sum of Units	Ship Date					
Region	1/31/2005	2/28/2005	3/31/2005	4/30/2005	5/31/2005	6/30/2005
East	66	80	102	116	127	125
North	96	117	138	151	154	156
South	123	141	157	178	191	202
West	78	97	117	136	150	157
(blank)						
Grand Total	363	435	514	581	622	640

Figure 11-9: Pivot type table.

A pivot-type chart does the same thing as a table except it presents the same information in chart form. Figure 11-10 is an example utilized to search out the spots in the month's maintenance activity for which there were variances of three types with respect to the annual workload-based budget: number of jobs, hours per job and overtime.

In this case, the user works the menus to search for up and down spikes of interest. Once again there is rollup, drilldown, slice-dice and add-remove capability. This particular presentation of information was the means to almost instantly find a few important needles in many haystacks.

Now rapidly emerging are dashboards. Furthermore, spreadsheet-type applications can be made to behave as a dashboard application.

Dashboards have been out there for some time. For a long time they seemed more like fiction than reality. Now they are widely available and layperson-friendly.

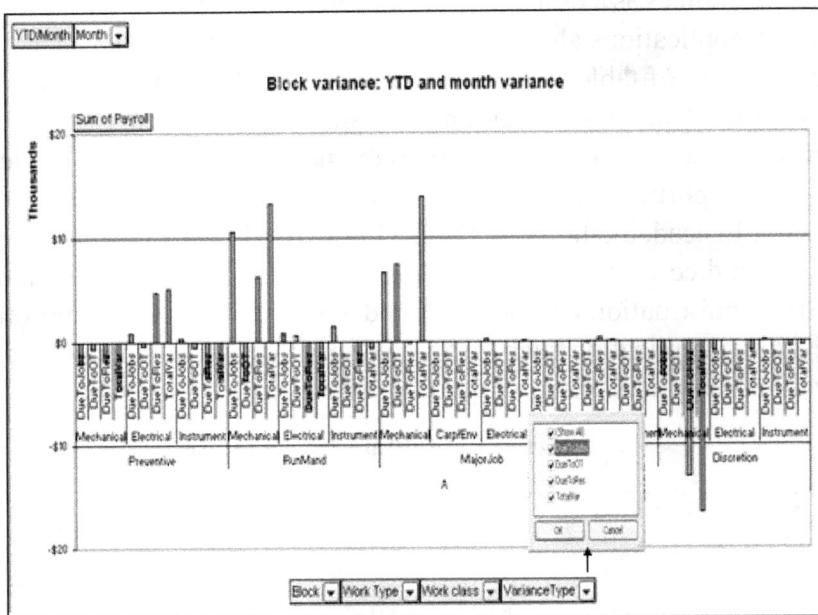

Figure 11-10: Pivot chart

Figure 11-11 is a dashboard that was built to demonstrate the conduct of what-if and sensitivity analysis for the returns from a maintenance improvement program. It is built on top of a financial-statements-based business model. Chapter 5 demonstrated the case of making a spreadsheet application dashboard-like. It too presented a simple financial-statements-based sensitivity model for seeking business strategies for managing maintenance as a part of the firm's business success.

However, the figure does not reflect the other great vision of a dashboard. It is to show information on a real-time basis. For example, a dashboard may be built to report productivity to-date as the month unfolds.

To strengthen our ability for ERP-type thinking, let's look at how information is delivered through a dashboard. First, it runs a query either periodically or on a refresh command. The result of the query may come directly to the backend of the dashboard. Alternately, it may pass through a home-grown application, subjected to a system of algorithms and pass into the backend of the dashboard. In a split second the objects on the frontend change.

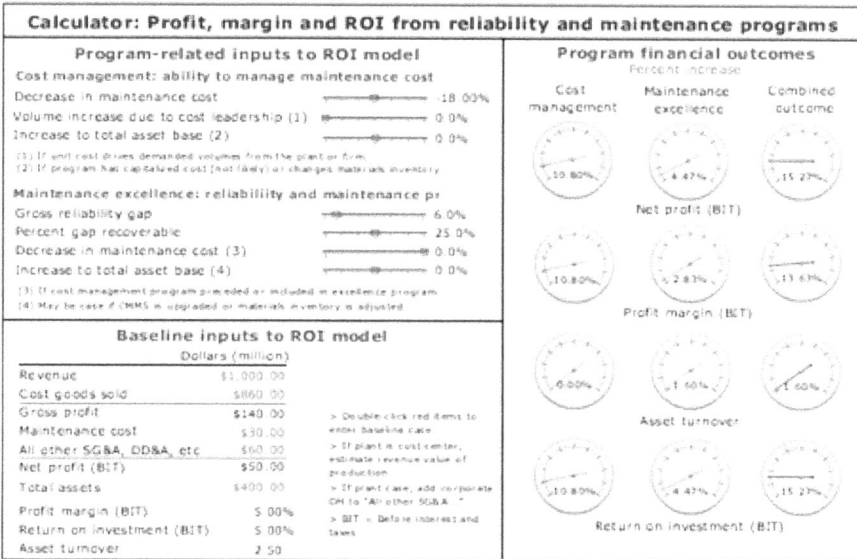

Figure 11-11: Dashboard on top of a financial-statements-based model.

Making the elephant dance

To fully tap into the possibilities for ERP applications in managing maintenance they are automated to conduct the business processes they make possible. For example, if we are looking at a data retrieval or entry in the conduct of a business process we often must be able to jump about amongst standard and home-grown applications as if it were a single application. This will be made to happen such that the user is unaware that it is happening.

We call this "making the elephant dance." The means is demonstrated by the Visual-Basic-based macro programming capability that is embedded in all of the Microsoft Office applications. However, we are not limited to the demonstrated capability. The purpose here is to set a point of reference.

A macro is a programmed action. When the user clicks a button or takes an action a macro may be set up to do something automatically. Visual Basic programming or other languages are used to build them.

An example at the most extreme is to pull data into the backend of a home-grown application such as a variance report. The data pulled in will have the same structure, but conceivably not bring all rows, i.e., days of the week, that exist in the formatted backend table; thus, distorting the information. A programmed macro would test for rows and insert a "dummy" row in the table brought into the application.

We can actually see this capability. It is made available at the same place, in all Microsoft Office applications. Figure 11-12 shows the path to reach it.

At the end of the path we can see the options. The first, Macros, is the set of macros that have been built already. They are activated by different means. One method is by button on an active form. Another may be when the user activates a worksheet. In the latter case, the user is virtually unaware of the macro but is its beneficiary.

The second, Record New Macro, is a tool that makes it possible to build macros without any knowledge of Visual Basic. However, it is not available in all Microsoft applications.

The person developing the macro turns the recorder on, actually goes through the desired steps and then turns the recorder off. The result will join the other macros on the list. It then only remains to set up a button or other event that triggers the macro. An example may be macros that change the content and format of report in response to a user's selection from a menu.

If the recording method is not adequate for a desired macro, the designer will go to the Visual Basic Editor and Microsoft Script Editor. These are the final options of the pull-down menu. In this setting almost anything is possible. This brings the applications for managing maintenance as part of the business to their maximum potential.

The overarching point is that home-grown applications to support business processes and their analyses for maintenance sometimes engage a collection of applications that must be brought together as if a single one in which its components are transparent to the user. A user may engage several applications and not be aware that they are no longer in the application they think they are.

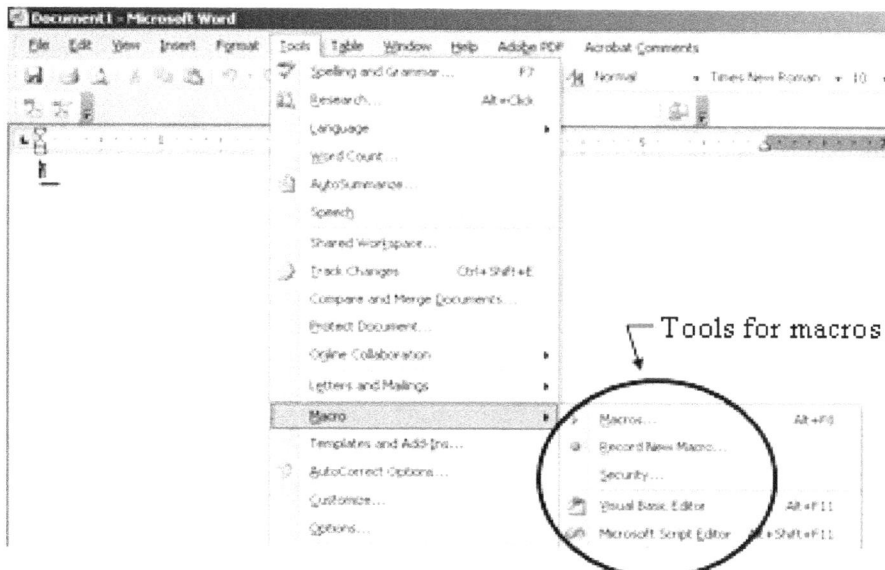

Figure 11-12: Reaching into the firm's database tables.

An example is a reporting application utilized by EAM/CMMS to generate work orders. When users pull up and print a work order while in the EAM/CMMS, they are actually in a reports application. It generates the work order and returns the user to the EAM/CMMS once the command is sent to the printer.

The other purpose of programmed macros is to automate the manual steps of the home-grown application. The time to take an action is reduced to zero and the likelihood of failing to do it correctly is eliminated. It follows that training is also reduced to the minimal and basic. All of this is especially valuable when the steps are beyond the skills of a non-IT professional.

Building business processes

The sections prior to this one explained where data comes from, how we get to it, how it is drawn into standard and home-grown applications, and how applications convert data to information. The sections also explained how different applications are made to talk to each other and how programming languages allow the user to move from one application to another seamlessly in the execution of a process's activity. Now let's take it to the next level: building business processes for maintenance as part of the firm overall business operations.

Subapplications to business process

To bring maintenance to be a part of the firm's business success we progress through the stages and methods explained throughout the book. After understanding the firm as a competitive, operational and financial entity, we ask ourselves a question with respect to sensitivity. Which returns, through line items and accounts of the financial statements, would be most moved by business strategies? In turn, we ask ourselves if there is a maintenance-based business strategy that would touch the revealed sensitivities.

As we detail the resulting business strategies for maintenance we identify and define the abilities the firm must acquire to conduct them. The abilities ultimately take the tangible, working form of business process.

Along any business process, there will likely be requirements for one or more of three types of applications: decision-support, management information and data-mining. Actually, all three have been evidenced in the chapters leading up to this one. However, the line is hazy at which one type ends and another starts.

Decision-support applications. Decision-support applications allow the maintenance function and greater firm to conduct the decision subprocesses of an ability. These can be exotic, but three are typical. They are sensitivity, what-if and goal-seeking analysis.

Sensitivity analysis allows the function to study how much changes in its competitive, operational and financial case would affect its returns or other outcomes. What-if analysis evaluates the impact for returns or other outcomes if the assumptions for the competitive, operational or financial case should change. Goal-seeking analysis determines what is required competitively, operationally or financially to realize a targeted level of returns or other outcomes.

The book has included these requirements as essential to managing the maintenance function as part of the business. The various financial-statements-based business models, the workload-based budget and work-load-based variance forecast for the remaining year are essentially deci-sion-support in nature. They have embedded in them sensitivity, what-if and goal-seeking analyses.

Management information applications. Management or executive information applications are a specialized type of decision-support appli-cation. They give function and firm management the information they need to manage maintenance as part of the business. A primary character-istic of management information applications is that they give users the interactive means to drilldown, rollup and slice-dice information. They also allow management to review information in the current and short-term.

These applications are also strongly evidenced in the overall approach to managing maintenance as part of the firm's business success. One case is the variance report with which the firm can spot and explore its vari-ances all the way to their sources.

Another case is the maps of interface measures explained in Chapter 6. Because they are nonfinancial measures linking activity to returns via the financial statements, they are the feedstock to presenting powerful infor-mation to management.

A large share of this type of information is made additionally powerful by delivering it through dashboard applications. This greatly contributes to the firm's opportunity to review and take action on information while it is still fresh.

Data-mining applications. A data-mining application sifts, almost instantly, through data to uncover patterns and relationships that would otherwise be too labor-intensive to discover.

Data-mining is an activity to seek insight and provide fact, rather than conjecture, to ongoing and ad hoc deliberations and decisions. However, it also operates behind almost all management information and decision-support applications. Data is mined and passed to them through their backend. Without the modern-day ability for sophisticated data-mining, the two other types of applications would be largely undoable.

An example is the workload-based budget. Much of its assumptions are built by mining the firm's data. In the first cycle data is heavily supplemented by the human sanity-check and conclusions. Quickly, with each passing budget cycle, data mining becomes increasingly dominant, making the budgeting process progressively easier and quicker. Subsequently, data is mined to report variance against the budget.

Form applications

All of the previously explained components of an ERP system make decision-support, management-information and data-mining applications possible and powerful along the business processes for maintenance. They are also engaged to automate and support the maintenance function's overall collection of business processes.

Maintenance has been limited to the management of a necessary evil because the EAM/CMMS is a special-purpose application. Its core business process is to administer work orders through their life cycle and capture equipment history as it does. Just as importantly, it does not make good sense to customize the system to conduct processes that is has not been designed to do.

What is especially important is that, as it supports the specialized processes it was intended for, an EAM/CMMS generates most of the data needed to manage maintenance as part of the business. Most of any other required data is available through other standard applications that reside both inside and outside of the firm's ERP system.

Anything needed beyond these data sources can easily be obtained by creating the ability to generate data not provided by any standard application. However, such cases do not begin with the issue of data. Instead, data needs are identified and fulfilled as a lead-ability to returns and its processes are defined and detailed.

Therefore, the importance of the EAM/CMMS for managing maintenance as part of the business is the data it makes available to home-grown business processes and the decision-support, management information and data-mining applications along them. The ERP-type technologies and methods described by the chapter make it possible for the firm to build these home-grown money-makers. When finished they will appear to the eye of "normal" people to be well developed applications. In many cases, they will not even be recognized as separate from a standard system.

In this vein it is necessary to look at one last type of application. It is what this book will call a "form" application and has only been mentioned in passing by previous sections of the chapter.

All professionals are very familiar with form applications working at their best. It is the frontend view (Figure 8-7) interacted with by a person who is logged onto an EAM/CMMS.

Now let's look at forms as an application in its own right, bringing with it a great deal of functionality. Figure 11-13 shows a form application. In this case it is Microsoft InfoPath; an application included in the Microsoft Office suite. Adobe offers an application it calls Adobe LifeCycle.

When the user of a home-grown application opens its frontend form, data is pulled by query from database tables into its boxes. Upon closing the application, the query-pulled data is dropped. As the user makes entries into the application via the form, they become data that flows to tables in a database. The tables may have been created to serve the home-grown application or already exist in the firm's database tables; serving standard applications in the ERP system.

As the user progresses through the form, at the frontend of the application, they are presented with requirements and decision points at each stage of the associated process. These are essentially "events." Some will cause another frontend within the form application to present itself to the user with respect to the continuing process.

The point of reference or comparison here is that, with form applications, we could do everything we have ever done in an EAM/CMMS. In other words, we can know from our experience with the power of EAM/CMMS, anything not served by a standard application can be easily achieved with the use of technology made available to us through form applications.

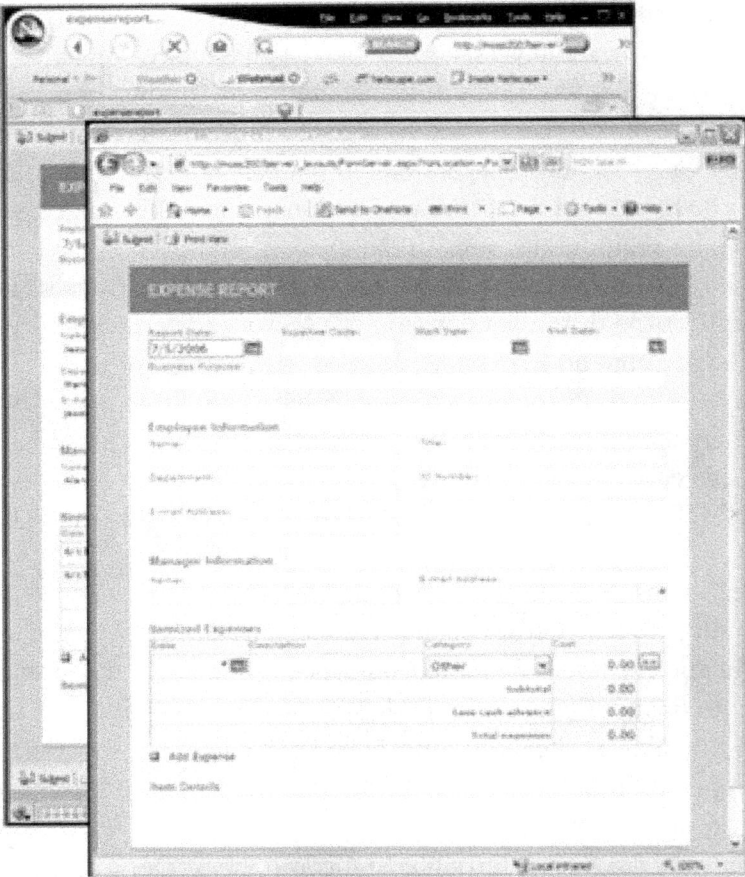

Figure 11-13: Example of a form-type application.

Pull it together

Let's now pull everything together. What if we need a business process with respect to a business strategy for maintenance? Figure 11-14 shows the solution in its design stage. In the case, a process is being designed for a work type that the standard EAM/CMMS does not well support.

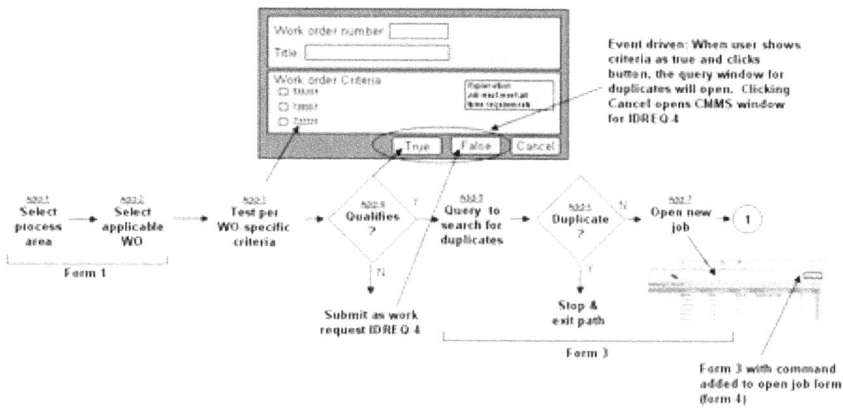

Figure 11-14: Process designed along with form to be its frontend.

The figure shows that flowcharting a process has changed to reflect modern ERP technology. Essentially, it is no longer good enough to flowchart steps. Instead, we must flowchart a process in accordance with the frontend or form view of the system through which it will be conducted.

In the figure, we can see each step being described with respect to the form-based frontend view through which the process will be conducted. Along with the charting we will define the database tables behind the process and any processing that must take place between data at the frontend and backend of the process. Along the process, the necessity and actions with respect to decision-support, management-information and data-mining are identified and charted.

Once detailed, it is simply a matter of setting up the overall business process. If computation with data is involved, a home-grown application will be built to do it. In many cases the built-in functions of the form application can be configured to apply algorithms; avoiding the need to build home-grown computational applications. If the process requires data not generated by other applications across the firm, we would set up data tables in the overall ERP-based database or a database located somewhere else on the firm's network. The final solution would look like a standard application to its users.

Chapter 11

A perspective of building applications for business processes that are not possible to support from standard applications opens another window for maintenance managed as part of the business. What if a process is important, but the investment in a standard system to conduct is extreme. It is much more than the firm requires: squirrel hunting with an automated assault rifle. When this is the case, the firm is not blocked from its possibilities because it can easily build an alternative application to conduct it. Something can be up and running in weeks with very little expense and energy to get there. This is not an infrequent case with respect to the functionality of EAM/CMMS.

The overarching point of this chapter is that we should focus on returns, financial statements, and business strategies and their processes. Given the state of the art of modern information technology, we should not limit ourselves for matters of technology. However, what we have not understood about that technology has been what has limited the field of maintenance to merely managing a necessary evil; end of story.

Now the environment is target rich with ERP-technologies. What once required a rocket surgeon to understand is relatively straight forward. Some like to say that database management applications are the new spreadsheet. As professionals, we do not need to be hands-on competent in all of the modern technologies; only conversant in their functionality. With that perspective we can recognize the firm's innovative, strategic opportunities to align the maintenance function to generating business returns.

Index

www.ingramcontent.com/pod-product-compliance
Lightning Source LLC
Chambersburg PA
CBHW060542200326
41521CB00007B/457